C000069738

# ORIGEN

# ORIGEN

The Bible and Philosophy in
the Third-century Church

JOSEPH WILSON TRIGG

SCM PRESS LTD

All rights reserved. No part of this publication may be reproduced, stored in a retrieval system, or transmitted, in any form or by any means, electronic, mechanical, photocopying, recording or otherwise, without the prior permission of the publisher, SCM Press Ltd.

Copyright © John Knox Press 1983

Unless otherwise indicated Scripture quotations are from the Revised Standard Version of the Holy Bible, copyright, 1946, 1952 and © 1971, 1973 by the Division of Christian Education, National Council of the Churches of Christ in the USA and used by permission.

*British Library Cataloguing-in-Publication Data available*

334 02234 7

First published 1983 by John Knox Press, Atlanta
First British edition published 1985
by SCM Press Ltd
26–30 Tottenham Road, London N1 4BZ

Typeset in the United States of America
and printed in Great Britain at
The Camelot Press Ltd, Southampton

To the Memory of
ALICE WOODSIDE TRIGG
and
MARY KING WILSON

Christianity is rightly dear to the best of mankind; yet was there never a young philosopher whose breeding had fallen into the Christian church by whom that brave text of Paul's was not specially prized: "Then shall also the Son be subject unto Him who put all things under him, that God may be all in all." Let the claims and virtues of persons be never so great and welcome, the instinct of man presses eagerly onward to the impersonal and illimitable, and gladly arms itself against the dogmatism of bigots with this generous word out of the book itself.

Ralph Waldo Emerson

# Contents

# Preface to the British Edition

Origen and Augustine tower above all other figures in the history of early Christian thought. Augustine has been well served by his recent commentators, especially by Peter Brown in his superb biography. But Origen has remained a much more shadowy figure, largely unknown except to the specialist scholar. Joseph Trigg's book should go a long way to remedy that state of affairs. It is hardly an exaggeration to say that his book does for Origen what Peter Brown did for Augustine. It weaves a study of the thought of Origen into the story of his biography and thereby quite literally brings it to life. In doing so he makes Origen more intelligible in terms of his own age, and at the same time more interesting to us and to our contemporary concerns. The sureness of Dr Trigg's interpretative touch means that the book has many things of interest to the patristic specialist. But above all it fulfils the invaluable task of making Origen's thought much more accessible to that far wider range of people concerned with the origins of Christian faith as the system of belief that has so powerfully moulded the world in which we live.

Maurice Wiles

# Foreword

Origen, Christian teacher at Alexandria and Caesarea during the early third century, was the first great theologian of the church. We know him and his thought from the surprising number of his works that have survived either in Greek or in Latin translations often adjusted for fourth-century orthodoxy. Though he wrote much more, enough remains for a synthetic picture.

There are difficulties, however, not least because of Origen's position in the life of the church and the life of the two important cities where he lived. To understand him means understanding him in his cultural settings, in relation to the history of Christianity, of Greco-Roman education and thought, and of the Roman empire. In each setting there were varieties, and Origen takes his place in relation to particular aspects of Christianity and "Hellenism" and in relation to the state.

Perhaps the principal merit of Trigg's fine study of Origen is its catholic character. He seldom neglects certain aspects of Origen's thought or overemphasizes others. This is a difficult feat in an area where—to oversimplify—Roman Catholic and Anglican scholars have tended to rely on the Origen of the Latin homilies and *De Principiis* while Protestants have often used Greek "fragments" of the *De Principiis* and restricted themselves to works preserved in Greek. In consequence there are sometimes two Origens, even beyond those whom Trigg mentions in his appendix. The virtue of this book is that there is one, even though some may suspect that he is a bit more Protestant than a third-century setting might suggest. *The Dialogue with Heraclides* gives us an Origen who seems more "orthodox" than the bishops with whom he confers.

Another merit of the book is its international character. Naturally there is work on Origen in many countries, but in recent years the books of Daniélou, Nautin, and Harl have added to the fame of Paris. Trigg's studies, begun at Chicago, took him to Paris for a time, and the seriousness of his work owes much to his knowledge of scholarship there.

Above all, his *Origen* owes much to the *Origène* of Pierre Nautin, without whose efforts modern patristic studies would be gravely impoverished. Trigg rightly follows Nautin much of the time.

His own purpose, however, is not to recover each detail of the life and thought of Origen but to put the whole into a framework. For this reason we find clear summaries of such matters as Alexandrian Platonism and Gnosticism, Greek education, indeed most of the matters with which Origen himself was concerned. The book will serve admirably as an introduction (and more) to the processes of Christian theological thinking. It shows that such thinking does not take place in abstraction but in reference to the biblical revelation and with use of particular logical systems for particular purposes called for by the life of the church.

Robert M. Grant

# Acknowledgments

Many people have helped me with their encouragement and criticism in the preparation of this book. My mother, Jean W. Trigg, helped me at all stages of its preparation. Robert M. Grant, my doctoral adviser at the University of Chicago, introduced me to the study of Origen and graciously wrote the foreword. My aunt and uncle, Emily and Alfred Wolfson, read the entire text and provided helpful criticism, as did my friends Richard E. Barnard, J. Patout Burns, Robin Darling, and Martin R. Kirby. Others, including Norma Burlingame, Carolyn Vogt Groves, Michael Hollerich, Allan E. Johnson, Rollin Kearns, Martin E. Marty, Alla McConathy, Bernard McGinn, Thomas Riddle, Joy Scheidt, Kristine G. Wallace, Robert L. Wilken, and Jon G. Wilkes gave assistance and advice at various stages of the book's preparation. No one listed above is, of course, responsible for any shortcomings here although all have helped make it a better book.

I also wish to thank Cambridge University Press for allowing me to quote material from Henry Chadwick's translation of Origen's *Contra Celsum* and *Church History* for permission to use material in Chapter VI that appeared in a different form in an article in that journal. I also wish to thank the editorial staff at John Knox Press over the years this book has been in preparation for their initial encouragement of my project and the care they have taken in seeing it through.

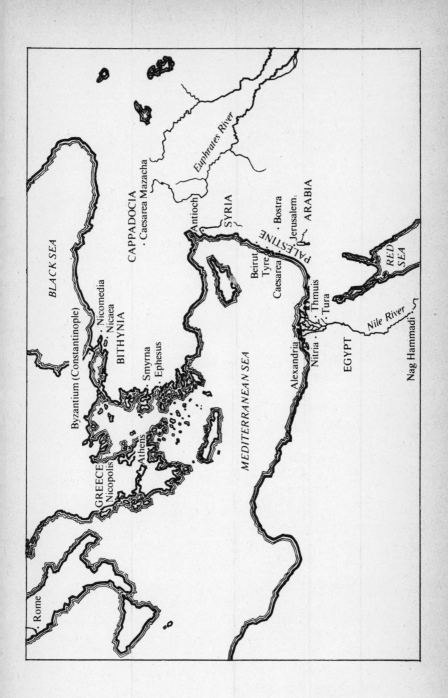

# INTRODUCTION

# Alexandria

If we did not know that Origen had spent his formative years in Alexandria, we would almost have to assume that he had. No place was better suited than Alexandria, the spiritual center of an aggressive Hellenism, to be the nursery of the person who would do more than anyone else to relate the Bible to Greek philosophy. Alexandria had been thoroughly Greek since 331 B.C., when Alexander the Great founded it.[1] In defiance of geography, it referred to itself officially as Alexandria "next to" rather than "in" Egypt. Ptolemy I (d. 282 B.C.), one of Alexander's generals, made Alexandria one of the world's great cities. It was the capital of that portion of Alexander's conquests he had managed to seize: an Eastern Mediterranean empire with Egypt as its chief province. He and his son Ptolemy II assured Alexandria's preeminence as an intellectual and commercial center. Their descendants ruled at Alexandria until the last of them, Cleopatra VII, committed suicide in 30 B.C. as the city passed with Egypt into the control of Rome.

Its founders made Alexandria a model planned city. They laid down a grid of broad streets on the city's flat and roughly rectangular site. The two chief avenues intersected at the center of the city, where stood the Soma, literally "the Body," a mausoleum of Alexander the Great, whose remains Ptolemy I contrived to obtain during the hectic days after his death. There Alexandrians still paid divine honors to their city's founder when Origen was a boy. Engineering works accomplished by the early Ptolemies assured Alexandria's continuing commercial prosperity by making it the chief port of Egypt. They created two sheltered harbors on the Mediterranean side of the city by building a breakwater

3

to the small island of Pharos, almost a mile off shore. On that island they constructed the marvelous four-hundred-foot-tall lighthouse that became known as one of the wonders of the world. A third harbor, landward of the city on Lake Mareotis, gave Alexandria access through newly improved canals to the Nile and the Red Sea. It was busier than the two sea harbors put together.

The Ptolemies, like the great princes of the Italian Renaissance, lavishly patronized learning to gain prestige. Ptolemy I founded the Museum, which functioned as an institute for advanced research, and gathered there the foremost scholars in the Greek world. The heart of the Museum was its great library, which probably survived largely intact until Origen's time. Zenodotus of Ephesus, the first curator of the library, laid the foundations of literary and textual criticism with his edition of Homer and his classification of other Greek literature. During the second century B.C. scholars consolidated, explained, preserved, and augmented the literary heritage of Greece. About a hundred years after the founding of the Museum, this effort culminated in the work of Aristarchus of Samos, one of the greatest scholars of all time.[2]

The Roman conquest of Egypt actually preserved the prosperity and literary culture of Alexandria, which the Romans made their seat of administration in Egypt. The Roman prefect and his entourage conducted official business in Latin, but Greek remained the city's language. In the second century A.D., the period of Origen's birth, the city throve as never before. Dio Chrysostom, a rhetorician, described Alexandria as the crossroads of the world, serving the world as a marketplace serves a single city.[3] Each spring the *annona*, a grain tribute from Egypt, sailed from Alexandria to keep the city of Rome alive. Through Alexandria passed the fruits, nuts, hides, cheese, papyrus, flax, emeralds, porphyry, and red granite that Egypt exported to the rest of the empire. Through Alexandria also, as the principal emporium for trade between the empire and the markets of Asia and Africa, passed pepper and muslin cloth from India, tortoise shell from Ceylon, frankincense from Yemen, and ivory and slaves from Abyssinia. Trade through Alexandria boomed in the second century because Roman mariners had recently discovered the prevailing monsoon winds in the Indian Ocean, which enabled them to travel from Egypt to India and back within a year, bypassing Arab middlemen in the process. In fact, shortly before

Origen was born, one of these mariners reached China, but deteriorating conditions in the empire kept this potential trade route from being exploited. Alexandria was a manufacturing as well as a commercial center. It practically monopolized the production of papyrus, the principal writing material in antiquity, and it was a major center for producing glass, textiles, leather goods, jewelry, and perfume.

This business activity supported a large and varied population. Dio Chrysostom also praised Alexandria for bringing together all manner of men and making them, as far as possible, a kindred people. Ethnic Greeks, some of them descendants of the original settlers brought in by the Ptolemies, were almost certainly a minority, but they set the cultural tone. The majority of Alexandria's residents were probably descendants of Copts from the Egyptian hinterland, who had assimilated gradually to the dominant Greek culture. Normally such persons would settle first in the Rhakotis, a quarter of the city on the site of an ancient fishing village, which had a definite Coptic flavor. From very early in the city's history until A.D. 115, Alexandria had a flourishing Jewish population concentrated in but not limited to its own quarter of the city. During that time the city was the center for a brilliant Hellenistic Jewish culture, which produced the Septuagint translation of the Old Testament, the book of Wisdom, and the monumental works of the Jewish philosopher Philo (c. 20 B.C.–c. A.D. 50). During the first century A.D., Philo's nephew, Tiberius Julius Alexander, forsook Judaism and became the Roman prefect of Egypt. Persistent enmity embittered relations between Greek-speaking pagans and Jews at Alexandria. In 115 the gentiles finally had their way and, in assisting the Romans to put down a Jewish revolt, destroyed the principal Jewish synagogue and inflicted frightful losses on the Jewish community, a community only beginning to recover when Origen was born.[4]

Alexandria's prosperity was, however, precarious since it depended on peace and prosperity in Egypt and the empire as a whole. The Coptic peasants, moreover, detested their Greco-Roman overlords, who left them little in return for the unequaled bounty their land produced.[5] Shortly before Origen was born, native auxiliary troops in the Nile delta mutinied and came close to capturing and devastating Alexandria, the hated seat of foreign oppression. Origen was, in fact, born just at the end of the period immortalized in Edward Gibbon's words:

> If a man were called to fix the period in the history of the world during which the condition of the human race was most happy and prosperous, he would, without hesitation, name that which elapsed from the death of Domitian to the accession of Commodus.[6]

Origen lived during the first and less severe phase of a century-long crisis that almost destroyed the Roman Empire. Even during Marcus Aurelius's reign, from 161 to 180, plagues and wars with barbarians on the Danube frontier sapped the human and monetary resources of the empire. His son Commodus, during whose reign Origen was born, paid off the barbarians and lavished money on the army and on personal display. From his reign dates the slowly accelerating rate of inflation that had created a major fiscal crisis by the time Origen died. By the time Egypt learned of Commodus' death in 192—a court conspiracy dispatched him after he had discredited himself by fighting as a gladiator—the next emperor, Pertinax, had already been killed by the Praetorian Guard. When the guard auctioned the empire to a rich fool, Didius Julianus, the three frontier armies each proclaimed its own commander emperor, and a terrible civil war ensued, which resulted in the destruction of several cities unfortunate enough to pick the wrong side. In 197 Septimius Severus, the commander of the Danube army, emerged as victor only to face a threat from the Parthians across the Euphrates to the east. Septimius Severus defeated the Parthians and kept an exhausted empire stable until his death in 211. After him, there were to be no powerful emperors with long reigns until the end of the third century.

The insecurity of this period of civil war and fiscal crisis caused trade to slump and existing trade routes to shift, curtailing Alexandria's era of phenomenal prosperity. Increased military costs and decreased customs revenue forced the Roman government to squeeze the peasants harder than ever before. In response, many Egyptian farmers simply abandoned land where their toil no longer rewarded them. We should not forget that Origen's very unworldly career took place against a backdrop of plagues, inflation, civil wars, foreign invasions, oppressive taxation, depressed trade, and the abandonment of productive land. On the other hand, Origen's career illustrates how, even in periods of crisis, people not directly affected manage to live reasonably normal lives.

The material prosperity of Alexandria ultimately made Origen's achievements possible by providing him with the means to pursue his intellectual inclinations. The second century A.D. witnessed a second flowering of Alexandrian scholarship, rivaling the period of the early Ptolemies. Claudius Ptolemy, working at Alexandria during the early second century, gathered the accumulated wisdom of antiquity in the fields of mathematics and astronomy and passed it on in works that remained authoritative for over a thousand years. Diophantius, the greatest Greek algebraist, and Hero, who wrote authoritative textbooks on geometry and ballistics and invented a functioning steam engine, may have been Origen's contemporaries. Pappus, whose work on solids was the last significant mathematical achievement of antiquity, demonstrates the continuing vitality of Alexandrian mathematics well into the third century. The literary scholars who labored at Alexandria during the same period are less eminent, but a number of them made lasting contributions to scholarship. Among those who carried on the tradition of Zenodotus and Aristarchus were the grammarian Appolonius Dyscolus, the commentator Valerius Pollio, the prosodist Hephestion, and the poet and antiquarian Ptolemy Chennus. Alexandria was thus easily the greatest intellectual center of the Roman Empire when Origen lived there. We have Alexandria to thank for Origen's compelling intellectual drive and his astonishingly wide interests.

# I
# The Church

(c. 185–c. 201)

When changed conditions call the church's message into question, a theologian must develop an all-encompassing religious vision that enables other Christians to interpret their experience. Two theologians, more than any others, have accomplished this for the entire Christian church. Paul of Tarsus is one of them. The other is neither Augustine, Thomas Aquinas, Luther, nor Schleiermacher, for none of them shaped the entire Christian tradition. The other is Origen, who lived at a time when the church's present divisions were, at most, only incipient. It may seem odd to mention Paul and Origen in the same breath. Paul was a leader and molder of institutions; Origen was a professional scholar. Paul could only hint at his thought in scattered letters; Origen could develop his at great length in volumes of treatises, commentaries, and published sermons. Paul was revered as an oracle of God; Origen was ultimately damned as a heretic. Yet their similarities are more important than their differences. Both men were conservative and radical at the same time. Paul intensely committed himself to preach faithfully the gospel message he had received; Origen was equally concerned to defend the Christian doctrine and morality his upbringing had made a part of him. But Paul's concern to preach the gospel faithfully made him willing, when the needs of the gentile mission faced him, to jettison the pious adherence to the Torah that was the earliest Christians' heritage as Jews. Similarly Origen, as a cultured and thoughtful Greek, found it necessary to transform the content of his received tradition in order to meet new issues that had arisen as Christianity became fully integrated into Greco-Roman culture. In pondering the dilemma that rejection of the Torah entailed, Paul reached insights into the human situation before God that still inspire us long after the actual issues he agonized over

8

have ceased to concern us. Origen, though again his immediate concerns may not be the same as ours, achieved comparable insights. Even if few Christians grasped Paul's profundity, the forcible divorce he effected between Christianity and the Jewish ritual law endured and made possible the spread of the church throughout the Greco-Roman world. Though few Christians, likewise, accepted Origen's entire theology, he made Christianity compatible with the highest aspirations of classical Greco-Roman culture. We have Origen, more than any other single person, to thank that Athens and Jerusalem belong equally to our Western heritage.

Knowing that Paul was a learned and pious Pharisee of the dispersion before he became a Christian and a zealous missionary afterward is obviously vital if we are to understand him. Similarly, knowing about Origen's upbringing at Alexandria and his subsequent career is essential to understanding what he was about. The church historian, Eusebius of Caesarea (c. 260–c. 340), to whom we are indebted for almost all of our information about Origen's life, presented him as an ideal Christian scholar and saint in the sixth book of his *Ecclesiastical History*. Unfortunately, Eusebius wrote fifty years after Origen's death, and had relatively little reliable information at his disposal about Origen's life, especially his early years. Furthermore, he suppressed some evidence that did not place Origen in the best possible light, accepted hearsay evidence that a modern historian would reject, and made questionable inferences from the information he did have. This has made it very difficult to write convincingly about Origen's life. Now, however, the scholarship of Pierre Nautin has sifted the reliable from the unreliable evidence in Eusebius and elsewhere with sufficient plausibility to make an account of his life possible.[1]

Nautin's research confirms Eusebius's report that Origen grew up as both a devoted Christian and a cultured Greek. This makes it most reasonable to assume that the reconciliation Origen effected between Christianity and Hellenism was, first of all, a resolution of tensions he found in himself. It is thus imperative to examine all the influences that made him the person he was. The first three chapters of this book are devoted to such an examination. Since relatively little literature survives from Origen's time, details about such things as Christian worship at Alexandria may not be precisely accurate, but the overall impression is reliable.

## Growing Up as a Christian

Origen's father must have been a prosperous and thoroughly Hellenized bourgeois since he had the ability and inclination to provide Origen, the oldest of nine children, with a Greek literary education. We cannot be certain of his name although tradition records it as Leonides. An ardent Christian, perhaps a convert, he personally taught Origen the Christian Bible. No doubt he led his family in private worship according to the custom of Christians at the time.[2] They prayed three times a day, reciting the Lord's Prayer and some psalms and adding their own petitions spontaneously. They stood to pray with their arms outstretched facing east, in the direction from which they expected their risen Lord to appear at the last day. On Wednesdays and Fridays they fasted.

At least on Sundays and fast days, Origen would have accompanied his parents to the common worship of the church at Alexandria. The city's Christian congregation probably still met together at one place. Although it must originally have met to worship in a large room in the home of one of its members, it almost certainly had a large building of its own for worship by the time Origen was growing up. Origen would have attended services of prayer and instruction. There were prayers and hymns, but the chief feature of these services was the exposition of the Bible. A qualified teacher read aloud extended passages from the Old and New Testaments. Immediately after each reading, he expounded the meaning of the passage to the congregation in a sermon. On Sundays at least, Christian worship continued with a celebration of the eucharist. At this point unbaptized persons, including most children, had to leave.

Origen's parents probably enrolled him as a catechumen—the word means "person under instruction"—as soon as he was old enough to learn. Since the church insisted that anyone about to be baptized should, if at all possible, have a firm grasp of its doctrines and of the obligations of a Christian life, this instruction usually took several years. If the evidence of Origen's own preaching many years later is a guide, the sermons in the ordinary services of instruction may have been designed to provide catechetical instruction. When thoroughly instructed and able to give an account of the faith, the catechumen was baptized and became a full member of the church.

## Instruction in Doctrine

The Bible was the principal source of Origen's instruction at home and in church. His Old Testament was the Septuagint, an early Jewish translation of the Hebrew Bible into Greek.[3] This included, in addition to all of the books the Jews accepted, a number of books, some originally written in Greek, that they did not consider part of the Bible (books which Protestants today exclude from the Old Testament as apocryphal and Catholics include as deuterocanonical). Christians in Origen's time, following Jewish legends that grew more impressive over the centuries, considered the Septuagint an inspired book in its own right. Supposedly Ptolemy II wanted a translation of the Jewish Bible for his newly-founded Museum at Alexandria. The Jewish community sent him seventy-two of its finest scholars—"Septuagint" comes from the Greek word for "seventy"—who accomplished the work in seventy-two days. In the form of the story that prevailed among Christians, these scholars worked separately and were kept from meeting with each other until they simultaneously completed their work. At that time it was discovered that a miracle had happened: each translation was exactly the same, proving that God had directly inspired each translator. This meant that the Septuagint was just as good as, if not better than, the Hebrew original. In fact, it was a competent translation but far from perfect, as Origen himself later came to see. By his time Jews had abandoned the Septuagint for more literal Greek translations and insisted that the Hebrew Bible was the sole authoritative text. They particularly resented mistranslations in the Septuagint that furthered Christian missionary purposes. The most notorious of these mistranslations was "Behold, a virgin shall conceive," the Septuagint translation of Isaiah 7:14, which Christians cited as a prophecy of the virgin birth of Jesus. Jews correctly pointed out that the Hebrew word translated "virgin" actually meant "young woman." But Jewish opposition, well informed as it was, only made Christians cherish the Septuagint all the more.

"Canon," which means "rule" or "measuring rod" in Greek, refers to the books included in the Bible. A book was considered canonical if an inspired author wrote it, and only canonical books could be employed in public worship or appealed to as authoritative in questions of doctrine. Christians throughout the empire accepted the entire Jewish canon as well as the books we classify as apocryphal or deuterocanon-ical. In its Old Testament Origen's church also accepted some books we call pseudepigraphal because, like the book of Daniel, they are falsely ascribed to great figures of the past: Enoch, Jacob's sons the Twelve Patriarchs, Moses, Jeremiah's scribe Baruch, and Ezra. Often these books are apocalypses, works that purport to explain the meaning and end of history or the nature of the universe in a symbolic or visionary form. The Jews rejected these books, and the main body of the Christian church followed suit eventually. Many pseudepigraphical books survive only because an isolated group of Christians like the church in Ethiopia continued to consider them canonical. By Origen's time these books, when not rejected outright, were considered doubtful. For all practical purposes, therefore, his Old Testament was the same as ours.

The same holds true for the New Testament. Origen studied the essential books—the four Gospels, Paul's epistles, and the Acts of the Apostles—and knew them intimately. His church probably accepted as canonical all the books in our New Testament except possibly 2 Peter and Jude. They also accepted as canonical but relegated in practice to a marginal status four books not in our Bible: the *Epistle of Barnabas*, the *Shepherd of Hermas*, the *Apocalypse of Peter*, and the *Acts of Paul*.[4] Supposedly either an Apostle or an Apostle's immediate follower wrote all of these books. The Alexandrian church in Origen's time no longer accepted as canonical two apocryphal gospels. One, the *Gospel to the Hebrews*, was Jewish-Christian; the other, the *Gospel to the Egyptians*, had Gnostic leanings. The latter book was strongly ascetical. In it Christ came "to destroy the works of the female," that is, to put an end to sexual intercourse. Neither survives except in fragments. We have no evidence that the church at Alexandria ever accepted as canonical other apocryphal gospels and acts of Apostles. Many of these, like the *Gospel of Thomas*, recently rediscovered in its entirety, had strong Gnostic overtones.

Tradition relates that Leonides had his son memorize Scripture daily. We may well believe it. As an adult Origen knew the Bible so well that he could recite extended passages at will and could associate verses throughout the Bible on the basis of key words as though he had a built-in concordance. But Origen did not stop at mere memorization.

We hear that

> he was not satisfied with reading the sacred words in a simple and literal manner, but sought something further, and busied himself, even at that age, with deeper speculations, troubling his father by his questions as to what could be the inner meaning of the inspired Scripture.[5]

Leonides supposedly advised Origen not to ask questions beyond his years but secretly marveled at his son's preternatural intelligence. At night he would uncover Origen's breast and kiss it, venerating it as the shrine of a divine spirit.[6]

Second-century Christians insisted that only the church could correctly interpret the Bible. Jews or judaizing Christians might claim that the Torah's ritual laws were valid for all time. Gnostic heretics might claim that the actions of the God of the Old Testament were unworthy of the loving God and Father of Jesus Christ and postulate that the two were different gods. Some might argue from the New Testament that Jesus Christ was only human, others that he was not human at all. Although the church rejected these interpretations, their proponents could make a case for all of them from the Bible. The Bible, after all, is not a tidy theological handbook. Christians therefore affirmed a second canon, in addition to the canon of Scripture: the canon of faith. This was a consensus of teaching that supposedly came from the Apostles. It was not entirely self-evident in the Bible, but the Bible as a whole testified to it. Origen, as a child, absorbed this canon of faith, and, as an adult, he took it for granted as the basis of the church's teaching. The canon of faith had no authoritative written exposition, but Christian writers of the second and third centuries agreed on its fundamental points.[7]

The canon of faith, as Origen learned it, probably included the following items:

(1) A doctrine of God. There is one God the Father, who created the universe and governs it by providence. Worship is due to God alone, who gave the Law to the Jews and sent God's son Jesus Christ to redeem the world.

(2) A doctrine of Christ. Jesus Christ, the Messiah whom the Old Testament foretold, was a man born of Mary, who as a virgin miraculously conceived him. In Palestine he taught and performed miracles, was crucified under Pontius Pilate, died, and was buried. He descended

into hell to liberate the righteous dead. He rose from the dead, appeared to his disciples, and ascended into heaven, where he reigns with God the Father. Christ will return to judge the living and the newly resurrected dead. Jesus Christ is divine and hence worthy of worship but not identical with God the Father.

(3) A doctrine of the Spirit. God's Spirit inspired the prophets and Apostles who wrote the Bible and continues to animate believers.

(4) A doctrine of spiritual beings. There are rational beings not confined, as we are, to earthly bodies. Some are angels who worship God and carry out God's commands. Others are demons—probably fallen angels—who follow the commands of Satan, their prince. The demons disguise themselves as gods, thereby deceiving the pagans into sustaining them with sacrifices, and they seek to entice believers into heresy and sin.

(5) A doctrine of last things. At the end of time, God will destroy the world God made. When this happens, all the dead will resume their bodies, and Christ will then welcome the righteous into everlasting happiness and condemn the wicked, along with Satan and the demons, to everlasting torment.

(6) A doctrine of sacraments. Baptism, a ritual washing with water, obtains forgiveness of all sins committed prior to it. The eucharist, a ritual meal celebrated with bread and wine, is a communion in the body and blood of Christ that obtains immortality for all who partake of it worthily.

This list obviously differs markedly, both in content and in emphasis, from what Christians today would offer as a summary of their faith. In particular, it is vague on matters which would later be carefully defined.[8] This is most evident in its doctrine of God and Christology. The three persons of the Trinity—Father, Son, and Holy Spirit—are affirmed, but their precise relationship is uncertain. The doctrine of the Spirit is particularly undeveloped, and the relation of God the Father to God the Son is defined only to the extent of affirming that the Son is divine but not identical with God the Father. The church affirmed Christ's divinity to justify worshiping him, but it denied his identity with God the Father because the human Jesus had a relationship as a separate person with God the Father and because he suffered and died, which God the Father could not do and remain the perfect ruler of the universe. Second-century Christians tended to consider Christ inferior to God the Father, a tendency later Christians branded heretical.

Although Christians in Origen's time affirmed that Jesus was in some sense divine, they did not formulate closely the character of that divinity. A common theological formulation was that Jesus Christ was God's Word or, in Greek, God's Logos. The Logos doctrine recommended itself because it harmonized with a long tradition of Jewish speculation on God's relation to the world, an issue to which Christian proclamation of Jesus Christ as mediator seemed to provide the definitive solution. In relatively early strata of the Old Testament the tendency to transform theophanies—actual appearances of God—to appearances of angels indicates an uneasiness with God's immediate relation with human beings. In later strata there appears a tendency to explain a transcendent God's creation of the world by making God's personified Wisdom the agent of creation as in Proverbs 8. Exposure to Greek philosophical concerns and terminology reinforced Jewish speculation along these lines. The tendency to posit a mediator between God and the world culminated in the writings of Philo, who identified the Old Testament theophanies and wisdom of God with the Logos, a Stoic term for the divine rationality immanent in the universe. Independently, it seems, the author of the Gospel of John applied this term to Jesus in the prologue to his Gospel. He thus gave an apparent apostolic sanction to second-century theologians like Justin Martyr (c. 100–c. 165) who applied Philo's full Logos theology to Jesus. Justin, in this spirit, identified the Logos as a second God. The Logos theology, for all its popularity in Origen's time, was transitional. The church ultimately rejected it because it limited Christ's dignity. The companion problem in Christology, the relationship between the divine and human natures of Christ, was also left vague. The church rejected docetism, the view that Jesus was a heavenly being who only seemed to be human, but it did not explain how he could be both human and God. Origen's work, as we shall see, advanced the definition of both issues materially.

The doctrine of grace was another area where the canon of faith had almost nothing to say. It affirmed God's providential governance of the world, an affirmation that contradicted the popular belief in astrological fatalism as well as the philosophical doctrines of Aristotelians and Epicureans, who ascribed earthly events to chance. It did not, however, in any way define the relationship between human initiative and divine grace in the accomplishment of salvation. The classical formulation of that doctrine did not occur until the early fifth century when Augustine of Hippo dealt with it. Only then did the church as a whole reject the notion that human beings have a natural capacity to do God's will. Augustine prayed that God would grant him the grace to keep the divine commandments. Christians in Origen's time simply taught the obligation to keep a strict moral code. Again this is an area to which Origen would make a significant contribution.

Another area of vagueness in the canon of faith was its doctrine of sacraments. The second-century church affirmed that baptism completely remits all sins and that the eucharist should not be partaken unworthily. It left the precise nature of those sacraments undefined, as they would remain until the Middle Ages. We have only the germ of a doctrine of sacraments other than baptism and the eucharist. Sacramental anointing with oil for healing, which is already found in the New Testament, is the most fully developed. Laying on of hands for confirmation was simply a part of the baptismal rite. The reconciliation of penitents and laying on of hands for ordination were practiced, but their meaning was not yet conceived sacramentally. Origen would have his say on a number of these matters.

In addition to its vagueness on issues later Christians would insist on defining with the utmost precision, we also notice a distinctive spirit in this canon of faith, a spirit best recreated in modern times by C. S. Lewis: it is intensely dramatic. Jesus' coming to the world, his death, descent into hell, resurrection, ascension, and expected return as judge are episodes in a cosmic battle, in the course of which God is overthrowing Satan's usurped authority over this world. This accounts for what we might otherwise consider a disproportionate attention to demonology. Early Christians were doing their part in the battle against Satan and the demonic legions. It is easy to see how this presentation of Christian teaching would appeal to a sensitive and imaginative boy; Origen came early to think of himself as an actor in the cosmic drama of redemption. He retained this identity of himself throughout his life although his exposure to a more sophisticated, philosophical understanding of reality greatly modified it.

## Instruction in Morality

Keeping in mind the dramatic spirit of second-century doctrine enables us to understand better the other aspect of Origen's instruction as a catechumen, instruction in Christian morality.

The Bible, as interpreted by authorized teachers, was again Origen's textbook. In many ways this morality was not distinctive; it had much in common with Greco-Roman ethics and still more in common with the ethics of Judaism. In 112 Pliny the Younger, as governor of Bithynia (the province on the Asian side of the Bosporus), wrote his friend the Emperor Trajan about Christians in his province. He had taken steps to eradicate their superstition, as he called it, but he noted that their moral teaching was unexceptionable. They bound themselves by an oath to abstain from theft, robbery, adultery, violation of oaths, and refusal to repay a deposit on demand, acts pagans proscribed as vigorously as did Christians. Christians and pagans also concurred in condemning quarreling, gossip, laziness, and abuse of wealth. Both groups stressed individual morality, paying little attention to societal and political injustices. The putatively benevolent autocracy of the *Pax Romana* smothered the passionate concern for social justice that once characterized Greek philosophy, and it did not encourage Christians to concern themselves with social issues either. Christians accepted the status quo. They defended private property, a possible early experiment in communism notwithstanding, and they supported established social distinctions including slavery and the subjection of women. An example of this social conservatism in Origen's time is one criticism which Hippolytus (c. 170–c. 236), an eminent Roman theologian, made against his bishop, Callistus (d. c. 222). He attacked Callistus for recognizing as legitimate marriages in the eyes of the church liaisons between slaves and women of high rank, which Roman law forbade.[9] Christians also, by and large, shared with their pagan neighbors a grateful acceptance of the peace and prosperity the Roman Empire secured. Christians had begun to make mutually favorable comparisons between the church and the empire and to remark on the providential conjunction of their origins in the reign of Augustus.[10]

Christians had even more in common with Jewish morality than with the conventions of Greco-Roman society. Christians repudiated the commandments of the Torah they considered merely ceremonial like the dietary and sabbath regulations, but they considered its moral commandments still in force. They thus adopted as their own the traditional Jewish abhorrence of idolatry, a sentiment that kept them from full participation in the social and political life of the empire and exposed them to persecution. Christians also adopted Jewish sexual ethics, something more significant in the long run since it shaped European legal and ethical traditions. The Jews had long distinguished themselves by forbidding practices such as prostitution, concubinage, pederasty, abortion, and infanticide that other peoples of the ancient Mediterranean world approved of or condoned. Christians, if anything, made more of an issue of their opposition to such things than Jews did.

While the content of Christian ethical instruction differed relatively little from that of other groups, its spirit differed greatly. The dramatic spirit of the early church's doctrine had as its corollary a heroic spirit in morality. This heroic morality was the Christian's participation in the drama of redemption. In this spirit, Christians during the time of Origen's boyhood exhibited a smiling contempt for life as usual, despising the most fundamental human impulses and flaunting their superiority to them.

One such impulse was the desire for possessions or at least for worldly security. In their attitude toward wealth, therefore, Christians stood out from the consensus of their larger society. Pagans and Jews agreed with them on the need to give alms to the poor and to abstain from wasteful indulgence and even on the ethical danger of excessive riches. But ordinary Greeks used the same word to say "happy" and "rich," and Aristotle considered moderate prosperity a prerequisite for a virtuous life. Jews, likewise, considered prosperity a sign of God's blessing on a righteous life. Contrast these attitudes with Jesus' exaltation of poverty in the Synoptic Gospels, a challenge to prevailing attitudes that influenced the early church enormously. An edifying story current in Origen's time exemplifies this influence. In an episode of the apocryphal *Acts of Thomas*, the Apostle acts out Jesus' sayings about obtaining treasure in heaven by giving to the poor. Gundafor, an Indian king, sent for Thomas, a renowned master carpenter, to build him a palace. Thomas took Gundafor's money and instead of building the palace gave it all to the poor. When the king inquired about his palace, Thomas told him he had built it in heaven. A miraculous vision persuaded Gundafor to spare his contractor's life. This exaltation of poverty and unsparing almsgiving does not mean that Christians were all poor. Many by Origen's time were rich, but such people often felt guilty about their wealth. This was true in Alexandria where Origen's mentor, Clement, reassured them that Jesus' commands to give away all possessions were not intended literally in *Who Is the Rich Man Who Is to Be Saved?* Origen's writings reflected this uneasiness about wealth and the business dealings that gain it. Later on, this uneasiness found powerful expression in the monastic movement.

The sex drive is at least as powerful as the desire for possessions, and here again the heroic spirit manifested itself, clearly setting Christians apart from the morality of other groups. The centrality of the family in Jewish ethics mutes this theme in the New Testament, but it appears very strongly in second-century Christianity. In apocryphal acts of Apostles we find an outright veneration of virginity. In the *Acts of Paul,* a book the church at Alexandria accepted, neither Barnabas nor Silas is Paul's principal companion; she is Thecla, a young woman Paul rescued from marriage on the eve of her intended wedding. Sexual abstinence, it seems, is the sum and substance of the gospel they preach, and virginity is a prerequisite for the resurrection of the body. During the second century some churches forbade marriage, and it seems that churches in the non-Greek-speaking areas of Syria restricted their sacraments to people heroic, or old, enough to commit themselves to complete celibacy. Even among those who rejected this position, which came to be labeled as the "Encratite," or "continent," heresy, few regarded marriage and procreation as an actual good. Most, rather, took the pragmatic position that the demand for total continence was too great a burden to lay on all Christians, and hence dangerous to the ethical life of the church. Practically all churches encouraged young persons to consecrate themselves to virginity and those widowed not to remarry. Christian apologists pointed to troops of Christian virgins as living proof that Christians participated in a higher realm of existence, one undominated by animal impulses.

Sometimes this heroic attitude toward sex went to extremes. In some places young men and women keen on virginity sought to prove their mettle by living intimately but chastely together. Soberer church leaders, alarmed by the inevitable failures, sought to end this practice, but it took a long time to eradicate. Our first record of Alexandrian Christianity is testimony to something more drastic. During the second century a zealous Alexandrian Christian, seeking to refute pagan allegations that Christians engaged in sexual licentiousness, asked the Roman prefect of Egypt for permission to have himself castrated (a certificate was required or he and his physician would be liable to prosecution). He was turned down, but he made his point. Bolder souls went ahead with the operation regardless. This sexual ethic shaped Origen all too well.

The second-century church's teaching on martyrdom testifies to their desire to rise above a still more powerful impulse, the urge for self-preservation. Christians believed that Christ, by triumphing over death on the cross, broke Satan's most effective weapon, the fear of death. The martyrs appropriated Christ's triumph when they chose death over apostasy. Their deaths had redemptive overtones and could cancel their own sins and, arguably, those of others because they participated in Christ's death. Ignatius (d.c. 107), an early bishop of Antioch, expressed his attitude to his impending martyrdom in a letter he wrote to the church at Rome as a military guard was conducting him there. The burden of his message was: "Do not attempt to arrange things so that I may be spared. By being a martyr I can become like Christ." He used eucharistic symbolism to link his own expected martyrdom with Christ's redemptive sacrifice. "Allow me," he wrote, "to be poured out as a libation to God. . . . I want to be his wheat, ground fine by the lions' teeth, to be pure bread for Christ."[11] This exultant tone in early Christian discussions of martyrdom often jolts us, but such Christians believed that God's power and mercy were nowhere more evident than in such atrocities. That belief gave them the ability to prevail.

The Roman government, which considered the regulation of religion one of its functions, treated obnoxious cults roughly.[12] It was particularly harsh on magic and necromancy because the supposed knowledge of the future so obtained could be politically subversive. Romans considered Christianity potentially subversive also because it was well organized, exclusive, and mysterious to outsiders. The fact that Christians worshiped a person whom a Roman governor had put to death as a partisan was not lost on them. The Romans also disliked

Christianity because it challenged the religious consensus of the empire. If Celts, Berbers, Armenians, Phrygians, Copts, and so on could not tolerate each other's practices, or if Mithraists, Druids, Baal-worshipers, Stoic pantheists, and stargazers did not respect one another's beliefs, the empire would fall apart. The Roman government would have preferred each group to stick to its ancestral religious practices, but societal changes made that impossible. Roman subjects continually abandoned their ancestral cults for new, more satisfying, modes of worship. The Romans therefore tacitly demanded that cults maintain a sort of religious free market. Any cult could advertise itself as the best product, but it should not try to destroy all the others. There thus arose in the Roman Empire a remarkable religious consensus much like the teeming pluralism of modern India but still more tolerant.

In theory, though, all Roman subjects shared a common observance of the imperial cult. In governing the empire, the Romans adopted, as the Macedonians had before them, the ancient Near Eastern practice of venerating rulers as gods. Actually only megalomaniac emperors like Caligula believed they were gods. Most were content for the senate to proclaim them posthumous divine honors. But emperors did consider it reasonable to demand that their subjects worship and swear by their divine genius, a loosely-defined entity something between an external soul and a guardian angel. This worship involved only throwing a pinch of incense on a civic altar, and it required no devotion beyond that. To refuse to render such worship, however, was an act of insubordination all the more serious because the demand itself was so trifling. Such refusal indicated contempt for the emperor and merited capital punishment.

Before the rise of Christianity, only the Jews rejected this Roman religious consensus. They obstinately insisted that their God was the only god, and was to be worshiped their way. Even a pinch of incense on a civic altar was an affront to their God which they would not commit. The Romans generally tolerated the Jews because it was clear that their fanatical intolerance belonged to their ancestral religion. The Christians rejected the religious consensus on the same grounds Jews did. They also exhibited an even more pronounced intention than Jews had to monopolize the religious free market. Mithraists or devotees of Dionysus could also patronize the mysteries of Isis, but Jews or Chris-

tians could only patronize their own cult. Christians pleaded for toleration as a "third race," distinct from gentiles and Jews, but they were
manifestly not a distinct ethnic group, so the Romans never granted
them such status.

The Christians' unauthorized refusal, on grounds of conscience, to
worship the emperor's genius provided Roman magistrates a legal
weapon. All a prosecutor had to do was arraign suspected Christians,
order them to worship the emperor's genius, and execute them if they
refused. The use of this weapon produced a common pattern in the
persecution of Christians, and some magistrates applied it with relish.
Others tried to save accused Christians in a way consistent with their
legal duties by giving them time to think things over or by torturing
them to make them recant. Torture was a routine judicial procedure, and
a magistrate could reasonably argue that it was better to bring fanatics to
their senses by twisting their thumbs than to kill them and rob society of
otherwise useful members.

Until the reign of Decius (249–251), persecutions were local and
infrequent, but they were always a possibility, and they claimed many
eminent Christians, among them the apostles Peter and Paul, bishops
Ignatius (c. 35–c. 107) and Polycarp (c. 69–c. 155), and the apologist
Justin (c. 100–c. 165). Even though there were relatively few martyrs,
martyrdom thus loomed large in the Christian consciousness as Origen
was growing up. The importance ascribed to martyrdom led Christians
to produce a new genre of literature, acts of martyrs. These were brief
works, often circular letters, that recounted the martyrs' deaths and the
circumstances surrounding them. Eyewitnesses often wrote such acts
shortly after the events described, and they frequently incorporated actual court records of the martyrs' trials or testimonies written by the
martyrs themselves as they awaited death. Christians in the church
where the martyrs died read the acts aloud annually on the anniversary
of their death. Christians elsewhere sought courage to face similar trials
from these testimonies to God's power.

The oldest surviving act of a martyr, and perhaps the first, is the
eloquent *Martyrdom of Polycarp*, written around 156.[13] It is characteristic of the genre, and it merits description in detail, not least because
Origen could have known it. The Roman proconsul of Asia sentenced a
group of Christians to death at Smyrna when they refused to recant. He

decided to make them a public spectacle by putting them to death in the gladiatorial games. He burned some alive and threw others to wild beasts, but the Christians did not blame the proconsul or the Smyrnan mob for the massacre. They knew that Satan was behind it and that Satan was being beaten. One martyr, Germanicus, contemptuously spurned the proconsul's pleas to recant and save himself; he went and provoked the beasts to kill him. Inspired by such displays of heroism, a Christian named Quintus from Phrygia, a hotbed of fanaticism, went to the proconsul with some other Christians he had recruited and offered himself for martyrdom. The proconsul, however, persuaded him and his followers to recant.

When the persecution began, Polycarp, Smyrna's aged bishop, allowed his congregation to persuade him to hide in a farmstead near town, close enough to attend to their pastoral needs. As other Christians died, the mob at the amphitheater called for Polycarp's blood, shouting, "Away with the atheists, go and find Polycarp!" The police discovered him easily since Polycarp did not try to escape. His captors generally treated him courteously although they made him bark his shins on their carriage. They allowed him a two-hour prayer before taking him off, and they tried to persuade him to recant. When he arrived at the amphitheater, the crowd was tumultous. "Have respect for your age," said the proconsul. "Swear by Caesar's genius, recant, and say 'Down with the atheists.'" Sighing "Down with the atheists," Polycarp gestured with his arm toward the crowd. When asked to revile Christ, he replied: "I have served him eighty-six years, and he has never harmed me. How can I now blaspheme my king, who saved me?" When the proconsul saw that his efforts at persuasion were in vain, he had Polycarp burned alive before a delighted mob. That night Christians gathered his ashes and buried them in a place where they intended to celebrate each year the "birthday," as they called it, of Polycarp's martyrdom.

*The Acts of the Martyrs of Lyons* is from Marcus Aurelius' reign. It recounts what amounted to a pogrom in 165 when a pagan mob actively searched out Christians in Lyons and nearby Vienne, dragged them from their homes, and brought them to the Roman governor. He tortured them to make them recant and thus succeeded with many although he unaccountably held all of them in prison together nonetheless. Those who held firm he sentenced to die as criminals in the games celebrating the union within the empire of the three Gallic provinces, saving money he otherwise would have had to spend on gladiators. There, to gratify the spectators, he put the Christians to death in a variety of painful ways. The crowd participated avidly and called for something called the "iron chair" to roast a beautiful young Christian name Blandina. The martyrs' unflinching courage inspired many of those in prison to abjure previous recantations and accept martyrdom for themselves. Thus, in the words of the *Acts*, the "living" martyrs brought their "dead" colleagues back to life. During the martyrs' trial another Phrygian, a physician named Alexander, conspicuously gestured his support for those arraigned. When his behavior aroused suspicion, and he was brought before the governor, he refused to give his name, saying only "I am a Christian." He thus joined the martyrs.

The early Christians were as aware as persecuted groups are now of the propaganda possibilities of an open trial. One would have expected Origen to have heard of *The Acts of Apollonius*, an Alexandrian Christian put to death in Asia Minor about the time he was born. Apollonius apparently considered himself, like Justin, a Christian philosopher. He parried the Roman magistrate's questions with a reasoned defense of the Christian faith. In one reply, he compared himself as a person unjustly persecuted, not just to Christ and the prophets, but to Socrates and to Plato's hypothetical "just man" of the *Republic*.[14]

Such works illustrate the prevailing ideas of martyrdom in the early church as Origen grew up. The insistence that Satan was the martyrs' real enemy is consistent with the dramatic character of Christian doctrine. The veneration of relics, implied in the *Martyrdom of Polycarp*, shows the extent to which martyrdom was perceived as redemptive. So does the fact that the martyrs at Lyons were credited with bringing their lapsed brethren back to life. Martyrs had a powerful motivation since martyrdom was considered a second baptism, procuring certain forgiveness of all sins the martyrs themselves had committed and, some thought, the sins of others as well. It was the one way an early Christian could be absolutely certain of salvation. Few Christians actively sought out martyrdom, but some, like the irresolute Quintus in *The Martyrdom of Polycarp*, and Alexander in *The Acts of the Martyrs of Lyons*, actually did so. The church in the second century was uncertain whether or not to approve of such actions, but as persecutions became more severe in the following century it came to disapprove of them, teaching that martyrdom was a gift only God could grant. Could anyone, the reasoning went, remain steadfast under torture and the threat of death unless one knew that God had summoned one to a martyr's crown? Were not volunteer martyrs, even if they held out, little better than suicides? Besides, how could Christians seek toleration and provoke death at the same time? The acts of martyrs also reveal the uncomfortable fact that many Christians did recant. What was to be done with them? They had committed apostasy, the most heinous possible sin a Christian could commit. As persecution sharpened during Origen's lifetime, this question became acute.

The exaltation of martyrdom was thus the capstone of Origen's training in the Christian life. Throughout his life Origen maintained the austere values he imbibed as a child. Eventually, when he knew the church's doctrine and morality well enough to affirm his faith in the one and to obligate himself to live by the other, Origen was baptized.

## Worship and Order

Baptism as Christians practice it today is pallid compared to the rite Origen underwent. Justin Martyr referred to baptism as "enlightenment," likening it to the initiatory rites of the pagan mysteries, rites that produced a sudden mystical insight leading to a sense of redemption and rebirth. Justin considered the pagan rites demonic imitations of Christian baptism but showed by comparing them that he considered them to produce similar effects. For Christians, baptism ritually confirmed the beliefs and values they learned as catechumens and, more than that, gave them a new and lasting identity. An examination of the rite itself will show how aptly it was suited to fostering the sense of spiritual rebirth.

Easter, the one festival Origen's church certainly celebrated, was the normal time for baptism. The timing emphasized the baptized person's identification with the dead and resurrected Christ. Catechumens about to be baptized prepared themselves for the rite by fasting for some days or even weeks before Easter, and the rest of the congregation joined them in solidarity. This is the origin of Lent. On Easter morning they went to a stream of "living" (flowing) water. The catechumens were exorcized, they renounced Satan, and they affirmed their faith publicly. Deacons baptized them, men and women separately, in the nude, in the name of the Father, the Son, and the Holy Spirit. Baptismal nudity, which reinforced the symbolism of new birth, was not awkward because early Christians were used to public baths. On emerging from the water, they put on a spotless new white garment. Its cleanness reminded them of their newly acquired purity and their need to keep it unsullied by sin. If they did so, they could expect to be among the saints clad in white at the resurrection of the dead. At the eucharist that immediately followed their baptism, the neophytes received milk and honey, the food of paradise, along with the bread and wine. The bishop then conferred on them the gift of the Holy Spirit by anointing and laying on of hands. They were then full members of the church. The elaborate preparation was not absolutely essential. Someone in imminent danger of death could receive baptism at any time, and if that person were an infant, parents could take the vows.

Having been baptized, Origen could participate in the other Christian mystery, the eucharist, which Christians celebrated each Sunday. Excluding from the service all but baptized Christians of good standing assured it a special character. The bishop and the presbyters of the church sat at a table at one end of the room where the service took place. The deacons stood nearby to serve the congregation. The believers sang hymns and psalms and offered petitionary prayers, including one for the emperor. They greeted one another ceremonially with a kiss, and then presented the offerings, bread and wine for the eucharist and gifts to be distributed as alms. Then the bishop probably initiated the familiar exchange:

> The Lord be with you.
> AND WITH YOUR SPIRIT.
> Lift up your hearts.
> WE HOLD THEM TOWARD THE LORD.
> Let us give thanks to the Lord.
> THAT IS WORTHY AND RIGHT.

In the ensuing prayer, the bishop thanked God for the gift of God's servant, Jesus Christ, recounted Christ's institution of the eucharist, called on God to bestow the Spirit on the bread and wine, asked for God's blessing on the congregation, and concluded with a doxology. "Amen," responded the congregation. The deacons then distributed the

bread and wine, and the believers dispersed. The eucharist made real
the solidarity of Christians with each other within the congregation,
with other Christians throughout the world, and with Christ.[15]

Precisely because the eucharist fostered such a strong sense of sharing in a common life, Christians did not want to partake of it along with
persons who did not meet their doctrinal or moral standards. In fact,
they considered themselves defiled if they partook with such heretics or
sinners. *The Didache*, a second-century book of church order, encouraged even those who so much as held grudges to abstain from the
eucharistic communion until they had gotten over them; one resentful
person present would endanger the purity of the whole congregation's
eucharistic sacrifice of praise. Denying communion was a powerful
instrument for maintaining church discipline. Being denied the fellowship of other Christians was terribly intimidating to anyone who had
adopted the church's beliefs and standards.

The church easily received heretics back into its fellowship once
they renounced their errors, but it had a harder time deciding what to do
with excommunicated sinners. Christians who had committed certain
grave sins—sexual offenses, murder, and apostasy are the ones usually
named—were thought to have forfeited the forgiveness they had obtained at baptism. How could they regain it? Only martyrdom could
incontestably restore it, but some communities also allowed a single
"second repentance" that enabled sinners who had atoned with fasting
and lamentation to rejoin the eucharistic fellowship. Other communities
allowed that such sinners might obtain God's mercy if they repented
continually the rest of their lives, but it would be presumptuous for the
church to readmit them to its fellowship. When, during Origen's lifetime and later, many Christians recanted their faith under duress, the
church split over what to do with them when they naturally begged for
readmission after having committed the sin of apostasy. We do not
know how rigorous the church at Alexandria was in Origen's time. At
any rate, the pitiful spectacle of penitents excluded from communion
and earnestly seeking readmission would have provided him a powerful
object lesson in the seriousness of Christian ethical obligations.[16]

The church had, by the time Origen was a boy, evolved a stable
organization. The three historic orders of ministry—bishops, presbyters, and deacons—had already appeared in the context of worship.

Their positions at the eucharistic service indicated their roles in the church. The bishop sat at the center of the table and presided over the ceremony. He alone, or a presbyter whom he designated, said the prayer of consecration that was the heart of the rite. Demetrius, who became bishop when Origen was a boy, brought Alexandria into line with a prevailing tendency in the second-century church by establishing himself as a virtual monarch, the ultimate authority in matters of doctrine, discipline, and practice. Congregations chose their bishops and conducted their own affairs. There was no formal hierarchy above the congregation. Ties of intercommunion, however, made the opinion of other churches important, so that no congregation was truly independent. Normally there would be a bishop in each important town, and the congregation that gathered under him would be that town's church. Thus the bishop was more like the pastor of a large parish than a diocesan administrator. As long as the church remained relatively small and concentrated in cities, this structure was the norm. In any given region of the empire, the bishops of the seat of Roman administration normally had considerable prestige and presided at gatherings of bishops called synods. Ordinarily these cities would be the largest in the province and have larger and longer-established churches. This explains the preeminence of the bishop of Rome among all the bishops in the empire. Bishops corresponded or met in synods to discuss such matters as how to define Christ's relation to God the Father so as to exclude heresy, whether or not to readmit penitent sinners to communion, and when to celebrate Easter. If a bishop faced opposition in his congregation, he would attempt to line up the support of other bishops.[17] Demetrius established, if it did not exist before him, a cordial relationship between the bishop of Alexandria and the bishop of Rome that their successors continued for centuries. Only other bishops could depose a bishop. If they wished to do so, they gathered in his city and tried him for heresy or misconduct before his congregation. If they found him guilty and deposed him, they withdrew their fellowship with him and with any of his congregation who still accepted him as bishop. The bishop was thus the congregation's link with the church as a whole in a flexible but resilient structure.

The presbyters sat next to the bishop at the table when he celebrated the eucharist. "Presbyter" literally means "elder." Originally they were simply the responsible, older persons in the congregation who collectively looked after its affairs. By Origen's time, though, it seems better to refer to them as presbyters rather than as elders since their function had become a well-defined order in the church for which ordination was a prerequisite. Etymologically, "presbyter" is the root of the English word "priest." That term is misleading, though, in describing the presbyters when Origen was a boy since it implies that the presbyters had a function regarded as the equivalent of the function of the priests of the Old Testament or of the priests of pagan cults, an idea that developed later. As a matter of fact, it began to develop during Origen's lifetime as Christians began to use the word for such priests to describe first the bishop and then later the presbyters of the church. In addition to advising the bishop on matters of congregational concern, the presbyters celebrated the eucharist in his absence and preached in the service of instruction that preceded it.

The deacons stood and served the congregation at the eucharist. This illustrates their role, not as counselors, but as aides to the bishop. Just as they distributed the bread and wine for him at the eucharist, they also distributed alms to the poor on his behalf. Bishops often employed deacons as emissaries in official correspondence with other bishops. Because they were the persons most familiar with the bishop's business, a deacon often succeeded to his office. In some churches women could be deacons, but we do not know how common the practice was, or if it obtained at Alexandria.

Certain laypersons also had distinct roles in the church. Lay teachers once expounded the Bible at Alexandria, but in the course of his episcopate Demetrius restricted the function to himself and the presbyters. Consecrated widows and virgins also served the church in official ways, looking after the poor and ill.

The doctrine, ethical standards and ideals, worship, and organization of the church did not change greatly during Origen's lifetime although the doctrine became more fixed, the ethical standards a bit less rigorous, the worship less spontaneous, and the organization more rigid. All these elements combined were a powerful set of internal and external controls on the behavior and views of the individual believer. These controls shaped the perceptions and values of those who grew up, as Origen did, in the second-century church. Christian doctrine was a

simple and readily understandable system that urgently demanded belief. The strictness and the heroic spirit of Christian morality set the
believer apart as a participant in a new and exalted mode of life. Christian worship assisted believers in making these doctrines and standards
their own and deepening their appropriation of them. The organization
kept believers in line, provided them stability, and made them part of a
universal movement.

The Christian church in this period was, indeed, what modern soci-
ologists would call a sect: a religious body that demands a high degree
of loyalty from its members and sharply distinguishes itself from the
larger society in which it exists. A sect is normally ambivalent toward
that larger society, despising its values yet yearning to be accepted by it.
This was certainly true of the second-century church. Origen's life work
demonstrates that he amply partook of this ambivalence. He remained a
devoted, perhaps even a fanatical, Christian, yet as we shall see Alexandrian Hellenism fully informed his outlook and categories of thought.

## The Death of Origen's Father

When he was seventeen, the event occurred that probably sealed
Origen's loyalty to the church. Laetus, the prefect of Egypt, acting on a
rescript from Emperor Septimius Severus that forbade conversions to
Christianity or to Judaism, arrested Origen's father and sentenced him
to death. As his father awaited execution, Origen wrote him exhorting
him not to waver out of concern for his family. Having put him to death,
the state confiscated Origen's father's property and left his widow and
nine children destitute.

# II
# Grammar and Gnosis
## (c. 201–11)

## A Hellenistic Education

Origen's education introduced him to the larger cultural world of
Alexandria. Christians, by and large, accepted the existing educational
system, which centered on the study of Greek literary masterpieces.
Christians did not establish their own schools when they were a persecuted minority, and they left the classical curriculum as it was when
they gained power. The civilization Origen grew up in cared very much
about education but very little about children.[1] The ancient Greeks despised elementary education, which normally began when a child was
seven, because it only taught a child rudiments: reading, writing, count-
ing, and doing sums. As a result they never modified what appear, at
least to us, to be terribly cumbersome methods of teaching. Children did
not learn to read and write words until they had memorized almost every
conceivable syllable. They got to sentences only after they had painfully
acquired an inventory of two- and three-syllable words. Doing sums
was more difficult than for a modern schoolchild because the Greek
number system lacks a zero. Corporal punishment supplied motivation.
Just because Hellenistic elementary education was so mechanical and
did not bear the responsibility our educational system attempts to assume for molding attitudes and values, Christians had no more reason to
establish their own elementary schools than to make their own shoes.

Children were ready, as soon as they mastered the content of this
curriculum, to pass on, if their parents could afford it, to grammar and
general education. Grammar was the more important of the two and
dominated the secondary curriculum. Grammar meant the study of
Homer and the other authors, chiefly Hesiod, Euripides, and Menander,

in the literary canon. General education was the study of arithmetic, musical theory, astronomy, and geometry.

The teacher of grammar, in approaching, for instance, Book IX of the *Iliad* or Euripides' *Bacchae,* took pupils through four stages of appreciation: criticism of the text, reading, exposition, and judgment. In the first stage, criticism of the text, the class went over their manuscripts together, letter by letter, to make certain they were identical. In the second stage, reading, they read the text aloud. This, of course, is still helpful in understanding poetry, but, as the Greeks wrote without lower-case letters or spaces between words and with minimal punctuation, it took an effort just to make sense of a passage. Rapid reading was impossible. In the third stage, exposition ("exegesis" was their term), the teacher helped students understand the text by giving them linguistic and historical background. In the case of Homer, this meant explaining the archaic dialect of his poems and identifying the stories behind his mythological allusions. In the final stage, judgment, the teacher assisted pupils to draw moral lessons from their reading. Plutarch's *On Reading the Poets,* a second-century treatise, is a work on judgment. In it Plutarch argued that reading about base behavior would debase children and reading about noble behavior would ennoble them.

Judging the works of Homer called for delicacy. The Greeks held the *Iliad* and the *Odyssey* to be inspired writings, but, whatever their origin, they were not composed to instruct Greco-Roman schoolchildren in morals. The indomitable courage of Ajax, the patriotic devotion of Hector, and the conjugal fidelity of Penelope were, to be sure, fine moral examples. But what were innocent schoolchildren to think when Achilles, the principal hero of the *Iliad,* sulked in his tent while his comrades died or later in the poem dishonored his noble adversary's corpse? The religious content of the poems was even more problematical than their morals. Homer, as the Greeks had long recognized, was the chief theologian of the Olympian gods.[2] But Greeks no longer believed as their ancestors had. Long before Origen's time, philosophy had transformed the religion of educated pagans into an ethical monotheism. What was the schoolchild to make of gods who quarreled among themselves, had limited knowledge and power, played favorites, wreaked frightful vengeance on often trivial grounds, and frequently violated the most elementary principles of morality? What sublime moral lesson could they learn from the notorious passage in the *Odyssey* where a bard regales his listeners with the story of how Hephaestus snared his wife Aphrodite in bed with Ares and called the other gods to come and see them?

As early as the sixth century B.C., Xenophanes attacked Homer's anthropomorphic depiction of the gods. Ethical and religious grounds led Plato a century and a half later to condemn the use of Homer in the education of children. By Plato's time Homer's admirers had come up with what was to be a standard defense: Homer's poems were symbolic, and were perfectly acceptable when read allegorically. Plato admitted this might be so but argued that the disgraceful literal meaning still would corrupt children. His strictures, however, neither removed Homer from the classroom nor discredited allegory as a way of justifying him. Among Homer's most zealous defenders was an otherwise unknown Heraclitus, who, perhaps in the first century A.D., wrote *The Homeric Problems*. Heraclitus considered allegory essential to the defense of Homer. Overstating his case, he wrote that in Homer "everything is impious if nothing is allegorical."[3] His book explains symbolically every scandalous passage in Homer. He offered alternative allegories of the contretemps in Aphrodite's bedroom. One of these explains the intercourse of Aphrodite and Ares in terms of the philosophy of Empedocles. In this reading, the ribald laughter of the gods at the hapless pair signifies their joy at the cosmic harmony that results from the union of love (Aphrodite) and strife (Ares, the god of war). The passage can also be interpreted metallurgically. Fire (Hephaestus) unites iron (Ares) with beauty (Aphrodite) in the blacksmith's art. Poseidon, the sea god, who ultimately releases the adulterers from Hephaestus' snare, is the water in which the iron is dipped after it has been tempered in the fire. Such interpretations make the meaning of the passage unexceptionable, but they do so at the expense of effacing the entertaining narrative. Although Plutarch recommended them, they could hardly be appealing to children. Even exposition, which should have made the poems live by clearing away difficulties, tended to bog down in trivial and pedantic details. The dryness of such approaches may explain why Origen came to know, but not to love, the classics of Greek literature.

General education, the other part of the secondary syllabus, was arithmetic, musical theory, astronomy, and geometry. These disciplines prepared the student for philosophy by making accessible apparently certain and unchanging knowledge independent of the uncertain and changing sensible world. Arithmetic was what we now call elementary number theory. It dealt with the relations between whole numbers. Many schoolchildren today learn that multiples of nine with any integer up to ten generate numbers, like 18 or 63, whose digits add up to nine. Schoolchildren in Origen's time learned that and a host of similar properties of integers. Such properties assumed an occult moral value. Seven, for instance, is mystically perfect because of its unique place among the first ten integers, the decad. It is the only number in the decad that neither generates (as two fives added together generate ten) nor is generated by (as nine is generated by adding together three threes) any number but the unit one. Musical theory, which taught that harmonic relations between notes on a scale could be expressed in terms of the ratios of integers, made the occult properties of whole numbers more credible. Numerological theories fascinated pagans, Jews, and Christians alike and frequently figured in allegorical interpretation. Astronomy seemed to make a transcendent reality accessible because it was believed that the heavenly bodies beyond the moon do not belong to our changeable world. Their ordered motion thus expresses an ideal rationality. Geometry also gave access to transcendent reality. A few simple and self-evident postulates generated, by logical inference, a grand series of theorems, all of which apparently described perfectly the actual relations of objects in space. The confidence such sciences inspired in the ability of theoretical reasoning to transcend sensible reality made reason appear to be an appropriate faculty for the apprehension of God, the basis of all reality.

## Alexandrian Paganism

Religion pervaded the larger culture of Alexandria into which Origen's education drew him. The Olympian gods, the principal objects of the state religion there, were not a serious alternative to Christianity. The dialogues of Lucian (c. 115–c. 200) make it clear just how dead those gods were by Origen's time. Lucian's bawdy literary ridicule of Zeus and his companions never rises to the level of blasphemy.[4] We should be glad the Olympians were dead. Had they not been, Christians

would scarcely have preserved, as they did, the literary legacy of
Greece.

The traditional gods of Egypt, unlike those of Greece, still lived in
Origen's time.[5] Egyptians in the hinterland still read the hieroglyphs,
practiced mummification, and worshiped animals as they had under the
pharaohs. Greek-speaking Alexandrians despised the way Egyptians
worshiped, but they respected their gods as figures with real power.
Alexandria's most well-known monument was not the Pharos lighthouse, but the Sarapeum, the temple of Sarapis. Sarapis was the Hellenized name of Osiris-Apis, the bull worshiped as a god at Memphis, the
ancient capital of Egypt. The immense precincts of the Sarapeum
housed sick persons who slept in the sanctuary in hope of a dream in
which the god would appear and provide them a cure. It also housed
devotees who vowed themselves to Sarapis until the god should release
them. The god's dark, monumental statue evoked extraordinary awe.
This awe momentarily infected the Christian mob who burst into the
Sarapeum to destroy it in 385. The Sarapeum was a cultural as well as
a religious center since it housed the daughter library which eventually
replaced the Museum library when the latter was destroyed, probably in
270. During Origen's youth the cult of Sarapis was at the apogee of its
prestige. Members of the ruling Severan dynasty were devoted to Sarapis
and depicted the god and the Sarapeum on their coins. Caracalla,
Septimius Severus' successor, built a Sarapeum at Rome.

Sarapis' sometime consort, Isis, was a still more awe-inspiring divinity.[6] She, unlike Sarapis, was one of the great deities of the ancient
Egyptian pantheon. Her cult, which the Greeks transformed into a mystery like that of Demeter at Eleusis, spread throughout the Mediterranean and even reached India. Her temple near the commercial sea harbor at Alexandria was the focus of colorful festivals in the spring and
fall which celebrated the opening and closing of the season for commercial voyages. Isis captured the devotion of Apuleius (c. 123–c. 180), a
rhetorician and Platonic philosopher from Africa, who described her
ceremonies and mysteries in the eleventh chapter of his Latin novel, the
*Metamorphoses* or *Golden Ass*. Lucius, Apuleius' feckless protagonist,
dabbles in magic and unintentionally turns himself into an ass. He has
many adventures as an ass but is about to drown himself in despair of
ever regaining his human form when Isis graciously reveals herself to

him, restores him, and calls him to be her devotee. Although reverence forbids him to describe what transpired as he was initiated into her mysteries, Lucius reports that he approached the boundaries of the earth, that he was transported to the spheres of the planets, that he saw the sun shining brightly at midnight, and that he conversed with the gods of heaven and of the underworld. There is not a touch of irony in this account, and we must assume that it reflects a genuine mystical experience common among initiates. Plutarch (c. 46–c. 120), another Platonist, also illustrates Isis' appeal to intellectuals. His treatise *On Isis and Osiris* expounds allegorically the ancient myth of her search for the dismembered body of her husband Osiris.[7]

After Origen's time, Egyptian Christians paid silent tribute to Isis by adopting the image of the goddess suckling her infant son Horus and employing it to depict their own Mother of God. Origen's own name probably means "of the race of Horus" although we should not assume from this that his parents had once been devotees of Isis and her son since Christians frequently gave their children names such as Demetrius and Dionysius which incorporated the names of pagan gods. In spite of its immense popularity, the cult of Isis may not have elicited much sustained devotion. Among sophisticated people it had a reputation as a racket. Unlike Christians who made baptism freely available to all who were willing to commit themselves to Christ, the priests of Isis demanded large fees from the initiate at each stage of progress in their mysteries. Lucius shells out several times in Apuleius' novel, but Isis assures him that he will more than make up the outlay in a brilliant career as a lawyer. Other similar mystery cults also flourished at Alexandria in Origen's time. Among them was the cult of Mithras, which had a rite of communion superficially similar to the Christian eucharist.

Magic, which gets Apuleius' protagonist into his predicament, was probably still more pervasive in Alexandria than the piety of the mysteries. Egypt was notorious as a center of magical lore, and people there and elsewhere employed magical practices habitually to protect themselves from sickness and the evil eye, to improve their chances at the races, or to enhance their sex life. A. D. Nock, a modern scholar, has also pointed to esoteric magical practices which amounted, in his words, to "private mysteries securing intimate relation to deity."[8] This esoteric magic appealed, like the mysteries, to some Platonic philosophers. *The Chaldaean Oracles,* written shortly before Origen was born, combined Platonism with magical practices known as theurgy.[9]

The belief that the mysteries and magic somehow offered release from an inexorable destiny fixed in the stars accounts for much of their appeal.[10] Astrological beliefs from Egypt and Mesopotamia had combined, by Origen's time, with Stoic belief in an inflexible destiny to produce an oppressive astral fatalism. Isis' highest cult title, "Queen of Heaven," expressed the hope that she could deliver her devotees from the dominion of the astral powers who enslaved them.

Neither the mysteries nor magic, much less astrology, actually explained how it occurred that we became subject to a destiny fixed in the stars or how we could conceivably be delivered from it. A radically dualistic world view made such an explanation possible. In this view the admittedly inexorable power of the stars extends only over the world perceived by our senses and humanity insofar as it belongs to that world. Human beings, however, are composite by nature. Our bodies, and the appetites and passions that bind us to our bodies, belong to the sensible world and are legitimately subject to the astral powers. Our minds and spirits, however, come from a realm beyond the stars and are trapped unnaturally and unjustly in this world. If our spirits can recognize their true origin and dignity and separate themselves from the body, they will be free from their enslavement to the stars. Such a dualism enjoyed a great vogue in Origen's time when many people apparently found the universe unbearably oppressive. There are traces of it even among philosophers committed to traditions opposed to it. In Egypt it reached full expression in the *Poimandres*, a second-century treatise. This is one of a number of works that purport to transmit the wisdom of Hermes Trismegistus, the Hellenized version of the ancient Egyptian scribe god, Three-times-great Thoth. The *Poimandres* recounts the creation of humanity far beyond the concentric heavenly spheres containing the stars and planets that surrounded our earth in the cosmology of the time. It then tells how Nature tricked humanity into the irrational matter of our world and trapped us here. The treatise proceeds:

> And that is why man, unlike all other living creatures upon earth, is twofold. He is mortal by reason of his body; he is immortal by reason of the Man of eternal substance [man as originally created]. He is im-

mortal, and has all things in his power; yet he suffers the lot of a mortal, being subject to Destiny. He is exalted above the structure of the heavens; yet he is born a slave of Destiny.[11]

## The Challenge of Gnosticism

Among Christians this dualism found expression in the movement we called Gnosticism, so termed because it claimed to offer a saving knowledge *(gnôsis)* of the human condition.[12] Origen, as a youth, encountered Gnosticism in the person of a teacher from Antioch named Paul. After Origen's father's martyrdom and the confiscation of his goods left his family destitute, a wealthy Alexandrian woman took Origen into her household and enabled him to continue his studies until he could support himself as a teacher of grammar. She was a Christian who considered herself capable of judging the contents of the faith for herself. Paul the Antiochene was also her protégé. He held meetings, at her house most likely, where he taught secret Gnostic doctrines to Alexandrian Christians. Origen, by his own account, attended these meetings but did not join in their prayers.[13]

We may assume that these meetings were an *ecclesiola in ecclesia,* a place where self-styled "spiritual Christians" could look for a deeper insight into their faith. Christians who did not belong to this group were "psychic" or soulish; they had advanced beyond purely material concerns, but they had not yet risen to spiritual ones. The psychics, people like Bishop Demetrius and Origen's father, adhered to a canon of faith that explicitly ruled out many doctrines taught by Gnostics. Theodotus, a second-century Gnostic, provides an example of the way Gnostics reinterpreted, or, as they would say, provided a deeper insight into, Christian teaching. Theodotus proclaimed baptism, in what is perhaps the quintessential statement of his school's ideal, as a liberation from the destiny fixed in the stars:

> Until baptism . . . Fate is effective, but after it the astrologers no longer speak the truth. It is not the bath . . . alone that makes us free, but also the knowledge: who were we? what have we become? where were we? into what place have we been cast? whither are we hastening? from what are we delivered? what is birth? what is rebirth?[14]

Compared to the legalism that characterized much teaching on baptism outside Gnostic circles, how much more satisfying Theodotus' interpretation must have been to persons who shared the anxieties of the devotees of Isis or the author of the *Poimandres?* One suspects that Origen's exposure to the fashionable gatherings in which such views were presented inoculated him permanently against Gnosticism. Though he himself displayed great independence of mind, he insisted throughout his life that genuinely spiritual Christians upheld the rule of faith.

To Origen Gnosticism meant, by and large, the schools of three Gnostic teachers he often spoke of in one breath: Basilides, Valentinus, and Marcion. Paul the Antiochene probably belonged to one of these schools, and Origen, in the course of his youth, must have come to know all three.

Basilides lived in Alexandria during the early second century. No works by him or his followers have survived, so we must reconstruct his thought from the hostile and often contradictory accounts of his opponents.[15] He apparently remained all his life in the good graces of the church at Alexandria. Had he been at Rome, as Valentinus and Marcion were, this probably would not have been the case, but the Alexandrian church was very tolerant of diversity until Demetrius became bishop.

Basilides apparently claimed that his doctrine came from one of two Apostles, Peter or Matthias, via a secret tradition. The most marked element in his teaching was an insistence on the absolute transcendence of God. God, he taught, so far transcended human categories of thought that nothing whatsoever could be said of God save by the crudest analogy. Even to say that God exists, in any sense of existence comprehensible to us, is to say too much. Even to say that God is ineffable is to say too much. Basilides affirmed, nonetheless, that we can say that the nonexistent God, out of a desire to create a world, deposited the world-seed. This world-seed, which Basilides compared to a peahen's egg, contained in its undifferentiated mass the principles of all existing things. Unlike Valentinus and his followers who posited a continuum of being between the transcendent God and the world, Basilides affirmed that the world, which came to be out of nothing, exists solely by the divine will.

Out of the mass of the world-seed bubbled, in Basilides' account, the First Sonship, the Second Sonship, the Holy Spirit, the Great Ruler, and the Second Ruler. The First Sonship, being of a refined spiritual nature, ascended immediately to God the Father in the transcendent realm. The Second Sonship, less refined, ascended to the Father with the aid of the Holy Spirit. The Holy Spirit, not sharing in the Father's transcendent nature as the two Sonships did, took its place just outside the transcendent realm in the outermost concentric sphere of what was to become the universe, the sphere which the Bible calls the firmament. The Great Ruler was still less refined and did not even know that the Holy Spirit or the transcendent realm existed. He begot a son, superior to himself, who sat at his right hand. Together, the Great Ruler and his son created the eight concentric spheres of the heavens, from the fixed stars to the moon. They then ruled in that realm. The Second Ruler, or Prince of the Air, was apparently the God of the Old Testament, who ascended to the region just beneath the moon, begot a son superior to himself, and with his son created our earth.

A Third Sonship, containing elements of the Father's substance but utterly unable to ascend, remained in the heavy central mass of the world-seed, the part that became our earth. This Third Sonship desires to return to the Father. Basilides interpreted Romans 8:22–23 "The whole creation has been groaning in travail together until now" as we "wait for adoption as sons," as a description of the situation of the Third Sonship. The gospel brought the possibility of deliverance from this tragic situation where portions of the Father's substance found themselves trapped in an alien universe. The sons of the Rulers received it from the Father by remote control, rather as naptha catches fire at a distance, since it would have been inappropriate for the Father to involve himself directly in our universe. The gospel provided the sons of the Rulers, and through them their fathers, with knowledge of the transcendent realm. In our world the gospel caught fire, as it were, in the person of Jesus of Nazareth as he was baptized in the Jordan River. Jesus Christ became the firstfruits of the third Sonship to return to the transcendent realm at his death on the cross. This is what Jesus spoke of in the words on the cross, "Father, into thy hands I commit my spirit" (Luke 23:46). When the gospel has fully accomplished its task, all of the Third Sonship, which consists of spiritual Christians, will have departed from the universe to the transcendent realm. When that happens, the world will undergo a sort of spiritual *Warmestod*. Forgetfulness will descend so that the creation will no longer be aware of the existence of the transcendent realm from which it is by nature excluded, and all spiritual striving will cease.

Why, if this is to be its fate, did the world come to be in the first place? Basilides believed that the world's purpose was to enable the Third Sonship to attain purification from the sins that had become attached to it. The sufferings of this world are ordained to this end and assist the Third Sonship in its ascent. If suffering often appears to bear no relationship to the sins any given person has committed, that is either because we do not know about that person's hidden sins or because he or she is expiating the sins of a previous life. Basilides believed that souls undergo transmigration and can, on account of their sins, return in a future life as animals or plants. The suffering that exists in the world is not God's punitive retribution for sin but God's ordained means of purification. It was, among other things, the punitive character of the God of the Old Testament that led Basilides to identify Yahweh as the inferior and ignorant Second Ruler. Basilides' understanding of the meaning of suffering and his recoil from attributing retributive punishment to God provided Origen a possible inspiration. Origen, however, sought to make such insights compatible with an acceptance of the Old Testament as a record of the transcendent God's dealings with the world.

Valentinus, the second of Origen's trio, may have been educated at Alexandria, but he exercised his influence at Rome during the middle decades of the second century.[16] He supposedly aspired to be bishop there, but he eventually found himself excommunicated. A vision of the Logos as a newborn child spurred him to develop a grandiose theological system out of earlier Gnostic speculations.

Valentinus' first principle, like Basilides', includes a transcendent Father, but from there on their systems diverge. Another name for the Father is Depth (*Bythos,* a grammatically masculine word in Greek). Depth is incomprehensible, invisible, eternal, and unbegotten. Alongside exists Silence (*Sigê,* a feminine word), the female aspect of the divine nature. Depth and Silence are the original aeons (literally, "eternities") in Valentinus' system. They are syzygies, "yokefellows," in relation to one another. Silence conceived by Depth and begot the second syzygy of aeons, Mind (*Nous,* masculine), also known as the Son, and Truth (*Alêtheia,* feminine). They in turn generated Word (*Logos*) and Life (*Zôe*) and Man (*Anthrôpos*) and Church (*Ekklêsia*), each of which was a masculine-feminine pair of syzygies. These eight aeons are the Ogdoad. Word and Life generated the Decad, five more male-female pairs of syzygies which include Unmoved, Unbegotten, and Union. Man and Church generated the Dodecad, six pairs which include Paraclete, Faith, Hope, Charity, and Understanding. The total of thirty aeons in these three groups constitute the Pleroma or "fullness." Although they function mythically as separate deities, the aeons apparently represent various aspects of a single Godhead. This series of emanated aeons bridges the gap between the utterly transcendent Father (Depth) and all other beings.

The lowest of the aeons was Wisdom (*Sophia*), the feminine partner in the last pair generated by Man and Church. In Jewish speculation God created the world by Wisdom (Prov. 3:19), and the aeon, Wisdom, is ultimately responsible for the existence of the world in Valentinus' system. Wisdom rashly attempted to know the Father, whom none of the aeons knew except for the Son (Mind). As she penetrated into the Father's unfathomable depths, she came close to dissolution, but Limit (also known as Cross) preserved her by halting her attempt. Limit then expelled Wisdom from the Pleroma. She was then known as Achamoth, from *hokmah,* the word for wisdom in Hebrew.

Wisdom generated a new aeon, Jesus, whose masculine nature enabled him to abandon her and ascend to the Pleroma. Abandoned, Wisdom, on account of her ignorance, underwent the emotions of despair, sorrow, and fear. She then repented and supplicated Jesus to intercede for her with the Father. Her attempt to reenter the Pleroma disturbed the other aeons. The Father calmed that disturbance by generating another new aeon, Holy Spirit, who provided the rest of the aeons with the knowledge of the Father that had formerly belonged only to the Son. The aeons gratefully generated Christ, another aeon, in the image of the Father. Christ descended with attendant angels to Wisdom. At their approach Wisdom underwent the emotions of longing and rapture.

Christ, for the time being, left Wisdom outside the Pleroma, but separated from her all the emotions she had undergone. The base emotions she felt at Jesus' departure were the unformed substance of the four material elements. Earth comes from her despair, water from her sorrow, air from her fear, and fire, which pervades the other elements, from the ignorance at the base of the other three emotions. The nobler emotions Wisdom underwent at the coming of Christ became, in the case of her longing, the psychic substance and, in the case of her rapture, the spiritual substance, the latter naturally akin to the substance of the Pleroma. Out of the psychic substance Wisdom fashioned the Demiurge or Creator, the God of the Old Testament, in the image of the Father. Because he was unspiritual, the Demiurge did not even know that Wisdom or the Pleroma existed, nor did he know that Wisdom had secretly deposited, in the world the Demiurge made, the spiritual substance that arose from her rapture.

Wisdom did what she did because the spiritual substance was entirely feminine in its nature and needed to be trained by sensory experience to be ready for its perfection by Christ, the masculine element, in spiritual marriage. Until Christ came into the world, Death reigned over these spiritual natures. At his descent, Christ redeemed them from Death and constituted them as the earthly church, the image of the aeon, Church, in the Pleroma. He accomplished this by assuming the earthly body of Jesus on the cross and revivifying it by a ray of power. He then subdued the Demiurge and provided the spiritual natures access to the place where Wisdom herself awaits her return to the Pleroma. Ultimately they shall put off their souls, known as wedding garments, and ascend to the Pleroma for the spiritual marriage, to which Wisdom will be admitted with them. They will then know the Father as spiritual aeons.

Valentinus' doctrine is Gnosticism *par excellence*. Ignorance brings the world into existence and traps a portion of the spiritual substance there, and it is precisely the knowledge of their true dignity and origin that enables persons who have that spiritual substance within them to attain deliverance. *The Gospel of Truth* is a sustained meditation on the Valentinian way of redemption that Valentinus himself may have written. It is one of a library of Gnostic documents translated from Greek into Coptic that were discovered in 1945 at Nag Hammadi in Upper Egypt. *The Gospel of Truth* states that the Father, in mercy, revealed Jesus Christ to enlighten those in darkness and to show them the way which "is the truth he taught them."[17] Knowledge is also central in its interpretation of Genesis 3, where the fruit on the tree of the knowledge of good and evil in the Garden of Eden symbolizes Jesus nailed to the cross. Ignorance, on the other hand, is the origin of our material world. *The Gospel of Truth* makes salvation depend on receiving the call of the Father, the call that reveals to human beings their true dignity. Those who do not receive this call are destined, not for eternal torment, but for oblivion. The treatise thus puts forward a doctrine of predestination that seems to exclude the possibility that all people will return to God or that those who do will do so by their own free choice.

A school of Valentinus' disciples in Asia Minor apparently adhered closely to their master's thought; an Italian school introduced modifications that often brought his system more in line with Christian beliefs. The chief representative of the former school was Theodotus, quoted above, who may have taught Clement of Alexandria. The latter school includes among others Ptolemaeus and Heracleon, both active, like Theodotus, in the second century.

Ptolemaeus' *Letter to Flora* is perhaps the only surviving Gnostic work that makes sense to the uninitiated on first reading. It was meant to.[18] Flora was evidently a refined Christian woman like Origen's patron. Though not a Gnostic herself, she asked Ptolemaeus about the continued validity of the Old Testament law. Ptolemaeus, on the basis of the Gospels, argued for multiple authorship of the Penteteuch. Parts of the law, he explained, come from God, parts of it from Moses speaking on his own behalf, and parts of it from the elders of the Jewish people. Those parts that come from Moses or the elders have no continuing validity for Christians. Of those laws that do come from God, some, including the Ten Commandments, are good laws which Jesus came, not to abolish, but to fulfill. They remain in effect. From God also come ritual ordinances like the law of circumcision, which Jesus abolished in terms of literal observance but fulfilled in terms of symbolic meaning. Since this second class of laws is good but not perfect, the God who gave them must have been the Demiurge who, lacking Jesus' spiritual discernment, is just but not truly good.

Ptolemaeus claimed that apostolic traditions substantiated his interpretation. He upheld sensible ethical standards, avoiding either excessive asceticism or libertinism. His letter betrays not the slightest historical awareness—it in no way prefigures Wellhausen's documentary hypothesis—but neither do the works of putatively more orthodox writers. It compares favorably with the *Letter of Barnabas*, a roughly contemporary document that deals with the same issue from a non-Gnostic perspective. We are fortunate that the *Letter to Flora* survived, because it enables us to see how Gnosticism could appeal to serious and literate Christians.

Heracleon, who probably died shortly before Origen was born, wrote a commentary on the Gospel of John that largely survives in fragments we can glean from Origen's commentary on the same Gospel.[19] Jesus' conversation with the woman at the well illustrated, to Heracleon, his dealings with spiritual natures. The spiritual woman hastens to call her neighbors, the psychics, out of their preoccupation with the material world. But significantly she leaves her bucket with Jesus. This symbolizes her inability as a spiritual person to convey her apprehension to them directly. Jesus' healing of the son of the royal officer illustrated his dealings with the Demiurge and with the psychics. The royal officer, whose title indicates that he rules in a subordinate capacity, is the Demiurge. He appeals to Jesus on behalf of the psychic natures, who are in danger of passing into oblivion because of their attachment to the material world, when he asks Jesus to rescue his son from death. Heracleon's interpretation of this passage in the fourth chapter of John indicates the extent to which he was willing to modify his master Valentinus' hostility to the God of the Old Testament, whom both of them identified as an inferior creator-god. In this way he made his own Gnostic theology somewhat more compatible with the tradition out of which Origen came.

Heracleon may also have written the work known as the *Tripartite Tractate* in the Nag Hammadi library. The mediating Gnosticism of that work, between conventional orthodoxy and the doctrine of Valentinus, apparently anticipated many of Origen's leading ideas. The *Tripartite Tractate* teaches a succession of aeons but largely suppresses the feminine elements in the Godhead and represents it as a trinity of Father, Son, and Church (the last being the totality of aeons or "holy spirits"). Logos, the inferior aeon who sought to know the Father, acted not out of ignorance but out of a voluntary and heroic choice. The Demiurge is the hand and mouth of the Logos, the means whereby it created out of nothing an essentially good world. The Demiurge is still the God of the Old Testament but no longer an incompetent deity working at cross-purposes with the transcendent God. (This is one detail that makes it plausible that Heracleon was responsible for the treatise.) The treatise solves the problem of the Son's relation to God much as Origen did; it posits the eternal generation of the Son from the Father, to whom he is, nonetheless, subordinate.[20] It also approaches Origen when it suggests that human beings go through a phase of earthly existence in order that, through growth and education, they may recognize God's existence and their need for God. The universe is thus the sphere of God's educative providence, where God employs all of the evils of this life, including death, to prepare us for unity with God, which is the greatest possible blessedness.[21]

Valentinus and his school confronted Origen with many issues. They claimed that the God of the Old Testament was an inferior deity, and although the *Tripartite Tractate* is an exception, they characteristically claimed that the world which that lower God created was a terrible mistake. How was Origen to justify his belief that the transcendent God who sent his son Jesus Christ to redeem us was also the Creator of the world and the giver of the Old Testament law? The Gnostics claimed that our salvation occurs when Christ reveals to us our true nature and dignity. Such a revelation can, of course, only come to those who do in fact share in the spiritual substance of the Pleroma. How was Origen to prove that what saves us is our response to the grace of God offered to all? They claimed that their teaching was the secret doctrine of the Apostles and the hidden meaning of the Bible. On what basis could Origen affirm that the church's publicly proclaimed rule of faith was the Apostles' real doctrine, and how could he counter Valentinian interpretation of the Bible without himself being a literalist? The Gnostics integrally related their message of redemption to a doctrine of God and an understanding of the world congenial to Origen's contemporaries. The rule of faith which he affirmed did no such thing. How could Origen meet the Valentinians with a persuasive, systematic account of the Christian faith fundamentally consistent with the rule of faith? All of these issues which the Valentinians raised are central to Origen's life work as a Christian theologian.

Marcion, a theologian from the city of Sinope on the Black Sea coast of Asia Minor, was the third figure who challenged Origen throughout his life.[22] As with Basilides, we must reconstruct Marcion's thought from hostile accounts, but in his case these accounts are reasonably full and consistent. Some modern historians do not consider Marcion a Gnostic since he did not proclaim a secret, saving knowledge, and he did not postulate the entrapment of a spriritual substance in the material world. Marcion, however, denied that the God of the Old Testament was the God and Father of Jesus Christ, so Origen consistently spoke of him in the same breath with Basilides and Valentinus. Celsus, the second-century philosopher who wrote against Christianity, would seem to confirm Origen's classification of Marcion. Although, naturally enough Celsus made no distinction between true and false Christian doctrine, he did consider an important distinction between Christians to be whether or not they acknowledged the Jewish Creator-God as the God and Father of Jesus Christ.[23]

In 144 the church at Rome excommunicated Marcion on account of his interpretation of the Gospel of Luke. He had taught that Luke 5:36, "no one tears a piece from a new garment and puts it upon an old garment," indicates the incompatibility of the Old with the New Testament. He had also taught that Luke 6:43–44, "For no good tree bears bad fruit, nor again does a bad tree bear good fruit; for each tree is known by its fruit," implicitly condemns the Creator of the world. The evident imperfections of the universe—the presence in it of crocodiles and locusts, for example, or the degraded and filthy procedure it provides for the reproduction of our species—indicate that its Creator was incompetent at best, slyly malignant at worst. The Creator, or Demiurge, could easily have been the jealous and imperfect deity of the Old Testament but certainly not the benevolent God whom Jesus Christ proclaimed as his Father. The need for this benevolent God to have no responsibility whatsoever for our miserable universe led Marcion to postulate that God and the Demiurge were, along with Satan and matter, independent and eternally existing first principles. The benevolent God, alien to our universe, was utterly unknown until revealed by Jesus. It follows that the Old Testament, the book of the Demiurge, is worse than useless for Christians since it keeps them in bondage to the Demiurge. That is why Paul so stridently berated the Galatians for keeping commands of the Torah after they had received the gospel.

Most of the New Testament was, in Marcion's opinion, as bad as the Old Testament, but the Epistle to the Galatians provided the key to separating the bad parts of the New Testament from the good. In Galatians Paul recounted his conflict at Antioch with judaizing apostles from Jerusalem and spoke of persons who preached a different gospel from his. Paul, Marcion reasoned, preached the gospel of the alien God of love and therefore advised the rejection of the Old Testament. By being circumcised in accordance with the law of Moses, the Galatians were submitting to the Demiurge. Paul's epistles survived, but the judaizers who preached a different gospel triumphed and, to consolidate their victory, they interpolated into the sayings of Jesus and the letters of Paul passages that identified Jesus as the fulfillment of Old Testament messianic prophecies. On the basis of this insight into the real character of the gospel, Marcion undertook the purification of the New Testament. Like those of Ptolemaeus, whose views paralleled his in some ways, Marcion's critical endeavors embody *a priori* theological judgments not founded on any historical, linguistic, or textual criteria we would recognize as valid. He produced two books which served his followers as Scripture. *The Lord* was his version of the Gospel of Luke, the only Gospel he considered at all genuine. *The Apostle* was his version of the epistles of Paul, from which he excluded the Pastorals and Hebrews entirely.

Marcion excised the first three chapters of Luke, which narrate Jesus' birth and present him as the fulfillment of Jewish messianic expectation. Jesus, according to Marcion, was not born. If he had been, he would have been a creature subject to the Demiurge. His body was an apparition, "in the likeness of men," such as angels employ to converse with us. Neither was Jesus the political liberator the Jews prophesied, an emissary from the Demiurge who, as the Jews themselves rightly believed, was yet to come. Jesus, by Marcion's account, appeared in the world for the first time in the fifteenth year of the emperor Tiberius (A.D. 29) at the synagogue of Capernaum, where he astonished everyone with his teaching. Presumably Marcion also excised, though we are not told so, the verses in which Luke narrates Jesus' actual sermon, in which he presented his ministry as a fulfillment of a prophecy in Isaiah.

Jesus, though he was not a real human being, nevertheless suffered and died on the cross. He thus propitiated the Demiurge and purchased the souls of the redeemed, to whom the alien God otherwise had no legitimate claim. Christ preached the good news of the alien God in hell. Abel, Enoch, and the patriarchs and prophets of the Old Testament assumed from previous experience that the Demiurge was testing their loyalty and stayed where they were on hearing Jesus' message. Cain, the Sodomites, the Egyptians, and the other peoples who had suffered from the enmity of the Demiurge heard Jesus gladly and obtained salvation.

In *The Antitheses* Marcion set forth his case against the God of the Old Testament. There he juxtaposed passages in the two testaments that could not, in his opinion, refer to the same God. Thus he put 2 Kings 2:23–24, where God obligingly sends a she-bear to maul some boys who have made fun of the prophet Elisha, next to Luke 18:16, "Let the children come to me, and do not hinder them; for to such belongs the kingdom of God." In addition to passages that reveal the cruelty and vindictiveness of the Demiurge, Marcion cited texts that portrayed the Demiurge as limited in knowledge and power. The Demiurge, for example, had to go in person to Sodom and Gomorrah to discover what was going on there. Marcion refused to acknowledge the legitimacy of interpreting such passages allegorically. This refusal was potentially devastating. In an age that lacked any conception of the historical development of religious ideas, allegory was the only way to reconcile the relatively primitive concept of God in some Old Testament passages with the more refined concept of God in the New Testament.

Hostility to the Demiurge was the guiding principle in Marcion's ethics. He advocated asceticism in order to make use as little as possible of the Demiurge's creation. In particular he forbade sexual relations even among those who had entered his church already married. Though he objected to reproduction on aesthetic grounds, Marcion commanded this for theological reasons: he did not want his followers to augment the realm of the Demiurge by having children.

Marcion did concede that the Demiurge was a just God, though not good like the alien God and Father of Jesus Christ. Separating love and justice was a weak element in his doctrine, and his opponents tellingly criticized it as ethically impossible. His followers, it seems, ultimately abandoned it in favor of the full-blooded dualism of the Manichees, who frankly ascribed the creation and governance of the universe to Satan.

Marcions' enemies have considered his doctrine ethically barren or even puerile. In modern times the great church historian Adolf Harnack attempted to rehabilitate Marcion's reputation. Harnack considered Marcion a witness, even if a mistaken one, to the New Testament message of salvation through God's grace. Could it be that Marcion alone took seriously the radicalism that can still shock us if we actually pay attention to such sayings of Jesus as Luke 5:31–32, "Those who are

well have no need of a physician, but those who are sick; I have not
come to call the righteous, but sinners to repentance''? Harnack cited as
evidence for his favorable view the extraordinary power of Marcion's
message, which quickly spread throughout the Greco-Roman world and
inspired a church that persisted for centuries solely by recruiting new
members. It seems plausible, though, that his message of salvation from
the universe, rather than his message of salvation by grace, accounts for
Marcion's appeal to the people of his time.

Marcion's forceful indictment of conventional Christian beliefs was
vital to Origen's intellectual development. Marcion denied that the Creator of our world could be both benevolent and all-powerful. Origen
sought throughout his life to reconcile the power and benevolence of
God to the sufferings we undergo in the world. Marcion denied that a
benevolent God would punish, even if that punishment were just.
Origen sought to show that God is both just and benevolent in dealing
with us and always seeks our good. Marcion threw out the Old Testament on account of the unworthiness of the God it depicted. Origen
retained the Old Testament and sought to interpret it in such a way as to
exclude from its depiction of God the qualities Marcion condemned.
Marcion denied the validity of allegory. Origen spent his life employing
allegory and seeking to justify the method. Most likely Marcion's ideas
never seriously appealed to Origen, but they undoubtedly haunted him.

Origen would have recognized that many Gnostic doctrines were
inconsistent with the rule of faith he learned as a child. That rule excluded them by insisting on the identity of Jesus' Father with the God of
the Old Testament, the applicability of messianic prophecies to Jesus,
and the authenticity of Jesus' humanity. This nascent orthodoxy did not
lack able defenders, and Origen may have read the fine anti-Gnostic
treatise by Irenaeus (c. 130–c. 200), *The Refutation and Overthrow of
the Knowledge Falsely So Called.*[24] "Knowledge falsely so called,"
*pseudonymos gnôsis,* is a reference to 1 Timothy 6:20. Irenaeus exposed the inconsistencies and absurdities of the principal Gnostic systems with wit and philosophical acumen and effectively challenged their
claim to present genuine apostolic teaching. When Irenaeus had no
answer to their more penetrating criticisms, criticisms such as Marcion
raised about the character of the God of the Old Testament, he denied
their right to make them and extrolled the virtues of simple faith. He

held, in fact, that there were many questions that simply should not be asked. If Irenaeus, the finest defender of the rule of faith, ultimately found himself reduced to that position, we may imagine that less penetrating intellects resorted to it very quickly. This could never satisfy Origen. It was not enough to expose the flaws in the teaching of Basilides, Valentinus, and Marcion, if the faith he professed was perhaps equally untenable. Origen ultimately answered the Gnostics by producing a comprehensive theological system of his own. In that system he sought to retain the rule of faith and the whole Bible while at the same time meeting rationally the Gnostic objections to them.

# III
# Platonism

## (211–15)

Alexandria exposed Origen to Christianity, Hellenism, and Gnosticism during his formative years. These ways of thinking and believing often conflicted. The Christian church hewed to its rule of faith as it taught and venerated the Bible. As far as Hellenism was concerned, the Christian rule of faith was just one more barbarian superstition. The Bible, by Greek aesthetic standards, was not worth serious consideration because it was written in highly unliterary Greek and none of its books conformed to accepted genres. Gnosticism offered answers to questions the church's rule of faith did not even envision and subjected the Bible to searching criticism, utterly transforming those parts of the Bible it did not dismiss. Origen had to come to terms with these conflicting demands on his allegiance, and the effort to do so must have caused him some anxiety. Nonetheless, he did not have to resolve them entirely on his own. Christians, and Jews before them, had already undertaken the task of reconciling the Bible to Hellenism, particularly the philosophy of Plato. Their legacy enabled Origen to turn to philosophy for answers, ostensibly compatible with the church's tradition, to the Gnostics' objections to the rule of faith and the Bible.

### Beginning as a Teacher

Origen completed his literary education, began to teach as a grammarian, and came to know the extravagant systems and probing questions of the Gnostics during a period when Alexandrian Christians enjoyed a temporary respite from persecution. The persecution that left Origen an orphan at seventeen occurred sometime during the procuratorship of Laetus, who governed Egypt from 199 to 203. The next persecution occurred under Aquila, who was procurator, as the prefect was sometimes called, from 206 to 211 while Septimius Severus was still emperor. Thus the church had from three to twelve years of peace before trouble resumed.[1]

It seems as if the policy prevailing among Roman authorities during the reign of Septimius Severus did not envision eradicating Christianity but preventing its propagation. For this reason the persecution would not ordinarily endanger someone who had grown up as a Christian, as Origen had, but would threaten new converts and those who instructed them in the faith. At any rate, during the second period of persecution, the Alexandrian church found itself without catechetical instructors. Because he was a zealous Christian, a professional teacher, and the son of a martyr, pagans wishing to be baptized sought out Origen to provide them such instruction. Even though his employment as a grammarian provided him a cover, Origen had to meet these prospective Christians at different houses in order to avoid detection. Although he himself was not arrested, a pagan mob almost lynched him and some of his students died as martyrs.

When the persecution ended, Origen found himself, by default, the principal Christian teacher in Alexandria. Bishop Demetrius probably did not care to have a young layman filling this position, but he could scarcely prevent Origen from teaching after he had met a pressing need at great personal risk. Demetrius therefore officially acknowledged Origen as a teacher. Origen soon abandoned his employment as a grammarian, selling his Greek literary works for a meager stipend that enabled him to subsist as he devoted himself to the Bible. It seems likely that this change of occupation was not just a matter of convenience. In the years after the persecution under Aquila, Origen adopted an extremely austere manner of life in imitation of the commands in the Gospels. He apparently went without shoes, possessed only one cloak, fasted regularly, and took what little sleep he allowed himself lying on the floor. A literal reading of Matthew 19:12, "and there are eunuchs who have made themselves eunuchs for the sake of the kingdom of heaven," led him about this time to castrate himself. Such an act would not have seemed as morbidly pathological in Origen's time as it does now: several pagan cults practiced self-castration and some Christians considered it praiseworthy. Nonetheless, Origen's enemies held it against him. Origen did not refer to this imprudent act in any of his own writings that have come down to us, but Eusebius' testimony about it must be reliable. Eusebius had no motive for passing on a piece of information to Origen's discredit, as it certainly was in his eyes, and would not have mentioned it had it not been notorious and beyond question. When, as an old man, Origen had occasion to comment on Matthew 19:12, he tacitly repudiated the literalistic reading he had acted on in his youth.

## Clement of Alexandria

A remarkable Christian teacher, Titus Flavius Clemens (c. 150–c. 215), whom we know as Clement of Alexandria, was one of the great formative influences on Origen during his youth. Clement was a learned and refined literary man for whom Christianity was the fulfillment of the aspirations of Hellenism. He came to Alexandria around 180 to study under Pantaenus, another Christian teacher about whom we know little except that his intellectual curiosity led him to travel as far as India and that his learning elicited the admiration of Clement and Origen. By 215 Clement had left Alexandria, and he was dead by 231.[2] Clement may have left Alexandria as early as 202 because his status as a convert or his activity as a teacher endangered him during one of the persecutions when Septimius Severus was emperor. It is possible that his departure is what led pagans to seek out Origen. There is no reliable direct evidence linking Origen to Clement, but it is inconceivable that he did not come under Clement's influence. Origen did not mention Clement in any work of his that has survived, but entitling one of his first works, now lost, with the same rare title as Clement's best-known book, the *Stromateis,* may have been intended as a tribute to his teacher. In addition, the continuity in their thought is so marked that is could not be coincidental. Practically all the elements which Origen was to weld into a magnificent theological system are present, if not coherently integrated, in the works of Clement.

Some of Clement's works have disappeared, but we probably have the core of his achievement in three books, the *Exhortation to the Greeks,* the *Pedagogue,* and the *Stromateis.* We also possess a few short works and fragments, including a fascinating treatise or sermon, *Who Is the Rich Man Who Is to Be Saved?*

Clement's *Exhortation to the Greeks* calls on pagans to abandon their traditional worship and accept Christian baptism. It belongs to a recognized literary genre. Philosophers, beginning with Aristotle, had composed "exhortations" to adopt the philosophic way of life as practiced in their schools. None of these works survive, but they were popular in Clement's time. One of them, Cicero's *Hortensius*, profoundly influenced the young Augustine. Clement, by this choice of literary form, advertised Christianity as a philosophy consistent with the ideals of Hellenism. The Logos who became incarnate in Jesus Christ spoke most clearly, he claimed, through Moses and Isaiah, but the Logos also spoke through Euripides and Plato.

Clement knew the classics of Greek literature and the Bible equally well, and he wove them together artfully in the *Exhortation*. Thus the legendary poet Orpheus became a symbol of Jesus, whose "new song" of salvation charmed, in Clement's presentation, even "the offspring of vipers" and "sheep in wolves' clothing." "Imitate Odysseus," he said in considerably more words, "ignore the siren-song of customary pagan religious practices so that you may arrive at the safe haven of the Logos." Especially since Clement was probably himself a convert, the *Exhortation* illustrates the factors that could lead a cultivated pagan to Christianity as well as the ways a Christian could assimilate Hellenism. What particularly repelled Clement in paganism was its worship, especially the sacrosanct Eleusinian mysteries which he considered obscene and its mythological depiction of the gods.

According to Clement, the principal activities of the Logos are, successively, to exhort people to believe and be baptized, to train them in morals and piety, and to initiate them into the knowledge of God. That means that the Logos is, in his terms, successively an exhorter, a pedagogue, and a teacher. The *Exhortation to the Greeks* presents the Logos in the first capacity. Another work, the *Pedagogue*, presents the Logos in the second. In it the Logos addresses newly baptized Christians.

Originally a pedagogue was the slave who accompanied a well-born child to and from school, carrying supplies and protecting from moral and physical dangers on the way. By Clement's time the pedagogue was recognized as the person responsible for the moral aspect of education, the person who taught a child everything from table manners to a sense of duty. In Clement's work, the Logos has the full range of pedagogic functions.

The first of the three books of the *Pedagogue* deals, in general terms, with the principles of divine pedagogy. In it Clement provided the answer that was to satisfy Origen to Marcion's question of how a benevolent God could inflict punishment. In Greek, perhaps because the rod was the characteristic means of providing motivation, the word we customarily translate "education" also meant "discipline" and "punishment." It was thus natural for Clement to conceive of God as a moral educator who frequently punishes pupils for their own good. God is also a physician who employs sometimes painful remedies to save patients. The vast majority of the human race, Clement argued, experiences God as a moral educator or physician, but God treats a select few in a very different way, conveying to them the joys of mystical knowledge. These persons are the genuine "gnostics." In using the word "gnostic" in this way Clement was not advocating the views of persons like Valentinus, whom the church condemned as heretics. "Gnostic," as the title of Irenaeus' great treatise made clear, was a word, like "catholic" or "evangelical" today, which clung to particular Christians but which other Christians were unwilling to consign to them alone. In order to avoid confusion, it will be left uncapitalized in this book when used in Clement's sense. The special status of the genuine gnostics does not indicate, as heretics claimed, that they are endowed with spiritual natures which differ from the earthly or psychic natures of other people. Rather, they have attained a level of spiritual growth toward which God sees to it that all people, willy-nilly, progress. If genuine gnostics and those who are actively progressing toward that state are saved by their obedience to God's precepts, this does not mean that others are not saved. Those who are at lower levels are saved eventually, but they require education in the hard and unpleasant consequences of disobedience. The heretical Gnostics, failing to perceive the beneficient intent of God's often harsh dealings with sinners, mistakenly characterized the God of the Old Testament as a tyrant. In fact, such differences as there are between the way God acts in the Old and in the New Testament only testify to different stages in God's plan of salvation.

The second and third books of Clement's *Pedagogue*, which deal with everyday life, illustrate Clement's assimilation of biblical morality to the humane tradition of Greco-Roman paganism. With a few digressions, these two books follow the Christian through a normal day, ad-

vising on how to act at each stage.[3] The day, computed in Jewish
fashion from sundown to sundown, begins with the evening meal. Here
Clement instructed simple Christians not to eat with their mouths full or
dribble their food and advised them on such matters as accepting invita-
tions from pagans (all right, depending on the nature of the entertain-
ment and the character of the people involved) and spending money on
tableware. Clement considered the simple meal of broiled fish Jesus ate
with his disciples after his resurrection the model for a Christian supper,
but he allowed for a reasonable compromise with prevailing standards.
This included moderate drinking for those mature enough to handle
alcohol.

The rest of the day follows the same lines. The night hours provide
an occasion to discuss sexual morality, where the guiding principle is
the Stoic criterion: what is according to nature. This criterion legit-
imates sexual intercourse within marriage for procreation but in no other
circumstances and for no other purpose. Although Clement's position
seems harsh enough today, it was actually liberal by Christian standards
in his time. Clement, at least, did not suggest that allowing sexual
intercourse was merely a concession to human weakness. Dress and
personal hygiene are the subject for the early morning hours. Wearing
clothes made of dyed fabrics and depilating the body do not meet Clement's standards. After giving advice on handling servants, Clement concluded his Christian day with a discussion of bathing, the normal activity at the end of the afternoon. We should keep ourselves clean, he
wrote, but not take hot baths simply for the pleasure of it and certainly
not engage in sexually mixed bathing. Prolonged bathing is clearly contrary to nature since it makes the human skin wrinkled like a prune. The
*Pedagogue* concludes with general considerations and a fine hymn to
Christ, the earliest Christian poem we know of composed in classical
meter.

It is clear from the *Pedagogue* that many Alexandrian Christians
were well to do. Poor people would have required no advice on how to
conduct themselves at sophisticated dinner parties or how to handle
servants. We find concern for relatively rich Christians in another of
Clement's works, the treatise, perhaps originally delivered as a sermon,
*Who Is the Rich Man Who Is to Be Saved?* Rich Christians who took the
gospel seriously found the passage in Mark 10 about the rich man dis-

quieting. The man in question, of course, went away sorrowing when Jesus advised him that if he wished to be perfect, he should sell all his goods, give to the poor, and become a disciple. Clement assured the rich that the passage was not intended literally: actual earthly goods do not hinder the achievement of Christian perfection.

Clement assumed, in accordance with the received wisdom of Greco-Roman civilization, that the attainment of psychological well-being and a beneficial role in society is a better ethical goal than ascetic renunciation. *Who Is the Rich Man Who Is to Be Saved?* is thus an attack on the extreme asceticism and rigorism of second-century Christianity. In an argument that closely paralleled that of a treatise *On the Good Life* by the first-century Roman philosopher, Seneca,[4] Clement made the point that moderate wealth is actually good for the soul: it relieves anxiety about subsistence and makes possible doing good to others. This being so, Jesus must have demanded that we disburden ourselves, not of actual wealth, but of the unruly passions that perturb the soul. The attainment of the soul's healing, not the renunciation of goods, was the object of Jesus' teaching.

To accomplish this psychological healing, Clement proposed a program of pastoral care. Those who are symbolically rich in unruly passions should give to the poor, that is they should entrust themselves to a pastoral adviser who could help them disburden themselves of passions. The person whom they should seek for this delicate task is the genuine gnostic, the elect of the elect of God. Finding such a person will not necessarily be easy since the genuine gnostic will be outwardly quite ordinary. Once they have found and tested the gnostic though, they should put themselves entirely in that person's hands. The gnostic deserves an implicit trust and obedience that otherwise only God would deserve because the gnostic participates, by good deeds, in God's saving activity, and has unmatched spiritual insight. By confessing sins to the gnostic and taking that person's advice, those in need of healing will eventually be liberated from the passions that are the root cause of their sins. As the conclusion of the treatise, Clement related a story in which the Apostle John exemplified the genuine gnostic. John, as an extremely old man, won back through love a youth who had joined a band of robbers, and even though the youth had sinned gravely after having been baptized, the Apostle restored him to the church.

Clement's stated intentions in the *Stromateis* were to justify the study of Greek philosophy, to establish the superiority of the Bible, to refute heretics, and, in the process, to preserve for posterity a "secret tradition of true gnosis" handed down by oral transmission from Christ. The handling of this secret tradition dictated the peculiar style of the *Stromateis* since it was necessary to restrict the tradition to the select few worthy of it. As long as the tradition was oral, this was no serious difficulty since the possessor of the tradition could convey it only to those ascertained to be worthy, but Clement did not want to entrust the tradition indefinitely to the memories of a handful of adepts. It was necessary, he was convinced, for the tradition to achieve the permanence only writing can convey. But, as Plato had written much earlier, "it is impossible for what is written not to be disclosed."[5] Clement took this dilemma very seriously. Just as in Exodus 21:33–34 God held the person who dug a pit responsible for injuries to domestic animals accidentally taken in it, God held the person who brought to light profound doctrines responsible for any harm that knowing them prematurely might cause simple people whom such doctrines might make stumble.[6] In order to preserve the secret tradition while restricting access to it, Clement proposed to scatter its contents throughout the *Stromateis* and to disguise them by passing continually from one topic to another and by hinting at one thing while demonstrating another.[7] Anyone already advanced in perception would immediately catch those hints, and they would pique the curiosity of those who were still progressing. The result is the most bafflingly and tantalizingly obscure work in early Christian literature.

In addition to the Bible, Clement, with the help of manuals and anthologies, ranged widely over the antiquarian and scientific lore, the poetry, and the philosophy of classical antiquity. In the midst of the wealth of allusions that characterize his work, we can detect four major influences: the ecclesiastical tradition, Gnosticism, Platonism, and the works of Philo. Clement came to know the ecclesiastical tradition at a time when its contours were ill-defined. As a result, it is often hard to sort the church's tradition from heretical Gnostic traditions ostensibly opposed to it. What, for example, are we to make of Clement's claim that Christ ate and drank, not because he required physical sustenance, but so that he might refute in advance the heretics who would claim that his body was an apparition?[8] The Platonism of Clement's time was a highly eclectic philosophy we shall soon examine in more detail.[9] Philo was the first-century Alexandrian Jewish philosopher whose Platonizing allegories of the Torah Clement often incorporated verbatim into his work.[10] Clement's ability to assimilate all these elements in his thought was perhaps, by the example it set, his most significant contribution to Origen.

Such unity as the *Stromateis* has is a unity of theme rather than a unity of structure. The central theme, around which cluster a number of subthemes, is the description of the genuine gnostic, the human exemplification of Christian perfection. Linked to this are five other major themes. Inasmuch as the genuine gnostic personally combines a profound knowledge of the Bible and a blameless manner of life, two themes in the *Stromateis* are biblical interpretation and ethics. In these areas the church's tradition, as Clement understood it, conflicted with the traditions of heretical Gnostics. Another theme, therefore, is the vindication of the church's tradition as opposed to those of the Gnostics. Such conflicts also occur frequently with pagans so that the vindication of Christianity as opposed to paganism is another theme. But Clement believed that God had inspired pagan philosophers through the Logos so that their ideas are valuable. A final theme, therefore, is the vindication of Greek philosophy as opposed to simple Christian obscurantism.

The genuine gnostic's goal is to become like God. This, Clement believed, was a goal Christians and pagans shared. The Apostle Paul said, "Be imitators of me, as I am of Christ" (1 Cor. 11:1), and Plato identified the goal of philosophy as "to take flight from this world to the other, and that means becoming like the divine so far as we can, and that again is to become righteous with the help of wisdom."[11] According to Clement, this ideal manifests itself in knowledge, a life free from the passions, and active care for others—three manifestations that will always be present together. Having all these traits, the genuine gnostic of *Who Is the Rich Man Who Is to Be Saved?* can assume a godlike role in dealing with immature Christians.

The knowledge that characterizes Clement's genuine gnostic is not the mastery of a body of doctrine but a process of learning that ultimately leads to the knowledge of God. Nothing is more typical of Clement than sheer exhilaration over the possibility of such knowledge. According to Clement, if the genuine gnostic had to choose between eternal salvation and the knowledge of God (it being understood that the choice is entirely hypothetical since the two are identical), the gnostic would unhesitatingly choose the knowledge of God.[12] It is hard to say which is more remarkable, the choice of the one over the other or the utter assurance that they are identical; no Faustian shadows haunt Clement's appreciation of the intellect. Clement constantly presented knowledge as superior to mere simple faith and presented the attainment of knowledge as a stage in the Christian's growth fully as important as initial adherence to the faith in baptism.

The path to the knowledge of God lies through the study of the Bible. The genuine gnostic has "grown old in the holy scriptures" and "lives and breathes" from them.[13] His study is the search for the mystical sense concealed beneath the letter of the Bible. According to Clement, the biblical authors, inspired by the Holy Spirit, used allegory for much the same purpose he had set himself in the composition of the *Stromateis:* allegory keeps simple Christians from doctrines they are not mature enough to handle and piques the curiosity of the more intelligent and spiritually advanced. Finding the deeper meaning is thus the process by which God gradually, by means of parable and metaphor, leads those to whom God would reveal himself from the sensible to the intelligible world.[14] In this way the genuine gnostic, pondering the obscurer passages of the Bible, takes flight from this world to the other and becomes like God. Such an understanding of the Bible and how it is interpreted easily enabled Clement to reconcile it to Platonism. Nonetheless, since few if any of the biblical authors had any actual inkling of Platonism, his interpretations are often strained. Frequently he borrowed, without necessarily acknowledging them, the Platonizing interpretations of Philo.

Although his interpretations, as in the case of Jesus' advice to the rich man about wealth, often appear arbitrary and even self-serving, it is unfair to question Clement's good faith. He was aware of the danger of arbitrariness in biblical interpretation and sought to avoid it. He proposed two fundamental principles as guides to biblical interpretation: first, that we can accept as literally true nothing that is unworthy of God, and second, that we can accept no interpretation that is inconsistent with the Bible as a whole.[15] The first principle eliminates jealousy and vindictiveness and, for that matter, human features from the Old Testament picture of God. The biblical God thus appears as the spiritual, passionless, and entirely benevolent deity of the Platonists. The second principle is a check. It rules out, in Clement's opinion, the attempts on the part of heretical Gnostics to deny the validity of the Old Testament or to put forward interpretations that testify more to the fertility of their imaginations than to the profundity of their understanding.

In his discussion in the *Stromateis* of the way of life appropriate to the genuine gnostic, Clement offered a fully developed ethical alternative to the rigorism and asceticism of second-century Christianity. Just as in *Who Is the Rich Man Who Is to Be Saved?* Clement offered an alternative, informed by Greco-Roman ethics, to prevailing Christian attitudes toward wealth, so in the *Stromateis* he offered an alternative to their views on sexual ethics and martyrdom. He also dwelt in more detail on the role of the gnostic as a spiritual guide.

Clement's *Stromateis* is more forthright in its defense of legitimate sexuality than any other important Christian work before the Reformation. Clement categorically denied that sexual activity, in and of itself, causes defilement, claiming that "even the semen of the sanctified is holy."[16] In striking contrast to prevailing veneration of celibacy, he considered marriage the preferred state for the attainment of spiritual perfection. The responsibilities of the family provide unique opportunities for spiritual growth, and even the continent widow is more noble than the celibate virgin since she despises temptations to do something she knows about from experience.[17] Clement held up the Apostles as paradigms of the married life and attacked the preference for celibacy as characteristic of the heretical Gnostic hatred for God's creation. This is not an area where Clement had much influence on Origen.

Clement exalted martyrdom as the acme of Christian perfection in the *Stromateis*, but he so spiritualized it as to transform it from a way of death to a way of life. We see this in his interpretation of Matthew 10:39, "He who loses his life for my sake will find it." Clement explained that we may lose our life when we expose it to physical danger, but overcoming daily the soul's habitual attraction to immoderate pleasures is also a "practice of death."[18] Winning salvation in one grand gesture thus cedes pride of place to life-long discipline of moderate asceticism as the ideal of martyrdom. The Christian must die, if necessary, rather than deny Christ, but one should seek to avoid that necessity. Seeking out martyrdom is worse than committing suicide since this not only brings about one's own death but makes one's judge a murderer.[19] The glory of martyrdom does not belong to persons who seek to make a spectacle of themselves but to those who, whatever their manner of death, have lived pure lives and attained to the knowledge of God.[20]

Genuine gnostics have a responsibility, according to Clement, "to impart to others the hidden things of truth" as teachers and spiritual guides. This is their highest calling, as it is in their dealings with others that gnostics have opportunity to imitate God's benevolence.[21] Their knowledge of God obtained through the study of the Bible and their purity of life obtained through self-discipline make gnostics, in this role, holy priests of God and successors to the Apostles.[22] Such qualities also make them, ordained or not, genuine deacons and presbyters.[23] Because God gives them the insight to meet each person's needs appropriately, gnostics can foster spiritual healing or, put differently, forgive sins.[24]

Clement's ideal of the genuine gnostic may recall Socrates or Epictetus more readily than Jesus, its ostensible model, but it is, in any event, a noble and compelling ideal, one that overcomes tensions between the active and the contemplative life and between the cultivation of the self and service to others. The study, self-discipline, and activity that characterize the true gnostic are not, in practice, separable. Only a person undistracted by unruly passions can obtain the knowledge of God, but the ardent love that increasingly dominates the soul as it comes to know God is the power that orders the soul's emotions. At the same time, the nobility of the gnostic's thought and conduct will inevitably attract less advanced Christians and will give the gnostic the means to assist them. As Clement himself put it, "works follow knowledge, as the shadow follows the body."[25]

Clement believed all three aspects of the genuine gnostic's activity—study of the Bible, moderate asceticism, and guidance of others—to be incompatible with heretical Gnosticism. In study of the Bible, the genuine gnostic confirms the unity of the Old and New Testaments and finds how utterly misguided is the depiction of the God of the Old Testament as a petty tyrant. In asceticism, the genuine gnostic does not neglect the body's legitimate needs since the gnostic considers the body a part of God's good creation. In this context, Clement confronted the Gnostics with Plato's belief that we must look after the needs of the body for the sake of the harmony of the soul.[26] Furthermore, the true gnostic, as a teacher and spiritual guide, participates in the educative activity of God which would make all the speculations of the heretical Gnostics needless if they understood it.

Clement's argument with the pagans in the *Stromateis* is not like his argument with the Gnostics. The Gnostics erred by distorting the truth, the pagans by neglecting it. He sought to prove that the profoundest doctrines of the philosophers, and Plato in particular, were really Christian. In so doing Clement adopted a line of reasoning which Jewish apologists developed and Christians adopted from them. Since, as it could be demonstrated, the writings of Moses were older than those of the Greek philosophers, the pagans must have borrowed from Moses those ideas which they shared with him. Whether this were so or if, as he had suggested in the *Exhortation to the Greeks*, the divine Logos directly inspired the philosophers as it inspired Moses and the prophets, the effect of Clement's argument was to demonstrate the fundamental identity of philosophy and the deeper Christian wisdom.

But was not an essential difference between Christianity and Greek philosophy that, whereas philosophy promised that one could attain truth through the unaided activity of the intellect, Christianity demanded faith in principles inaccessible to proof as a starting point for progress in knowledge? Clement responded by attempting to show that some sort of faith is the unavoidable basis of philosophical inquiry since all reasoning begins from postulates that are not themselves arrived at by logical proof but accepted, as it were, on faith. But why should one choose to have Christian faith? The high standard of morality Christians practice and the wide dispersion of their doctrines, far wider than the dispersion of Greek philosophy since they are not restricted to an intellectual elite, testify to the superiority of the faith they espouse.[27]

Clement's concern to defend philosophy in response to Christians suspicious of it proves that his argument for the superiority of Christianity was not intended to exclude philosophy. Christians in Clement's time must have quoted against him Paul's statement, ''See to it that no one makes a prey of you by philosophy and empty deceit, according to human tradition, according to the [elements] of the universe, and not according to Christ'' (Col. 2:8). Clement neutralized the verse by centering on the phrase "according to the elements of the universe." This he interpreted as a restrictive phrase, limiting that philosophy Paul condemned to materialism such as that of Epicurus, which denied the existence of anything but the material elements. Such philosophy was truly "according to human tradition" and "not according to Christ." But Paul's statement did not in any way touch on the sublime idealism of Plato, which could, by implication, be given by the Logos.[28]

Provided we set aside the impious doctrines of the materialists, philosophy can prepare us for the truth embodied in Christianity, and, Clement argued, that has been its historic function. Just as the law of Moses was God's covenant with the Jews and a pedagogue to train them until Christ came, philosophy did the same with the Greeks.[29] The Apostle Paul wrote a sentence usually translated as "Has not God made foolish the wisdom of the world?" (1 Cor. 1:20). Clement reinterpreted that sentence in a grammatically dubious way to say, "God has not made foolish the wisdom of the world."[30]

Origen did not ostensibly share Clement's serene confidence in the compatibility of Christianity and Greco-Roman culture. He could not have spoken of Christ and Orpheus in one breath, and he did not feel at all inclined to moderate the world-denying tenor of early Christian ethics. Although he frequently employed technical terms from Greek philosophy, Origen, in all but one of his works, cited practically no book but the Bible. The exception is the *Contra Celsum*, where Origen displayed his formidable literary and philosophical erudition in order to establish his credentials for defending Christianity against a pagan opponent.

Having made such reservations, however, it is almost impossible to overestimate Origen's debt to Clement and the outlook he represents. This is especially apparent in Origen's intensely optimistic estimate of the possible achievements of the human intellect. Like Clement, Origen believed that diligent study can enable us, with God's aid, to pass from mere faith in the essential doctrines of Christianity to an intimate knowledge of God, and no one is more likely to have mediated this optimism to Origen than Clement. It seems likely, as well, that it was Clement who showed Origen the possibility of a reasoned defense of the ecclesiastical tradition against heretical Gnostics and fired Origen with the desire to produce the theological system he himself hoped to achieve. Clement may have been more systematic than he appears to have been, his baffling and diffuse style only a subterfuge to protect profound teaching from the vulgar and them from it, but it seems more likely that Clement's style mirrored his mind better than he would himself have cared to admit.

## Ammonius Saccas and Middle Platonism

The other great teacher whom Origen knew during his formative years was an even more remarkable man than Clement, although, unfortunately, it is much harder to estimate just how he influenced Origen. The Platonic philosopher Ammonius Saccas (c. 175–242) wrote nothing, and it is notoriously difficult to reconstruct his doctrines, but he taught Origen and Plotinus, the two most influential thinkers of the third century, as well as other men eminent in their time. The historical record is confusing, but it seems that Origen could not have met Plotinus since Origen had left Alexandria permanently before Plotinus became Ammonius' student.[31] Ammonius had no objection to teaching Christians although he was almost certainly a pagan himself; in addition to Origen, he taught Heraclas, a future bishop of Alexandria.

Origen's decision to study with Ammonius Saccas would not be difficult to explain even if Clement had not been around to urge on him the value of philosophy as a preparation for the deeper Christian mysteries. Philosophy and rhetorical training were the two principal ways to complete an education in Origen's time, and studying philosophy was less likely to offend Christians than the study of literature he had already completed. When the poets wrote of Zeus, Hera, Bacchus, and Aphrodite, Christians were reminded that those otherwise admirable authors were the victims of demonic deception on the part of beings who were not gods. Vague philosophical terms such as "the One" or "the Idea of the Good" struck Christians, on the other hand, as legitimate, if inadequate, ways of speaking about divine reality. Philosophy, in addition to being free of pagan mythology, also had the advantage over poetry of having no necessary link to pagan worship. Plotinus' reply to a student who invited him to a festival is famous: "It is for those Beings to come to me, not for me to go to them."[32] Philosophy's disdain for popular religion should not disguise the fact that it was, by Origen's time, a way of salvation as well as what it had always been, a way of life. Justin Martyr, before he became a Christian, went from one school to another with a single purpose, to obtain the knowledge of God. Having found all the schools inadequate, he announced "Now I have become a philosopher" when he became a Christian. In token of this he wore the distinctive philosopher's cloak as a Christian teacher.[33] Origen, by his own testimony, did not go that far, but Heraclas did wear the philosopher's cloak during the years they studied under Ammonius.[34]

It is impossible to say just what Origen learned from Ammonius. It may be that, like other great teachers, Ammonius influenced his students more by instilling in them a sympathetic yet critical approach to a great tradition than by passing on his own particular doctrines. Platonism, the school to which Ammonius belonged, came closer than any other to meeting Justin's standards, and it continued until the thirteenth century to be the favored school, by and large, among Christians. It has been said, "When the church fathers 'think' their mysticism, they Platonize."[35] Platonism had undergone considerable changes since the death of its founder.[36] Increasing doubts among its adherents about the possibility of obtaining certainty culminated in the skepticism of Carneades (c. 213–129 B.C.), who countered the doctrinaire Stoics with arguments demonstrating the impossibility of obtaining infallible knowledge. But reliable knowledge, the best Carneades could offer hope for, did not satisfy those who sought in philosophy an authoritative explanation of reality and a guide for conduct.

When Antiochus of Ascalon (c. 130–c. 60 B.C.), the chief representative of Platonism at Athens, rejected skepticism even though he had not convincingly refuted Carneades' arguments, that rejection decisively changed the course of Platonism. Antiochus accepted Stoic claims to the possibility of obtaining absolute certainty and accounted, with the Stoics, the existence of the gods among the things about which such certainty is possible. Antiochus, in fact, taught an eclectic Platonism, borrowing freely from Aristotelians and Stoics on the grounds that they also were heirs of Plato. Antiochus' eclecticism and dogmatism persisted in Platonism down to Origen's time. Antiochus established a position on free will that was distinctively Platonic. He rejected the determinism of the Stoics and the Aristotelian and Epicurean denial of God's providence in human affairs. He founded his affirmation of free will on an argument developed by Carneades to the effect that the soul's ability to generate its own impulses rules out the possibility that its actions are externally determined. Origen was to make use of this argument himself to attack the predestinationism of Valentinus.

In Antiochus' younger contemporary, Eudorus of Alexandria (fl. c. 25 B.C.), Platonism emerges as a complex of ideas that were to remain fairly stable until Origen's time, the complex that modern historians know as Middle Platonism. Eudorus rejected two important elements of Antiochus' Stoicizing Platonism. In contrast to the Stoic doctrine that God is immanent in the universe by virtue of being composed of particularly subtle matter, he proposed the authentically Platonic doctrine that God is absolutely transcendent and incorporeal. He also replaced the Stoic ideal of human conduct as life according to nature with the ideal, taken from Plato's *Theaetetus,* of likeness to God. In each case Eudorus appealed beyond even Plato to the authority of Pythagoras, the sixth-century philosopher whose mathematical discoveries did much to initiate the Greek fascination with numbers as a key to ultimate reality. It was particularly easy to ascribe Plato's cosmological ideas to Pythagoras since Plato himself had employed, in the *Timaeus,* a Pythagorean as a mouthpiece for them. The function of philosophy was thus, for Eudorus and Platonists after him, to provide the intellectual discipline needed to attain likeness to God, and Eudorus insisted that the intellect was the faculty by which such a goal was to be reached.

Plutarch of Chaeronea, whom we have already seen as a moralist and allegorist and who is best known for his *Parallel Lives* of Greek and Roman statesmen, was one of the few Middle Platonists from whom actual works have survived intact. Such is not the case with Antiochus or Eudorus. Plutarch's *On Isis and Osiris* is interesting in this connection because it showns how pagans, as well as Jews and Christians, could use allegory to find Platonism in the religious legacy of the ancient Near East. In Plutarch's case, the sacred myth of Isis was an exercise in Platonic cosmology with a strong dualistic element. The philosophy made the crude myth acceptable and the myth reinforced the philosophy with the allure of ancient wisdom and popular devotion. Plutarch's *On the Delays of Divine Vengeance* grapples with the issue of theodicy which the Gnostics posed for Origen. Epicurus posed the issue for Plutarch by asking how a benevolent and all-powerful God can reasonably allow the wicked to prosper. Plutarch responded that God is like a physician whose concern is for the ultimate best interests of every individual soul, no matter how sick with wickedness that soul may be. We laypeople in art of divine healing, Plutarch held, are in no position to evaluate the curative measures God chooses to take, but we should bear in mind a few basic principles of divine therapy. In the first place, a wicked soul is its own punishment, so that God at no point actually allows the wicked to escape the consequences of their evil character. If God withholds further punishment for a while, it may be so as to give the wicked an opportunity to become disgusted with their infirmity and freely repent. In the second place, the soul is immortal, and the lives we witness are only a brief phase of a process that includes the chastisement of disembodied souls and their reincarnation in bodies appropriate for their purification. Origen's approach to theodicy belonged to the tradition Plutarch represents.

Origen knew and respected the works of Numenius of Apamea, a Platonist who lived during the second century A.D., but only fragments of Numenius' works survived. Numenius' most important contribution to the Middle Platonic tradition was his contribution to the Platonic doctrine of God. His principal work was *On the Good*, which takes its title from the Idea of the Good in the sixth book of Plato's *Republic*, which later Platonists identified as God. Numenius taught that there is a first God, ineffable, incorporeal, unmoved, and, indeed, utterly separated from sensible reality, who through the mediation of a second God, communicates eternal order to the sensible world. He justified this doctrine by appealing, not just to Plato and Pythagoras, but to the ancient traditions of the East. In doing so Numenius, unlike other Platonists, gave the Jews a prominent place beside the Indians, Persians, and Egyptians. Thus he readily conceded the most cherished claim of Jewish and Christian apologists, that Moses arrived at the concept of a transcendent God before Plato did. "Who is Plato," Numenius asked, "but a Moses speaking Attic Greek?"[37] In the course of *On the Good*, Numenius used both the Old and the New Testament, interpreted allegorically, to substantiate his thesis. Thus, just as Philo and Clement reached out to Platonism to understand the deeper meaning of the Bible, Numenius appealed to the deeper meaning of the Bible to buttress the authority of

Plato. Origen found Numenius' doctrine of God helpful in his attempts to describe the relationship between God the Father, God's son Jesus Christ, and the created world. He also welcomed Numenius' interpretation of the Bible as a powerful confirmation, all the better because it came from an unexpected quarter, of his own principles.

Origen's debt to Ammonius and to the Platonism he mediated appears at every level of Origen's thought, from the language and style he employed to express himself to the deepest convictions he had about the way we can come to share in the being of God.

Simply at the level of expression, Origen found it impossible to do without the rich and subtle fund of terminology that his study of philosophy put at his disposal. Such terminology appears on every page of Origen's writings, and he clearly found terms like *asômaton*—"incorporeal," an attribute of God—and *to hêgemonikon*—"the governing faculty," a component of human nature—essential if he was to say what he had to say. Origen's careful, discursive style, in addition, owes more to the writings of Plato and Aristotle than to other models. In this style we may see one of the most important legacies of Ammonius' instruction. In approaching any subject, Origen was careful to bring to bear all relevant evidence, to weigh competing hypotheses, and to allow no more certainty to his conclusions than careful scrutiny warranted. Flaws in Origen's conclusions usually stem, not from his arguments, which are reasonable and undogmatic, but from his premises. Such consistent mental discipline and intellectual integrity do not arise spontaneously; a skilled teacher instills them. Since it was a philosopher's calling to be such a teacher, and since such intellectual integrity is as conspicuous in Plotinus as it is in Origen, it is most likely that Ammonius was that teacher in Origen's case.

We catch a glimpse of the process of discipline that produced such character and intellect in the figure of Epictetus (c. 50–c. 130), a Stoic philosopher whom Origen admired for his effectiveness as a teacher of practical morality. Epictetus taught that our actions are morally worthless unless we have logically determined that they are appropriate. When rebuking one student for intellectual sloppiness, he recalled an occasion when his own teacher, Musonius Rufus, criticized him for a small error in logic. At that time, Epictetus had said, "It isn't as bad as if I had burned down the Capitol,'' and Musonius had shot back, ''Slave, the omission here *is* the Capitol.''[38]

While it is hard to overestimate the importance of the mental discipline and questioning approach Origen learned from Ammonius, the conviction he acquired that Platonism was the best antidote to Gnosticism was, perhaps, still more important. In spite of Clement's example, this was not a foregone conclusion. Hippolytus, the Roman theologian who was Origen's older contemporary, saw philosophy simply as a breeding ground for error and attempted to demonstrate how each Christian heresy took root in the tenets of a particular philosophical school. Furthermore, though Origen was schooled in Greek literature, he was quite ready to reject Clement's veneration of it along with Clement's modifications in the church's ethical ideals.

The tendency for modern theologians, particularly Protestants, to accentuate the incompatibility of Platonism with biblical thought may make it seem paradoxical to us that, in spite of a manifestly critical attitude toward Greek learning, what struck Origen was their compatibility. It is not, however, difficult to understand Origen's attitude if we bear in mind that when he came to philosophy, the central issues for him were those the Gnostics raised.

Basilides, Valentinus, and Marcion deprecated the church's account of God's dealings with the world as a fable fit only for the unspiritual or as a deliberate lie. They could not allow that the God of the Old Testament, declared there to be the Creator of the world, was either beneficent or transcendent. Marcion, in particular, disparaged the morality of the Creator of the universe with such searching arguments that they haunted Origen throughout his life. Origen must, therefore, have welcomed what he read in Plato's *Timaeus:*

> This question, however, we must ask about the world. Which of the patterns had the artificer in view when he made it—the pattern of the unchangeable or of that which is created? If the world be indeed fair and the artificer good, it is manifest that he must have looked to that which is eternal, but if what cannot be said without blasphemy is true, then to the created pattern. Everyone will see that he must have looked to the eternal, for the world is the faires. of creations and he is the best of causes.[39]

There Plato concurred with the guardians of the church's rule of faith
that to deny the goodness of the Creator was not just an error, it was
blasphemy. The world was not the dregs of a spontaneously created
world egg, as Basilides held, nor was it an incompetent copy of the
spiritual realities above it, as Valentinus taught, much less, as Marcion
thought, the cruel joke of an utterly unloving God. Rather, God made
the world because God "desired that all things should be as like himself
as they could be."[40] Thus far, as Origen saw things, Plato and the Bible
as the church interpreted it were in profound agreement in their rejection
of the Gnostics, but there was far more to their compatibility than simply their agreement on the goodness of the world and its Creator. The
Christianity of Origen's time, even as it rejected the Gnostics' hatred of
the world, taught its followers to despise the fundamental cravings for
comfort, sex, and the continuation of life itself that tie us to the world.
Plato's dictum that we should take flight from this world to become like
the divine so far as we can found its echo in Paul's "Set your minds on
things that are above, not on things that are on earth" (Col. 3:2). If
Plato complained that the body was a prison house in which the soul
was tightly bound like an oyster in its shell, Paul asked who would
deliver him from this body of death (Rom. 7:24).[41]

Ammonius may have made a particular point of the incompatibility
between Plato and the Gnostics. Certainly no one more fully agreed
with Origen in this regard than did Plotinus. Plotinus unambiguously
affirmed the goodness of the created order while being aware of its
limitations. In a portion of a treatise that Porphyry (c. 232–c. 303), his
editor, labeled "Against the Gnostics," Plotinus contrasted Platonic
and Gnostic attitudes to the created order:

> But perhaps they will assert that those arguments of theirs make men
> fly from the body since they hate it from a distance, but ours hold the
> soul down to it. This would be like two people living in the same fine
> house, one of whom reviles the structure and the builder, but stays there
> none the less, while the other does not revile, but says the builder has
> built it with the utmost skill, and waits for the time in which he will go
> away, when he will not need a house any longer.[42]

Another area where Origen found Platonism and Christianity singularly compatible was in their simultaneous insistence on the activity of
divine providence and on human freedom and moral responsibility.

Platonists seconded the church's rejection of Basilides' perfectionism, which taught that sins are external appendages, and Valentinus' predestinarianism, which meant, at least as Origen understood it, that what saved a soul was the nature with which it happened to be endowed. We have seen how, in the Middle Platonic tradition, this insistence alike on divine providence and on human free will clearly marked Platonists off from rival schools. But, though the school tradition which Ammonius mediated to him and to Plotinus elaborated and emphasized these doctrines, Origen could read them in Plato himself. Indeed, Paul's "in everything God works for good with those who love him, who are called according to his purpose" (Rom. 8:28) almost reads like an echo of Plato's "all things that come from the gods work together for the best for him that is dear to the gods."[43]

Yet Platonism, besides agreeing with Christianity on the goodness, if limitedness, of the created world and on the compatibility of God's providence with human free will, provided Origen with what Christianity manifestly lacked, a rational understanding of God's purpose in which all of these seemingly disparate and contradictory doctrines formed a coherent whole. That is what he needed to answer the Gnostics effectively. Here again, the Platonic tradition, as exhibited in a work like Plutarch's *On the Delays of Divine Vengeance,* elaborated on what was already in Plato and directed Origen to find it there. From the viewpoint of Plato and his followers, Marcion's inability to reconcile the pain and agony he found in the world with its creation and governance by a loving God stemmed from a failure to view the occurrences of this life *sub specie aeternitatis.* Had he been able to do so, Marcion would have seen that the evils each soul suffers depend not only on what we can to some extent perceive, the way that soul has acted morally in this life, but upon the consequences of its actions in previous lives. Likewise, rewards and punishments which may seem to be due but not received in this life will be amply paid in subsequent lives. Furthermore, it is by pain and agony that souls in need of cleansing derive the benefits of God's healing correction, and, according to Plato, "it is impossible to be rid of evil otherwise."[44] It is impossible because the soul can only become good if it ascertains the good and voluntarily chooses to seek it. Divine chastisement, like all punishment, seeks to benefit sinners or, if they are incurable, at least to benefit those whom the example of their punishment will deter from evil. One of Plato's chief grievances against Homer and the tragedians was that they ascribed to the gods entirely vindictive chastisements. The stories told by such poets are not at all acceptable to him unless they can show how those who paid the penalty were actually benefited by their chastisement.[45]

Such correspondences between Platonism and the needs of Christian theology in its battle with the Gnostics help explain the extraordinary power of Platonism over Origen's thought, a power greater than he himself was aware. He became convinced that false doctrine was bad philosophy, that true doctrine is good philosophy, and that good philosophy is Platonism. Origen knew how important Platonism was to his understanding of God and God's relation to the world, even if he ostensibly considered philosophy, as Clement did, a preparatory discipline, useful for making the Christian aware of what was already there, beneath the veil of allegory, in the Bible. He does not always seem to have been aware, even as aware as Clement was in his own case, of the extent to which Platonism molded his understanding of the Christian life.

However much he knew it, Origen, as is evident in his treatise *On First Principles,* was, in the words Plato used to describe the philosopher-king of his ideal city, "a mind habituated to thoughts of grandeur and the contemplation of all time and all existence."[46] Just as Plato distinguished the great mass in whom "we may tolerate mere conformity to the tradition embodied in the laws" from the elite whose business it is "to master every proof there is of the being of gods,"[47] Origen distinguished between simple believers who accept the Christian faith on authority and the tiny elite of spiritual Christians who seek to know the deep things of God. For Plato, as for Origen, the intellectual elite is a spiritual elite because the intellect is the faculty of the soul which alone can attain to the vision of true being.[48] Moreover, just as Plato transformed and spiritualized the external rites by which simple believers sought to attain salvation into symbols of the purification that comes through intellectual striving,[49] Origen, as we shall see, understood the rites of the church in the same light. The only place where we shall find a better living example of the Platonic ideal than we find in Origen is, significantly, in Plotinus, whose entire work, from the earliest treatise,

*On Beauty,* onward breathes a spirit of intellectual holiness.

We in the twentieth century who tend to look on religious fervor, whatever its value, as irrational almost by definition, find it hard to appreciate the way of salvation through the activity of the intellect that Origen exemplified and took for granted. Admittedly Origen, like Plotinus, had more than a little of the distinguished professor in his makeup, but the depth and fervor of his commitment to the study of the Bible differ in quality from anything we could find in the most dedicated biblical scholar today. Origen was as much a hierophant as a teacher, a person convinced that intellectual activity was the means of initiation into the ultimate mysteries of existence. We can only marvel at the sheer optimism of a person who was convinced that by such means he could come to *know* God. We should never pretend that Origen's philosophical concerns and his mysticism were two separable and perhaps even incompatible sides of his character: they were one and the same.[50]

# IV
# Christian Scholarship
(215–22)

The period in Roman history from the accession of the fratricidal emperor Caracalla, the son of Septimius Severus, in 211 to the accession of his cousin, Alexander Severus, in 222 witnessed Origen's emergence as a mature scholar who commanded respect well beyond Alexandria. During this period also Origen became familiar with current theological issues, fell under the lasting influence of rabbinic Judaism, gained a lifelong friend and patron, and made his first permanent contribution to scholarship, his effort to establish a reliable Greek text of the Old Testament.

## A Journey to Rome

At some time before 217 Origen left Alexandria "desiring," in his words, "to see the most ancient church of the Romans." We know nothing about this journey to Rome except that he attended a lecture by the theologian Hippolytus, who acknowledged his presence.[1] Perhaps Origen, already finding his relations at Alexandria with Bishop Demetrius strained, had hopes of establishing himself elsewhere. If so, his hopes of finding Rome congenial did not materialize, and he did not stay there long. Rome was a place that would attract someone with Origen's interests. It was, along with Alexandria and Athens, one of the empire's foremost intellectual centers. Galen, the great physician and philosopher, had lived there within living memory, and Plotinus was to prefer it to Alexandria as a place to teach philosophy. Rome, when Origen visited it, was not only an extraordinarily wealthy and splendid city but was the real seat of imperial power, even if within two generations the city that had boasted that its defenses were on the Rhine and

76

the Danube would feel the need to construct the massive defensive walls that still encircle it, and the emperors would actually rule from barracks cities closer to frontiers.

"The most ancient church of the Romans" was the largest and most prestigious body of Christians in the world. Unlike Alexandria its credentials as a center of apostolic Christianity were impeccable. As we know from Paul's Epistle to the Romans, there was already a sound and flourishing congregation there before he arrived. The Roman church claimed the Apostle Peter as its founder, and its special claim to glory was as the place where both great Apostles met martyrs' deaths and were still interred. Nor, for that matter, was the glory of the Roman church restricted to the apostolic age; it could boast of a continual succession of martyrs down to Origen's time. The Roman church had long displayed the characteristically Roman genius for organization and concern for properly constituted order. One of the earliest pieces of Christian literature outside the New Testament is a letter from the presbyters at Rome to the church at Corinth seeking, as Paul had done, to settle internal disputes there. The letter, which we know from the name of its author, a Roman presbyter, as the *First Epistle of Clement,* tells the Corinthians that they had no right to depose the regularly constituted leaders of their church, and, whatever the ins and outs of the situation might be, they should repent and reinstall them. By the middle of the second century, Rome put itself organizationally in the vanguard of the church by concentrating ecclesiastical authority in the hands of a single bishop, and Victor, bishop from 189 to 198, had already begun to claim for Rome the position of primacy that was to play such a fateful role in the subsequent history of Christendom. Victor sought to coordinate the day on which churches throughout the world celebrated Easter with the usage at Rome, although he was at the time unable to prevent the churches in Asia Minor from following their own calendar. Because of this concern for proper worship at Rome, our earliest accounts of Christian worship, after the *Didache,* those of Justin and Hippolytus, come from Rome. Rome also took the lead in organizing charitable works. By Origen's time it had acquired a burial place for its members, the Catacombs of Callistus, in addition to looking after the poor and the sick.

Rome would have attracted Origen as the center of Christian theological activity. Since the middle of the second century, Rome had been the place par excellence where competing theological ideas battled for the allegiance of Christendom. There Valentinus and Marcion sought to make their views acceptable and found themselves excommunicated. There Justin Martyr, the Christian philosopher, wrote the first full-scale treatise against Gnosticism. The work is now lost, but its principal ideas must survive in the work of Justin's disciple, Irenaeus of Lyons. There, during Victor's episcopate, theological controversy took a portentious new tack. Although it had not yet become apparent in places like Alexandria, the Gnostic crisis was over. Gnosticism was still, and would remain, an enemy, but it had become an enemy outside, rather than within, the church. The real struggle, one that would continue to occupy the church in ever subtler forms for hundreds of years, was over the relation of Jesus Christ to God the Father. Was Jesus Christ "God the Son" as well as the "Son of God"? If so, how was this affirmation consistent with monotheism? If not, how was Christ's salvific activity to be accounted for? Origen's exposure to the controversy over these issues while he was in Rome provided him with new issues for his own theology and, because of the centrality of those issues to the life of the church, greatly increased the relevance of his work.

The issues first became objects of controversy during the episcopate of Victor, when Theodotus the Leatherworker, a Christian from Asia Minor, was excommunicated for teaching that Jesus was not a preexistent divine being. He taught that Jesus was a person adopted as the Messiah and the Son of God at his baptism in the Jordan. At that time God also bestowed the Holy Spirit on Jesus to make him an instrument of salvation. Zephyrinus (d. 217), Victor's successor, who was bishop of Rome when Origen went there, felt it necessary to excommunicate a namesake, Theodotus the Moneychanger, for teaching the same doctrine that Jesus was merely human, but he managed to reconcile most of the followers of the earlier Theodotus to the church. Although similar views would appear later in the theology of Paul of Samosata, bishop of Antioch in the period shortly after Origen's death, their inconsistency with the tendency of devout Christians to worship Christ as God denied them a significant following.

This was not true of the views of Sabellius, another teacher at Rome when Origen visited there. Sabellius held that Jesus Christ was God in the fullest sense, and he challenged the view, upheld by Justin as well as by the theological tradition which Origen had inherited from Clement of Alexandria, that Christ was God's preexistent Word or Logos. The Logos Christology, in Sabellius' opinion, inevitably compromised the church's proclamation of monotheism or, as he spoke of it in the theological terminology of the time, the monarchy of God. Rather, Christ was simply a mode of the divine activity. Sabellius coined the term "Son-Father" (*huiopator*) to express this unity of God. Proponents of the Logos Christology found this view utterly unacceptable because it contradicted the clear sense of the Gospel accounts which depict Jesus as a separate person whose relation with the Father is not one of identity but of mutual love. They found it philosophically unacceptable also to speak of God the Father, the transcendent Maker of the universe, as actually suffering on the cross as Jesus Christ. For this reason they called Sabellius and those who agreed with him "Patripassians," believers that the Father suffers.

At the time of Origen's visit, Hippolytus, a prolific if unoriginal theologian whose *Commentary on Daniel* was one of the first extended Christian commentaries on a book of the Bible, was the chief proponent of Logos Christology. As the advocate of the theological tradition that bore the greatest kinship to his own, Origen was naturally attracted to him, and he would have had no trouble following his lectures since Hippolytus, like Galen and even the Stoic emperor Marcus Aurelius, wrote and spoke in Greek. (Victor was probably the first bishop of Rome even to speak Latin as his native language.) Hippolytus was carrying on a vigorous polemic against Sabellius and against Bishop Zephyrinus for not repudiating Sabellius' views and excommunicating him. Zephyrinus, no theologian but a pastor concerned for the unity of his church, scarcely mollified Hippolytus by stating as the official position of the Roman church: "I know only one God, Christ Jesus, and none other Who was born and suffered," with the qualification, "It was not the Father Who died, but the Son."[2] By doing so Zephyrinus, in Hippolytus' opinion, simply compounded heresy with incoherence. The controversy, which was simmering during the episcopate of Zephyrinus, broke out into open schism when Callistus (d. c. 222), Zephyrinus' protégé, became bishop in 217. In addition to hating him for his supposed acquiescence to Sabellius' views, Hippolytus despised Callistus because of his birth as a slave and his allegedly limited intellectual abilities. When Callistus made it the policy of the church at Rome to accept as legitimate in the eyes of the church marriages forbidden in Roman law between noble women and men of servile origin and to allow all penitent sinners to return to the church's fellowship, Hippolytus refused to accept him as the true bishop of Rome. Although Hippolytus' own way of reconciling the Logos Christology to monotheism by conceiving the Godhead as an organic unity in which the substance was distributed between the Father and the Son had little influence on Origen, he no doubt made Origen fully aware of the issues at stake. He also gave him an example of the way in which an intellectually gifted theologian could hold his own against bishops more concerned with pastoral duties and the enhancement of their own authority than with delicate doctrinal issues.

## A Teacher and a Patron

Although we cannot speak of Hippolytus, much less any other figure at Rome, as a major influence on Origen's theology, one person whom he probably met at Alexandria during this period of his life exerted a very great influence: the man whom Origen referred to as "the Hebrew." We do not even know his name. All we know is that he knew Hebrew, that he had been trained as a rabbi, and that he had fled his native land when he became a Christian—indications that point to a Palestinian origin. As a Hebrew speaker he would have been an anomaly in Alexandria, where the Jewish community spoke Greek. It is not difficult to understand why Origen found such a person's knowledge of the utmost interest. The Hebrew was someone who knew and could teach him the language in which the Old Testament was originally written. He could also acquaint him with a rich tradition of biblical interpretation, a tradition that allowed a wealth of meaning beneath the surface of the Bible. It is doubtful that Origen really mastered Hebrew, perhaps because his teacher died before he could complete his instruction, but he knew more Hebrew than any other Christian theologian of gentile birth before Jerome. In several cases he mentions interpretations of Scripture he learned from the Hebrew, one of which, that the two seraphim in Isaiah 6 represent the Son and the Holy Spirit, was probably the Hebrew's own contribution. Perhaps more important than the traditions he relayed to Origen was the fascination with Jewish lore that he provoked, a fascination that led Origen to make full use of the opportunity to learn from Jewish rabbis when he himself lived in Palestine.

The Hebrew's interpretation of Jeremiah 20:7, "O LORD, thou hast deceived me and I was deceived," struck Origen so forcefully that he recalled it spontaneously in a sermon decades later.[3] The Hebrew boldly identified the deception of which Jeremiah complained with the narrative of Jeremiah 25:15–18. God, the Hebrew took as his premise, acts as a king rather than as a tyrant, always seeing to it that people do God's will voluntarily rather than by necessity. In the case of Jeremiah, God knew that he would not willingly pronounce against Jerusalem and the Kingdom of Judah the prophecies of doom he intended him to utter. God therefore said to Jeremiah, "Take from my hand this cup of the wine of wrath, and make all the nations to whom I send you drink it." Jeremiah, assuming that God intended to send him to prophesy against Judah's enemies, took the cup from God's hand. Only then did God command him to make Jerusalem and all the cities of Judah drink from the cup of wrath, having deceived Jeremiah into committing himself to prophesy against his own people. Origen valued the interpretation because it opened up a way in which the Bible dealt, in mythic terms, with an issue at the heart of his theology: how it is that God accomplishes divine designs while respecting the free will of rational creatures.

Another person whose acquaintance Origen made during this period of his life was Ambrosius, a wealthy and cultured Alexandrian. Ambrosius was a householder whose entire family, including his wife Marcella, also became Origen's friends. We do not know what his occupation was, but a statement by Origen that he was "honored and applauded in many cities" led ancient historians to assume that he was a functionary of the imperial court. A more recent, and perhaps more probable, conjecture is that he was a professional rhetorician.[4] That profession, one for which there is no real parallel in our culture, was the most honored and influential in the ancient world. Professional rhetoricians, like Dio Chrysostom and Aelius Aristides in the second century, were in demand throughout the empire to adorn civic occasions with their powers of oratory, powers which the great mass of citizens fervently appreciated. Such men, even if not formally trained as philosophers, often had keen philosophical interests, and, whether or not he was a rhetorician, this was certainly true of Ambrosius.

His dealings with Ambrosius gave Origen an object lesson in the need for Christians to present their faith in a rationally satisfying way. When they originally met, Ambrosius was a Valentinian Gnostic who despised the narrow-mindedness and obscurantism which he took to be characteristic of defenders of the rule of faith. Origen converted him from Gnosticism but considered his earlier adherence to heresy understandable. In an aside to Ambrosius in his *Commentary on John*, one of the many works which Ambrosius commissioned, Origen wrote:

> You yourself, through lack of persons espousing better things, and because your love for Jesus did not permit you to put up with an irrational and ignorant faith, once gave yourself over to doctrines which you later rejected when, having accepted the intelligence which was offered to you, you properly judged them to be false.[5]

Origen's conversion of Ambrosius, besides providing him with a lifelong patron and colleague, must have encouraged him that his own rational approach to the Christian faith could, indeed, assist the church in its battle with heresy.

### The *Hexapla*

Origen was now committing himself entirely to what would be his life work, the study of the Bible. Having been trained as a grammarian, this meant, first of all, establishing the correct text to serve as the basis for interpretation.[6] In the case of the Septuagint, the Greek translation of the Old Testament which the church employed, this was a major task because manuscripts differed significantly among themselves. Origen knew how the task was to be carried out; he needed to compare as many manuscripts as possible, preferably old ones from disparate sources, and then determine by accepted critical means the reading most likely to be the original in cases where the manuscripts differed. This was the method Aristarchus had developed at Alexandria five centuries or so earlier to ascertain the best possible text of Homer. In the case of the Septuagint there was a complication. The Septuagint was not, like the *Iliad*, an original composition in Greek but a translation from Hebrew. A translation, that is, but supposedly not just a translation, for in the face of Jews who protested that the Septuagint was not a real Bible, the church had come to rely increasingly on the legend of the Septuagint's

miraculous origin. The church thus taught that the seventy-two translators were, in effect, not just translators but prophets, inspired authors in
their own right of a definitive replacement of the Hebrew text. Had he
accepted this belief as in fact he ostensibly claimed to, Origen could
have dealt with the Septuagint as if it were an original work in Greek.
Nonetheless, he did not do that. Rather than seeking merely to find the
best possible approximation to the original text of the Septuagint,
Origen revised the Septuagint with the aid of other translations of the
Old Testament into Greek, so as to arrive at the best possible text in
Greek of the Old Testament.

Perhaps the Hebrew influenced Origen in this direction, but he
could have arrived imperceptibly at the conclusion that the Septuagint
was inadequate by critical means. Even if the Septuagint were the divinely inspired replacement for the Hebrew Bible, it was a translation,
and manuscripts of the Septuagint differed among themselves. It would
therefore have been critically advisable, in cases where there were variant readings among Septuagint texts, to consider as authentic those that
most closely translated the original Hebrew. Even if one allowed for
inspired mistranslation, abridgment, and supplementation where the
translators improved on the original, the possibility that copyists unfamiliar with Hebrew would substitute a variant reading closer to the
admittedly obsolete original for the authentic Septuagint reading was
negligible. Knowledge of the Hebrew Bible was thus an indispensible
critical tool for recovering the original text of the Septuagint, and to
seek it as such would have been legitimate for a scholar convinced of
the Septuagint's inspiration.

Since Origen never actually mastered Hebrew, his only practical
resources for obtaining knowledge of the Hebrew original were second
hand, by consulting Jewish scholars and comparing the Septuagint to
other translations of the Old Testament into Greek. Three such translations were available to Origen at Alexandria, two of which were accessible in a highly useful format. Once the church had adopted the
Septuagint as its Old Testament, Jews abandoned it and proclaimed the
sole authority of the Hebrew Bible. It alone, in their terminology,
"defiled the hands," that is, had the quality of holiness peculiar to
sacred Scripture. Thus only the Hebrew Bible could be read as Scripture
in synagogues. This was an understandable position, but in Alexandria

and in much of the Greco-Roman world including some parts of Palestine, the fact was that few, if any, Jews actually understood Hebrew. There were many places where it was impossible even to find one person capable of reading aloud the vowelless Hebrew text. This forced a compromise. If the synagogue contained no one who could read Hebrew, the lector could read the lesson from a Bible transcribed into the Greek alphabet, and, since such a reading would make no sense to anyone present otherwise, it would have to be accompanied by a word-for-word translation into Greek. Aquila, a Jewish translator, supplied such a Greek translation in the second century. Nonetheless, since Hebrew and Greek are utterly different languages, Aquila's slavishly literal translation, which preserved Hebrew word order and idiomatic turns of phrase, was not much more comprehensible than the original and quite barbarous. A second Jewish translator, Symmachus, therefore produced a translation in more acceptable Greek. Apparently synagogues at Alexandria used a three-columned Bible in which, to the right of each transliterated Hebrew word was, first, its translation by Aquila and, second, its translation by Symmachus. Such a Bible was a ready-made tool for someone seeking to compare the Septuagint with other translations of the Hebrew. Origen apparently acquired a copy and transcribed it or had it transcribed so as to leave room to the right of the Symmachus column for the best text of the Septuagint that conventional means could produce and another Greek translation, that of Theodotion, a shadowy character who may have been a Jewish Christian. Origen himself then added these two other versions in parallel columns. When completed, the resulting work was an enormous manuscript that contained the entire Old Testament written out five times. It enabled anyone consulting it to tell at a glance where the Septuagint differed from the other translations and, presumably, from the Hebrew original. Where the Septuagint lacked words present in the Hebrew, Origen supplied them from other versions and marked the additions with an asterisk. When the Septuagint contained words not in the Hebrew, he marked them with an obelus. These were standard critical marks developed by the Alexandrian textual critics of the second century B.C. and still in use today. The work, known from its four Greek versions, was called the *Tetrapla* or "Fourfold Bible." Origen had much of it completed before he seriously began publishing the commentaries for which it served as the textual foundation, so that he must have begun it in the period we are now studying.

Later after he had settled in Palestine, Origen supplemented the *Tetrapla* with two other translations of the Hebrew Bible into Greek. One of these translations was an anonymous version he acquired at Nicopolis during a visit to Greece. Another anonymous version, this one only partial, he acquired in Palestine, where it had been discovered in the neighborhood of Jericho in a jar that contained a number of Hebrew and Greek manuscripts. Presumably the circumstances of its concealment and recovery were similar to those of the Dead Sea Scrolls found not far away in 1947. The version from Nicopolis Origen placed in a column to the right of Theodotion's, calling it the Fifth Version. The version from Jericho he placed to the right of the Fifth, calling it the Sixth Version. The resulting work, with six versions of the Bible next to the transliterated Hebrew, was known as the *Hexapla* or "Sixfold Bible," the name by which the product of Origen's text-critical labor is known in modern scholarship. Origen frequently referred to it in his commentaries and even sermons on the Old Testament, often preferring versions other than the Septuagint.

Origen's *Hexapla* is a milestone in biblical scholarship that makes him the father of textual criticism of the Bible in the Christian tradition. The work itself did not survive; in fact, no one may ever have made a full copy of it because of its sheer bulk and specialized function. It remained at Caesarea in Palestine until the Arab conquest, where a number of scholars, including the church historian Eusebius, and Jerome, the translator of the Bible into Latin, consulted it. It seems as if Eusebius had the column with the revised Septuagint copied, without the critical notations, as a text for use by the church. Some modern scholars have regretted the way in which the Hexaplaric version of the Septuagint has contaminated the textual tradition of that translation, which is valuable to them precisely because it witnesses to Hebrew traditions older than the Masoretic text on which the other translations Origen used were based. For this they should not blame Origen, who was fully aware that the Septuagint could be useful that way, but the subsequent tradition that failed to maintain his critical standards. Origen's *Hexapla* was chiefly important for its example. Because of Origen's work, Jerome translated his new Latin Bible, the Vulgate, from the Hebrew rather than from the Septuagint. And because of Origen's and Jerome's examples, the Hebrew Bible became the standard for Protestants when the Reformation adopted the revived critical scholarship of the Renaissance.

It may, at first, appear surprising that Origen, whose real devotion was to the mystical sense of the Bible hidden under the veil of the letter, paid such painstaking attention to the minutiae of textual criticism and, in fact, to other matters pertaining to the letter such as biblical geography, but this was entirely consistent with his presuppositions. Origen was convinced that the Holy Spirit inspired every jot and tittle of the Bible, so that it contained the oracles of God. Knowledge of the Bible was the royal road to the knowledge of God, and any attempt to gain such knowledge was vain, his Alexandrian grammatical background taught him, without knowing just what the text of the Bible was and just what it said. Origen's lifelong devotion to textual scholarship, which began to bear fruit before he began to write any of the great speculative works that have come down to us, is only the first example of an astonishing coherence and integrity in his work that brings together categories of thought we moderns take for granted as disparate: textual study and allegory, scholarship and personal piety, Greek philosophy and the biblical tradition.

Probably around 222 Origen answered a highly unusual summons: the governor of the Roman province of Arabia, an area that corresponds roughly to the modern Kingdom of Jordan, sent a military officer to Alexandria with letters to his counterpart, the Prefect of Egypt, and to Origen's superior, Bishop Demetrius, requesting that Origen travel to Arabia to see him. Origen went, but we do not know what the two men discussed. The incident shows that Origen's reputation had begun to spread well beyond the church at Alexandria. Within about a decade he would receive a similar summons from the seat of imperial power.

# V
# A Theological System

The period from 222 to 230 marks Origen's emergence as a great teacher and writer. Although very little of the work he wrote at that time survives, the one treatise, *On First Principles (De Principiis)*, which does survive more or less intact would suffice to assure his reputation if all of his later work had perished. About this time Origen attracted so many students that he had to restrict himself to those whose intellectual qualifications would enable them to profit from his teaching. His teaching on the Bible so impressed Ambrosius that he took steps to preserve it for posterity. He therefore, out of his personal resources, provided Origen with the backing to publish extensively. This backing took the form of a trained staff of stenographers, copyists, and calligraphers. As Origen lectured, the stenographers took down his words in shorthand. The copyists then produced a fair copy for Origen to revise. Finally, the calligraphers reproduced in a clear, elegant hand as many copies of the original as were called for. This system enabled Origen to compose very rapidly although it perhaps encouraged him sometimes to be prolix. As a result of Ambrosius' patronage, Origen became one of the most prolific authors of all time, not the least because Ambrosius constantly pressed new commissions on him and badgered him to complete works he had not finished.

## Early Works

Origen had to overcome misgivings about committing his interpretation of the Bible to writing. Clement, after all, hesitated to write on more profound subjects, and Ammonius did not write at all. Like them, Origen took if for granted that not everyone had any business knowing advanced doctrines and that, misunderstood, such doctrines could harm those unready for them and discredit their propagators. He had cause to be concerned since some of his ideas, intended as explanations of the ecclesiastical tradition, seemed instead to modify it. Moreover, Origen did not find congenial the diffuse and allusive style that so suited Clement. Origen may have tried his hand at such a style of writing in his now-lost *Stromateis,* but in all the works by him that survive, his writing is clear and analytical. Origen, instead, exercised reserve in his written works by claiming that ideas which fellow Christians might find offensive were set forward merely as speculations.[1] He also attempted to restrict the circulation of his writings to persons he considered responsible.

Origen's first extended work was apparently a commentary on the Psalms, the book which Christians knew best because it was their principal hymnal. He probably intended to comment on the entire psalter, but he began the work with such a minute examination that he was able to complete it only through Psalm 25. This commentary has almost entirely disappeared, but we do have a fragment that reveals Origen's view on biblical interpretation. In it Origen adopted as his own a Jewish tradition he learned from the Hebrew. According to it, the Bible in its obscurity resembles a series of locked rooms. Outside each room is a key, but it is not necessarily the key that fits the lock to that room. All the keys are available, though, even if they are not in the first place one would seek them. Thus the obscure texts of the Bible can only be properly understood by comparing them with other texts, the process Origen understood Paul to be referring to when he wrote of ''comparing spiritual things with spiritual'' (1 Cor. 2:13 KJV).[2] For Origen this key was often a particular word or concept which, examined in the light of similar words and concepts elsewhere in the Bible, suddenly shed unexpected light on the text in question.

Among the other works Origen wrote around 222 were his *Stromateis,* treatises *On the Resurrection* and *On Natures,* and a *Dialogue with Candidus.* The *Stromateis,* at least by its title, attests Origen's debt to Clement, but we do not know for certain what it contained. *On the Resurrection* combated what Origen considered a crude understanding of the resurrection of the dead as the reconstitution of the fleshly body. *On Natures* combated the Valentinian doctrine that the sort of nature a person has determines whether or not that person is saved. The *Dialogue with Candidus,* like the *Dialogue with Heraclides* which Origen published much later, was apparently the actual transcript of a debate in which Origen participated, in this case with a Gnostic teacher. Candidus, the Gnostic, cited Satan as a case of a rational being who had no free choice since Satan was everlastingly condemned to be God's enemy. Origen responded that not even Satan lacked free choice of the will, and that even Satan could, by choosing to do good, return to God's favor. Orthodox critics of Origen quickly took this statement that Satan could be saved as an indication that Origen was heretical since the Bible consigned Satan eternally to the Lake of Fire at the end of time.

Origen's concern with the question of human nature led him to abandon his commentary on the Psalms in favor of a commentary on Lamentations.[3] This book, with its poignant laments over the plight of Jerusalem during the Babylonian exile, a city humiliated and subjected to its enemies, struck Orgien as an allegory for the soul's plight in this world. When the biblical author lamented that Jerusalem was no longer full of people, he spoke symbolically of the soul's loss of the fullness of theoretical wisdom. When he lamented that Jerusalem was no longer great among the nations, he spoke of the soul's loss of preeminence in good works. When he cried, "The ways of Zion mourn," he referred to the conventional divisions of philosophy: the sciences of contemplation, physics, ethics, and logic. They mourn because they cannot conduct the soul to truth since the passions, inimical to philosophy, dominate it. Origen painted a bleak picture of the soul's situation, but he held out the hope that its sufferings are a purgative interlude in God's overarching drama of redemption. Although Lamentations has only five chapters, Origen completed his commentary on only four of them. Abandoning commentaries before the end of the book was a habit Origen maintained for the rest of his life; we cannot be certain that he ever commented on a book of the Bible all the way through.

The disappearance of Origen's next project, his *Commentary on Genesis,* is most regrettable. In it Origen must have addressed many of the issues the Gnostics raised in the one section of the Old Testament they took seriously. A recently discovered *Commentary on Genesis* by Didymus the Blind (c. 313–98), a writer who relied heavily on Origen, does at least provide us some notion of Origen's interpretation, but even there the pages on the all-important first chapter of Genesis are heavily damaged.[4] We have only one significant fragment left of Origen's Genesis commentary, the section that dealt with one verse, Genesis 1:14, which states that the stars shall "be for signs." Origen picked up on the intention of the biblical author to repudiate the Babylonian ascription of the government of the universe to the stars although he was less radical in his attack on astrology than the Bible would have allowed him to be. Belief in astrology, and the attendant belief that the stars rigidly determined all events, was, as we have seen, extremely widespread in Origen's time. Early Christian authors emphatically denied the doctrine of astral fatalism because it fundamentally contradicted the Christian message of redemption, but before Origen only Gnostics had attempted to provide a rational argument against astrology, and they were only concerned to argue for the freedom of the spiritual part of a person from the control of the stars. Because, as a Christian and as a Platonist, he believed in free will, Origen felt compelled to undertake such an argument.[5]

Here is a case where Origen's background in Platonism was clearly helpful in defending the church's teaching. We may conjecture that the use of the word "signs" in Genesis was fortuitous; it is the term which Plotinus, also an opponent of astrology, used to indicate the genuine, nondeterministic function of the stars in the overall scheme of the universe,[6] and we may presume that he inherited it from Ammonius. In Genesis 1:14, therefore, the Bible for once spoke to Origen in the technical language of Middle Platonism. Origen willingly affirmed that God knows all events in advance and even revealed some of them to the prophets, but even God's foreknowledge does not produce events, which spring from the free choice of responsible, rational creatures. If even God does not cause events to happen, much less do the stars, who are God's servants, cause them. Nonetheless, the stars are the book in which God reveals knowledge of events; Origen, as opposed to the author of Genesis (who sensibly restricted the role of the stars to determining the calendar), will admit this much. But the stars are a book which only angels, not humans, can read; there are insuperable barriers to the interpretation of the stars by grossly corporeal spirits such as we are. To prove that astrology is useless, Origen repeated an argument, perhaps not entirely consistent with his assumptions, from Carneades:

since differing laws and customs of people born with the same horo-scope around the world will necessarily cause them to live very different lives, astrology is insufficient. Origen also argued that the inability to know the exact second of birth renders it impossible to draw up a suffi-ciently accurate horoscope to be of any use. Similarly, the precession of the equinox, which gradually shifts the position of the zodiac with respect to the planets, makes astrological calculations theoretically un-sound, an argument Origen was the first to use. We may presume that the rest of Origen's *Commentary on Genesis* exhibited the same em-ployment of philosophy and even natural science to defend the church's doctrine.

## The Character of *On First Principles*

Soon Origen's use of philosophy and allegorical interpretation of the Bible exposed him to criticism from the anti-intellectual Christians at Alexandria about whom Clement had complained. After completing a number of volumes of his *Commentary on Genesis*, Origen, therefore, felt a need to explain and justify his procedure of interpretation. The result was his treatise *On First Principles*. Though this is the earliest work by Origen we possess in anything resembling completeness, it was not a youthful work. Origen probably composed it in 229, when he was more than forty years old, and it presents a mature theological vision that he never altered significantly. Although only fragments survive in Greek, we possess a Latin translation of the entire treatise by Rufinus, a fourth-century admirer of Origen. Unfortunately, however, we must use Rufinus' text with caution. In addition to the loss of subtlety inevitable in a translation, we know, because Rufinus said so, that he altered passages which he considered of doubtful orthodoxy in order to make the work accessible to Christians in the West. The principal fragments that survive in Greek are the discussion of free will in the third book of Origen's treatise and the discussion of biblical interpretation that takes up all of Origen's fourth and last book.[7]

Recent research has done much to illumine the nature and purpose of Origen's treatise.[8] It is now clear that Origen did not intend to write a *summa*, a systematic presentation of all Christian doctrine, but to deal with the key issue of God's relationship to the world. His treatise be-longs to a recognized genre of philosophical literature dealing with questions of "physics," as the study of such issues was known in Origen's time. An example of this literature is a treatise by the fourth-century pagan philosopher Salutius (or Sallustius), *On the Gods and the World*.[9]

Origen's choice of title for his treatise was a stroke of genius because it integrated the two fundamental purposes of his work. *On First Principles* is an excellent translation into English of the Greek *Peri Archôn*, in which *archôn* is a plural form of the noun *archê*. *Archê*, the root meaning of which is "beginning," is a word with an extraordinarily wide range of meaning and associations in Greek, a range Origen fully exploited. The foundation of philosophy was the search, begun by the so-called "physicists" of the sixth-century B.C., for a first principle *(archê)* or limited number of first principles of the universe, and the term continued to be used in this sense down to Origen's time. Thus, although Origen recognized God as the sole ultimate first principle of the universe, it was appropriate to entitle a treatise on physics *On First Principles*. This would have seemed all the more appropriate to Origen, as *archê* is intimately connected to God's relations with the world in the Bible. The first important word in the Bible, "in the beginning *[en archêi]* God created the heavens and the earth" is *archê*, and it also appears in Proverbs 8:22, "the LORD created me [Wisdom] at the beginning *[archê]* of his work," and in John 1:1, "In the beginning *[archê]* was the Word." Since Origen had only recently completed his commentary on the opening chapters of Genesis, the word would have been fresh in his mind. Shortly after writing *On First Principles* Origen spent half of the first book of his *Commentary on John* discussing the manifold senses of the word *archê*.

Origen also exploited, as, in his opinion, the Bible did, a second range of meaning of the word *archê*. In philosophy the logical premise, or first principle, of an argument is an *archê*, and Christians used the word somewhat similarly to refer to the rudiments, or first principles, of the faith. Although the preface to *On First Principles*, in which Origen enumerated the rudiments of the faith in the church's tradition, has come down to us only in Rufinus' Latin translation, Origen almost certainly referred to them as *archai*. These first principles of the faith were, for Origen, the foundation of his treatise and of his whole theological enterprise. Thus *On First Principles* announces itself as simultaneously a philosophical treatise on the relation of God to the world (*archê* in the first range of meaning) and as a development of a coherent body of doctrine from the logical elaboration of the implications of the rudimentary doctrines of the Christian faith (*archê* in the second range of meaning), the implication being, as Origen intended, that the two procedures are identical.

*On First Principles*, as we now have it, consists of Origen's preface and four books, which later editors divided into thirty short chapters that obscure the overall structure of the work.[10] The first major part of the treatise, extending through the third chapter of the second book, provides an overview of topics within the purview of physics. In this part, a first section deals successively with God the Father, Christ, the Holy Spirit, and the Trinity as a whole. A second section discusses the four types of rational creatures Origen recognized. These are the heavenly bodies, which he, along with most of his contemporaries, considered animate beings; the angels; the hostile powers; and human beings. A third section of the first part deals with the world and with the return of all creation to God. The second major part of the treatise, beginning with the fourth chapter of the second book, deals with special topics under each of these headings in the same order. These issues are the identity of the God of the Old Testament and the God of the New, the incarnation of the Savior, the identity of the Spirit that inspired the Old Testament with the Spirit that inspired the New, free will, the war of the hostile spiritual powers against human beings, the corruptibility of the world, the end of the world, and the interpretation of the Bible. The last topic, though not strictly speaking a part of the series, provides the theoretical undergirding for the whole. Finally, the last chapter of the fourth book is a recapitulation of the principal subjects touched on in the rest of the treatise. The effect of this highly complex structure is to provide a dramatic rendering of how the diversity of our world came into being and how it shall eventually return to the divine unity which Paul prophesied when he declared that "God may be all in all" (1 Cor. 15:28 KJV).

In the preface to *On First Principles* Origen set forth the ecclesiastical tradition which he declared to be authoritative in faith and doctrine and explained why it was necessary to go beyond it. The church's canon of faith is insufficient by itself because it simply states baldly the doctrines necessary for a person to believe while leaving to the philosophically trained theologian the responsibility to seek the inner rationale of those doctrines and to develop their implications. In his summary of the canon of faith, Origen therefore pointed out the limitations of each article of faith as he listed it. Thus, for example, he gave as the church's teaching on cosmology "the doctrine that this world was made and began to exist at a definite time and that by reason of its corruptible nature it must suffer dissolution." Then he pointed out that "what existed before this world, or what will exist after it, has not yet been made known openly to the many, for no clear statement on this point is set forth in the Church teaching," leaving such matters as legitimate topics for theological investigation.[11] In order to justify his own far-reaching allegory, Origen unconventionally included in his summary of the canon of faith the doctrine that the Bible has a spiritual sense, a doctrine the church as a whole used only to justify keeping the Old Testament while rejecting the Jewish ceremonial law. He summed up his theological intentions in the last paragraph of the preface:

> Everyone therefore who is desirous of constructing out of the foregoing a connected body of doctrine must use points like these as elementary and foundation principles, in accordance with the commandment which says, "Enlighten yourselves with the light of knowledge". Thus by clear and cogent arguments he will discover the truth about each particular point and so will produce . . . a single body of doctrine, with the aid of such illustrations and declarations as he shall find in the holy scriptures and of such conclusions as he shall ascertain to follow logically from them when rightly understood.[12]

We must not minimize Origen's claims here. Although his work is, formally, an elaboration on the canon of faith he received from the church's tradition, it is also a systematic presentation of the most profound doctrines of the Christian faith. He wished to replace the faith that relies unreflectingly on dogma with a genuine insight into God's truth. If, in the preface to *On First Principles*, Origen was indirect about this intention, it was to prevent unsympathetic, and presumably less advanced, Christians from accusing him of teaching as doctrine ideas not found in the canon of faith; spiritually advanced Christians would recognize *On First Principles* for what it was and profit from it accordingly.

## The Divine Triad

*On First Principles* proceeds in the first chapter of the first book to discuss the doctrine of God, a discussion in which Origen quickly began to interpret the Christian faith in Platonic categories. The doctrine of God par excellence was the doctrine of God the Father since for Origen the Son and the Spirit are "God" only by attribution. Like other Platonists, Origen was concerned to defend the incorporeal nature of God against the Stoic doctrine that God is a particularly rarified body called "spirit." In the process, he strove to demonstrate that biblical language calling God "spirit" or "a consuming fire" was not intended in the Stoic, materialistic sense. Sharing in the Holy Spirit of God, he argued, is not like sharing in a material substance that can be divided up into parts; it is like sharing, as physicians do in a science like medicine, by participating in the whole. Drawing on traditional Platonic vocabulary to describe God's transcendence, Origen described God as imcomprehensible, immeasurable, and incomposite as well as incorporeal. He also employed the Neopythagorean term *henad*, which expresses the utter unity and simplicity of God in contrast to the multiplicity of the world.

In the section of the second book that dealt with the identity of the God of the Old Testament and the God of the New Testament, Origen stressed, in equally Platonic fashion, the beneficence of God. This meant that he could not allow any suggestion that God actually experienced wrath. He therefore took pains to interpret allegorically passages in the Bible that, taken literally, presented an unworthy or incoherent image of God, providing fuel for Gnostic criticism. Since Origen lacked the notion of progressive revelation that enables us to accept as primitive but still genuine the concept of God in early strata of the Old Testament, the allegory could be drastic. He also argued against Marcion that it is quite consistent for God to be both just and good.

Origen's stress on the absolute transcendence of God, sharpened by Platonism, made it all the more necessary to postulate some sort of mediator between God and the world. Here again Origen's philosophical background enabled him to present coherently and systematically the nature and role of that mediator, whom he naturally identified as

Christ. The resulting Christology, the subject of Origen's next principal discussion, was incalculably important for later Christian theology.

Origen's first endeavor, in his discussion of Christ, whom he identified as the Son of God, was to define the Son's relation to the Father. This meant showing how it was possible for the Son to be a separate divine hypostasis, hypostasis being a philosophical term for what we might call an individual entity. How is it that we can speak, for example, of the Son as God's Wisdom? When we speak of a person's wisdom we do not in any sense imply that that wisdom has an existence apart from the person who is wise; wisdom in that case is not a hypostasis. In the case of the Son, however, we cannot simply identify him, as Sabellius did at Rome, as a mode of the Father's existence. To do so would, among other things, make it impossible for the Son to mediate between God and the world. At the same time, Origen could not allow for the Son to be a completely separate being from the Father; to do that would be to admit the existence of two separate Gods. Platonic categories also enabled Origen to arrive at a formula, "eternal generation," to describe the Son's relation to the Father. We need to take a close look at both words in the formula.

Generation indicated that the Son shares the same essential characteristics as the Father, since like always begets like. It is his participation in these essential characteristics of God—characteristics such as goodness, truth, life, and power—that distinguishes the Son, along with the Holy Spirit, from all other beings. But the manner of the Son's generation, unlike the generation of the aeons in Valentinus' system, bears no resemblance whatever to ours. It resembles, rather, the way in which a thought proceeds from the will or the way that brightness proceeds from light. Origen justified these metaphors from Platonism on the basis of the one book in his Bible that displayed marked Platonic influence itself, the book of Wisdom. In it Wisdom, which Origen identified with Christ, is "a pure emanation of the glory of the Almighty" (Wis. 7:25).

The adjective in the formula, "eternal," is at least as important as the noun. It means that there was no time when the Son did not exist. Origen found it necessary to affirm this in order to safeguard the changeless simplicity of God. There could not be a time when the Father lacked a Son since if there had been, the Father's nature would have to have changed in order to be a Father. This is good Platonic reasoning, and we find it in Plotinus' description of the first and second hypostases in his philosophical system.[13] Later, in the fourth century, the application of "eternal" to the Son became controversial because of its implication that the Son and the Father are essentially similar, but Origen seems to have used the term more with the Father in mind than the Son. The notion of eternal generation does repudiate, however, the view of the two Theodotuses at Rome, who held that the Father, at Christ's baptism in the Jordan, adopted him as his Son.

Within the context of Origen's system, the Son, as the second divine hypostasis, is the necessary link between the Father and the world. The Father is absolutely simple, but the Son is multiple and accounts for the diversity of the creation.[14] Origen expressed the Son's nature as multiple in terms of "aspects," *epinoiai*, a philosophical term that implies an entirely conceptual distinction as opposed to *hypostasis*, which implies a real distinction. Since Origen more fully discussed his Christology in the first two books of his *Commentary on John*, a work written only a short time later, that work will supplement the discussion here. The aspects are traditional Christological titles such as Logos and resurrection, titles of which the Gospel of John is especially full. The Valentinians ascribed these titles to separate aeons, but Origen held that they were ways in which a single divine hypostasis appears to us. The *epinoiai* fall into two groups which correspond to the Son's activity in creation and in redemption. The first group, involved in creation, belong to the Son's eternal nature. The second group are the Son's response to the fall of rational creatures and provide them the means to return to union with the Father. There are four *epinoiai* in the first group: Wisdom, Word, Life, and Truth.[15] Conceived as Wisdom, the Son is the Demiurge or Artisan of Plato's *Timaeus* who created the world according to the pattern of preexistent ideas,[16] ideas which Origen, in company with Plotinus, believed to exist within the second hypostasis itself, not as independent entities. Conceived as Word or Logos, the Son is the immanent rationality that animates the cosmos and is the basis of human rationality. This is a concept which Middle Platonism borrowed from the Stoics and applied to the world-soul of Plato's

*Timaeus*. The *epinoiai* of the Son as Life and Truth express two functions of the Son as Logos. As Life the Logos animates the cosmos; as Truth it is the source of rationality.

Those *epinoiai* of the Son that characterize his role as redeemer correspond, like those that characterize his role as creator, to roles of the second divine hypostasis in Platonism. Platonists, like Christians, conceived of the second hypostasis as the means by which the creature can reascend to the simplicity of the first hypostasis as well as the principle accounting for the diversity of the world. The Son's *epinoiai* in the order of redemption are far more varied than in the order of creation. There need to be as many *epinoiai* here as there are needs which their fallen state imposes on rational creatures and as there are stages in the ascent of those creatures back to God. Most Christological titles, therefore, fall into this group; a few examples are Resurrection, Good Shepherd, Way, and Vine. Christ is the Resurrection in delivering us from mortality. Chirst is Good Shepherd to those who have fallen so far as to become brutish in their understanding. Christ is the Way as an intellectual and moral guide. Christ is the Vine in making possible at the highest level of the rational creature's ascent the mystical contemplation of God. This last epithet requires a little explanation. Taking his cue from the wine that makes glad the heart in Psalm 104, Origen argued that Christ as the Vine causes the rational faculty, which the Hebrews knew as the heart, to be glad by transporting it in ecstasy beyond ordinary human concerns.[17] It is fascinating to see how the rather dry philosophical concept of the diversity of the second divine hypostasis acquires life and color in Origen's hands as it becomes the organizing principle for the teeming variety of Christological titles that were his legacy in the Christian tradition. The Valentinian use of those titles, by contrast with Origen's, appears artificial and lifeless, as no doubt Origen intended it to.

A corollary to Origen's identification of Christ with the second divine hypostasis of Platonism is the Son's inferiority to the Father. As an emanation outward from the utter simplicity of the Father toward the utter multiplicity of the world, the second hypostasis is, necessarily, less perfect than the first or, as Plotinus said, "the offspring is always minor."[18] Because of this, Origen, although he insisted on Christ's divinity and utter difference from all lesser beings, was unwilling to ascribe to the Son the same dignity he ascribed to the Father. The Son as a mediating hypostasis is inferior to the Father and represents a lower stage in the cosmological scale. Only the Father, Origen said, is truly God; the Son is God only by participation in the Father. He found in the opening verse of the Gospel of John a grammatical construction that confirmed his evaluation of the Son's lesser divinity. There the biblical author makes use of the Greek definite article in referring to God but leaves off the article in referring to Christ, the Word, as God.[19] The Son, for Origen, is not God but the image of God, the archetype of all rational creatures. In a sense, what we are in relation to the Son, the Son is in relation to the Father.[20] Thus knowledge of the Father is superior to knowledge of the Son, and it is knowledge of the Father, arrived at through the Son, that distinguishes spiritual Christians from simple Christians who know only the Son. Similarly, it is appropriate to pray to the Father through the Son but not to the Son by himself. This tendency to subordinate the Son to the Father caused Origen no trouble theologically during his lifetime since most Christians took such a subordination for granted. Later, when the development of Trinitarian theology in the fourth century made subordinationism untenable, it brought Origen's theology into disrepute.

As long as he dealt with the Son's relation to the Father and his role as a cosmological principle, Origen found it easy to be simultaneously a Christian and a Platonist. This was not so when he came, in the sixth chapter of the second book of *On First Principles*, to the doctrine of the Incarnation. An anecdote from Augustine's *City of God* illustrates the dilemma. According to Augustine, a Platonist once told a Christian bishop that the opening verses of the Gospel of John—"In the beginning was the Word, and the Word was with God, and the Word was God," etc.—should be written in gold and set up in all the churches. But the Platonist did not include the fourteenth verse, "And the Word became flesh and dwelt among us," which he blushed to say.[21] The Christian doctrine that the Son of God became human, as the Platonists viewed it, absurdly united the highest mode of existence, God, with the very lowest mode, matter. For God to become human, assuming a body, was for them an inconceivable degradation of the divine nature, and they charged Christians with boorishness and irreverence for even suggesting that such a thing had happened. Gnostics found the Incarnation, if anything, even harder to accept than Platonists did. Their belief that matter was the creation of an inferior deity made them speculate that what appeared to be Jesus Christ's human body was only a phantom or that Jesus was simply a person inspired by a power sent from above. The church, however, held to the belief that Jesus Christ was God come in the flesh, and in this doctrine Origen fully concurred. This was so even though, as a Platonist of sorts himself, he was aware how seemingly paradoxical was the doctrine that Jesus Christ was both God and human. He wrote:

> When . . . we see in him some things so human that they appear in no way to differ from the common frailty of mortals, and some things so divine that they are appropriate to nothing else but the primal and ineffable nature of deity, the human understanding with its narrow limits is baffled, and struck with amazement at so mighty a wonder knows not which way to turn, what to hold to, or whither to betake itself. If it thinks of God, it sees a man; if it thinks of a man, it beholds one returning from the dead with spoils after vanquishing the kingdom of death.[22]

Although Origen's acceptance of the doctrine of the Incarnation sharply distinguished him from non-Christian Platonists, the problem which was for them the central objection to Christian doctrine was for him the central issue to be resolved. In resolving it, Origen, as elsewhere, made the fullest use of his philosophical background. He felt the need of a mediatory element to explain the union of the second divine hypostasis and Christ's human body. This mediatory element he found in Christ's human soul since the soul, according to Plato's *Timaeus* and Aristotle's *On the Soul*, is dual: being rational it could be united to the Godhead, but it also had the capacity to be united with a human body. By postulating the union between Christ's body, human soul, and divine nature, Origen explained the Incarnation and allowed for Christ's full humanity. The Son did not just become a body, but a human being, body and soul. Since Origen believed that human souls do not come into existence with the body but are preexistent rational spirits, it was possible for him to postulate a preexistent union between Christ and a human soul. Christ's human soul, Origen believed, was the one rational spirit who did not in the least depart from God in the primeval fall that gave rise to our world. Through its willing adherence to God, when all other spirits fell, this human soul became associated with the Son. By its steadfast union in the ages before the Incarnation, it eventually acquired natural goodness which otherwise belongs only to God and became one personality with the Son. When this soul, therefore, joined a human body in the person of Jesus of Nazareth, the result was a complete union of God and humanity. Condescending as he did to take human flesh, the Son provides a supreme example of loving service. His doing so enabled us to apprehend the nature of God in a manner within our grasp, and Origen would insist, against the claims of the Platonists, that this was the only way God could really accomplish such a purpose. Origen, however, did not consider God's activity in the Incarnation an end in itself but the means to bring us to the knowledge of God. We should seek not simply to know Christ after the flesh but to progress from the knowledge of the incarnate Son to the knowledge of the Son as the second divine hypostasis and ultimately to the knowledge of God the Father.

*On First Principles* does not deal specifically with what we call the doctrine of the atonement, the way in which Christ accomplished the salvation of the human race. Like other writers of the time, Origen described Christ's death on the cross and subsequent resurrection as the definitive defeat of Satan and conquest of death. He also described Christ's death as a sacrifice. This raises the puzzling question, to whom was the sacrifice directed?[23] It could not have been a propitiatory sacrifice directed toward God since the sacrificial atonement of Christ has long been conceived of in Western Christian theology. A propitiatory sacrifice would be one in which Christ died to propitiate God's righteous wrath against sinful humanity, but God, Origen taught, had no wrath to be propitiated. Although Origen could speak of Christ's sacrifice in such a way as to suggest that it was a sacrifice intended to avert the machinations of Satan, he seems to have conceived of it primarily as an offering directed toward us. Christ's self-giving life and sacrificial death transform us into beings worthy of the knowledge of God. Christ heals us of our sin by providing us an example of perfect love and obedience and by teaching us, at whatever level of comprehension we are capable of receiving it, the way to ascend mentally to God.

Origen followed his discussion of the doctrine of Christ with a discussion of the doctrine of the Holy Spirit. He taught that the Holy Spirit is a third eternally existing divine hypostasis, subordinate to the Son, whose function is the inspiration and the sanctification of believers. Like the doctrine of Christ's Incarnation, the doctrine of the Holy Spirit owes nothing to Platonism. Origen stated that while some pagan philosophers knew of the Father and of the Son, none knew of the existence of the Holy Spirit as a third divine hypostasis (a statement which implies that Plotinus, whose doctrine of three divine hypostases does bear a superficial resemblance to the Christian Trinity, probably did not derive that doctrine from Ammonius). As with the case of the doctrine of the Incarnation, Origen, though affirming the traditional doctrine of the Holy Spirit, had some difficulty with it. Since Christ is the link between God and the world in Origen's Platonic system, the Spirit has little obvious place. It is the Son, as we have seen, who contains the ideas which are the pattern of the sensible world, who created the world according to the pattern of those ideas, who animates the universe, and who provides other creatures with the possibility of rationality. Though later Christian theologians gave the Holy Spirit a role in creation, Origen did not. Genesis 1:2, "and the Spirit of God was moving over the face of the waters," the biblical warrant later cited to prove the Spirit's role in creation, only proved to Origen that the Spirit, like the Son, existed eternally.

Uncertainty about the nature and role of the Holy Spirit, however, was not peculiar to Origen. While Christians in his time had a general idea of the Spirit's function, they affirmed little else about it. In 325 the Council of Nicea, which spared no pains over the doctrine of Christ, affirmed in its creed only "and I believe in the Holy Spirit," leaving even the Spirit's place in the divine Triad a matter of conjecture. What Christians did affirm was that the Holy Spirit inspired the prophets and Apostles and that it was given to believers at baptism to keep them from sinning. Christians also worshiped the Holy Spirit along with the Father and the Son, a practice that implied its status as a third divine hypostasis. Within these modest limits, Origen provided the doctrine of the Spirit with theological elaboration.

Origen, denying the Spirit a role in creation, limited its role to the inspiration and sanctification of believing Christians. As the inspirer of the biblical authors, the Spirit played an important role in Origen's understanding of biblical interpretation. Just as the Holy Spirit gave the authors of the Bible insight into divine mysteries that enabled them to compose their writings, so the same Spirit inspired interpreters of the Bible to understand those mysteries. Without the Spirit it would be impossible to get beyond a simple, literal reading of the Bible. Before the coming of Christ, the Jewish people, uninspired by the Spirit except in special cases, failed to comprehend those mysteries, and those of them who reject Christ still fail to comprehend them. The coming of Christ, however, made the inspiration of the Spirit accessible to all believers through the bestowal of the Spirit at baptism. The fruit of this is that all Christians have at least a minimal grasp of the spiritual sense of the Bible. Thus all Christians are able to understand that the ceremonial law of the Old Testament should not be literally obeyed. Christians more advanced in the knowledge of God receive a special gift of the Spirit to comprehend on a far more profound level the hidden mysteries of the Bible. In Origen, as in Clement, this knowledge of God is intimately tied to holiness of life, so that the Spirit's role as inspirer and sanctifier is fundamentally the same.

Origen discussed only briefly what we call the doctrine of the Trinity. Actually the word "Trinity" is anachronistic when speaking of Origen's doctrine since it implies a more fully developed doctrine than the church in his time proclaimed. "Triad" is the word Origen used. Although he considered the doctrine of the Holy Spirit peculiar to the church, Origen employed Platonic concepts to explain the structure of the divine Triad. He thus explained the relation of the Holy Spirit to the Son on the analogy of the relation of the Son to the Father in terms of separate hypostatic existence, eternal generation, and subordination. The doctrine of the Trinity, however, was not one of Origen's major interests, and he made little contribution to the church's understanding of it.

## Rational Creatures

Origen followed his discussion of God with a discussion of rational creatures. These beings have the gift of reason as their principal attribute, and since they are rational, Origen, who accepted the arguments of Plato's *Phaedo* on the immortality of the soul, considered them to be naturally immortal as well. The spiritual world of rational creatures was, Origen believed, God's original creation, and the creation of the material world came later. He claimed biblical warrant for his doctrine of two creations in the puzzling first verse of Genesis, "In the beginning God created the heavens and the earth." He accepted the interpretation of Philo that this verse, which would seem to be superfluous in light of the detailed description of the creation in the rest of the first chapter, actually applies to the creation of the spiritual world, the rest of the chapter being the description of the material world. God, Origen held, must have created a limited number of rational creatures, as an infinite number of them would be incomprehensible even to God, and to allow that the All-knowing could fail to comprehend anything would be to postulate what is not possible, a self-contradiction in the nature of God. Origen may have learned of the problem of the incomprensibility of the infinite from Numenius, who wrote that if matter is infinite, it is unbounded; if unbounded, irrational; if irrational, unknowable; if unknowable, without order.[24]

Since they are not God, these rational creatures are not good essentially, as only God is, but they do possess free will to choose the good and the concomitant moral responsibility to do so. There are four major types of rational creatures: angels, the powers of wickedness, the animating spirits of the heavenly bodies, and human souls. The human soul of Christ, as we have seen, is a rational creature that is a uniquely special case. The thrones, dominions, principalities, and powers of Paul suggested to Origen that within these four large groups there are a multitude of ranks, each with its proper dignity and authority. Angels and devils, much less animated heavenly bodies, are scarcely prominent in theological thought today, but Christians, Gnostics, Platonists, and Jews all affirmed their existence and importance in Origen's time.

What explains the diversity of rational creatures? To suppose that God created them in the ranks they now occupy would, Origen argued, make God partial and thus impugn divine justice. God alone cannot be responsible, therefore, for the gradations of angelic authority, the varying brightness of the stars, and the multiplicity of intellectual and physical endowments that characterize the human race. It would not only be irrational but impious to suggest that God made the powers of wickedness evil by nature because this would make God responsible not only for their condition but for the evil they commit. We must assume, therefore, that each rational creature has precisely the position it merits on the basis of its free and responsible conduct. This assumption made it necessary for Origen to postulate the fall of rational creatures from an original unity with God, a fall that, in his opinion, accounted for the very existence of the material world. In this fall all rational spirits, with the exception of the human soul of Christ and perhaps the very highest angels, declined to some extent from the pure contemplation of God that had been their original condition. Those that fell least far are angels; those that fell farthest are the powers of wickedness. But this fall in no way removed from rational creatures their ability freely to choose the good, so that it is always possible for them to turn again toward the contemplation of God and reascend to their former estate. Because of this the present rank of rational creatures is not static. We might better consider their ranks as stages in their progress toward or away from God. Here Origen departed from many Platonists who seem to have given these ranks a permanent status.

Theoretically this process of ascent or descent of rational creatures could be interminable, but Origen was confident that while descent from God is always possible, the general trend is for rational creatures to ascend toward God. This is Origen's interpretation of the eschatological hope that finds such eloquent expression in Paul's "that at the name of Jesus every knee should bow, in heaven and on earth and under the earth, and every tongue confess that Jesus Christ is Lord, to the glory of God the Father" (Phil. 2:10–11). To Origen this meant that, in the end, all rational creatures will be saved and restored to their original state of contemplative union with God, "for the end is always like the beginning."[25]

Angels are the highest rational creatures. Origen believed that angels direct nations and churches as well as acting as the guardians of individual people. Angels of higher rank have charge of more important functions. In his homiles at Caesarea, Origen claimed, for example, that angels of higher rank are assigned to persons of higher intellectual stature and consequently greater responsibility, than are assigned to the common run of folk. Persons who failed to behave worthily of their high calling could be divorced by their heavenly guardians and assigned to an angel of lower rank.

The powers of wickedness are the mirror image of the angels. They are the rational creatures who sinned most grievously and are, as a consequence, the farthest from God. They retain the aerial bodies which are the privilege of the angels at the highest end of the scale of creatures, but for the powers of wickedness this form of embodiment is not a privilege but a penalty. Our embodiment in grossly material bodies is a punishment for sin, but it is also a means whereby we can be disciplined and trained for our return to God; the devils do not merit this concession. Because they are conscious of the enormity of their punishment and despair of returning to God, the devils take a malign pleasure in hindering, by temptations to sin, the ascent of other rational spirits to God. In Ezekiel's description of the fall of the Prince of Tyre from an original, paradisaic splendor, Origen found Biblical justification for his belief that the powers of wickedness were originally good and are where they are on account of a fall from grace. In this belief Origen was faithful both to the Bible and to the ecclesiastical tradition. He tacitly departed from that tradition in his teaching that their fall has not deprived the powers of wickedness of their freedom to return to God, the position he took in his discussion with Candidus.

Origen denied that the powers of wickedness can actually cause us to sin. Though they tempt us, God always gives us the gracious help to resist their blandishments, and resisting them actually does us good since it trains us to control our lower nature. The existence of the powers of wickedness, therefore, gives us no legitimate excuse for sinning. The powers of good, the angels who assist us against the devils, and the powers of wickedness work in different ways. The angels sharpen our intelligence, enabling us better to perceive the nature and consequences of our actions. The devils, on the other hand, darken our understanding. We can be confident of God's assistance, but it is up to us to be vigilant.

Origen's belief that rational spirits animate the heavenly bodies was fully in accord with the scientific beliefs of his time since Aristotle had explained the regular motion of the stars by such an assumption. Origen simply repeats his arguments:

> No movement can take place in any body which does not possess life, nor can any living beings exist at any time without movement. And since the stars move with such majestic order and plan that never have we seen their course deflected in the slightest degree, is it not the height of stupidity to say that such order, such exact observance of rule and plan, is accomplished by things without reason?

Origen found biblical warrant for the belief that the stars are animate, rational beings in Isaiah 45:12, which read in his translation, ''I have given precepts to all the stars," and proof of their fall in Job 25:5, "the stars also are not clean in his sight." Like us, the heavenly bodies desire to put aside their material bodies to be entirely united to God. He could picture the sun saying with the Apostle Paul (Phil.1:23), "I could desire to be dissolved . . . and be with Christ; for it is far better," yet, like Paul, the sun and stars abide in the body for the sake of the service they render to other rational creatures.[27] The stars, however, ultimately will be released from the futility of their bondage to material bodies when in the consummation God is all in all.

Human souls, as already mentioned, have grossly material bodies as a punishment and a remedy for their fall from God. Origen's teaching that the human soul exists eternally before it enters the body was later condemned as inconsistent with the church's teaching though he certainly did not think it so. Souls were once minds, but they lost their purely intellectual character in the process of their fall from God. This descent Origen described as a process of cooling from the ardor of the mind's original contemplation of God, an account of the soul's origin he may have borrowed from Valentinus.[28] In fact, Origen derived *psychê*, the Greek word for soul, from a verb, *psychô*, that means "to cool." It is the extent of the soul's fall from God that determines the diversity of human capacities and situations. "Jacob I loved but Esau I hated" (Mal. 1:2–3 as cited in Rom. 9:13), a text Paul used to demonstrate God's unmerited election of one person instead of another, proved to Origen that souls must preexist the bodies they animate. How, he asked, could God, whom we know to be just and good, prefer Jacob to Esau even before either was born except on the basis of the relative merits of their preexistent souls?[29] Though for most souls embodiment is a remedial punishment, some souls have taken on bodies in order to serve their fellows. This is preeminently true of the human soul of Christ though Origen hinted in his *Commentary on John* it may also be true of John the Baptist. The logic of Origen's position is consistent with a doctrine of continual reincarnation such as Plato at least envisioned mythically, but Origen seems to have considered corporeality as a single, unrepeatable stage in the road of spirits back to God. He raised the issue of the possibility of some souls descending so far from God as to lose rationality altogether and become embodied in brute breasts, but this speculation runs counter to the logic of his system which demands the possibility that all rational creatures can return to God.

## The World and the Return to God

Chapters one to three of book two and chapters five and six of book three of *On First Principles* deal with the beginning and end of the world. Origen's belief that the end is like the beginning made it appropriate for him to deal with these subjects together. We have already seen how Platonism and the church's tradition each taught that our world is good but not the ultimate good. In one breath both Christians and Platonists praised the beauty of the created order; in the next they directed human aspirations toward a higher realm of reality. Although they stood together against world-hating Gnostics as well as against any materialists who might still be around, Christians and Platonists had reached a similar position from very different basic assumptions.

Platonists considered the world and the human body good because they reproduced, in so far as possible, the unchangeable, supersensible world of the ideal forms. Their materiality, which made them subject to change, kept them from being an ultimate good because what is ultimately good is always the same. Furthermore, most Platonists, including Plotinus, believed that the material world had to be eternal since its creation in time would imply change in the eternally existing divine hypostases. They could find no possibility that a new circumstance could have arisen to cause God to create the world, and they could not imagine what God could have been doing before God created the world, assuming it was created in time. Platonists by and large, therefore, assumed that the existence of the world was a necessary reality, not a contingent one. Platonists also denied that God, strictly speaking, created matter. Matter was a principle independent of the ideal realm although it in itself was not so much something existing as it was the absolute limit to the genuine existence of the ideal forms. In the Platonic system of emanation outward from the One to lower and lower forms of reality, matter marks the farthest border of the divine activity. Matter was not so much, as we might assume, the substance out of which God made the world as the principle that prevented the order that God imposed on the world from being an unchanging and ideal order. Though the divine providence has so arranged matters that this material world can serve the soul as a preliminary stage in its ascent to God, the world and the body by which the soul participates in the world are essentially hindrances. The soul's goal is the abandonment of materiality, a goal for which the Platonic dialectic prepared it by enabling it to grasp intellectually the truths of a higher level of reality.

Christians disagreed seriously with Platonists over the source and effects of materiality. Christians considered the material world and the human body good because God made them so. They taught unambiguously that the world came into being in time, that it owed its existence entirely to God, and that it would cease to exist at the day of judgment. Thus they rejected the Platonic beliefs in the eternity of the world and in the independent and necessary status of matter. The world's admitted limitations came, Christians believed, not from its participation in materiality, but from its bondage to sin, the sin of human beings and angels who had freely chosen to disobey and reject God. Christians also hoped for a resumption of material existence in the resurrection body which would inhabit the new heaven and new earth which they expected at the end of time. It was Origen's task to reconcile, as far as possible, these fundamental differences.

Characteristically, we find in Origen's teaching on the world a number of specifically biblical phrases and ideas that have their place in a structure more Platonic than biblical. Origen's discussion is saturated in biblical language, but the context often gives that language a very new meaning. An example is the biblical phrase, "foundation [*katabolê*] of the world." Etymologically, *katabolê* comes from words which mean "cast down," and in an agricultural context it can refer to the sowing of seeds. Origen took the term to imply that the world came into existence by being "cast down," a meaning more in keeping with Platonic emanationism than with anything in the Bible as Christians had traditionally read it. Origen agreed with the church's tradition in ascribing the current limitations of the world to the fall of rational creatures, but the fall had a very different place in his system from its place in more conventional Christian teaching. The fall, for Origen, did not impair an already existing material world but brought it into existence. The material world for him is God's provision for rational creatures who have failed to abide with God. Origen seems to have followed Philo in interpreting the expulsion of Adam and Eve from Eden as the expulsion of human souls from the supersensible ideal world to the material world and the coats of skin God mercifully provided them as our gross, material bodies.[30] Origen thereby ascribed our bodily nature, in Platonic fashion, to our separation from a higher, supersensible realm. Similarly, Origen argued for the creation of the world in time, a position at odds with that of most Platonists. Yet if we were to ask, "What was God doing before God created this world?" Origen would not declare the question meaningless but would affirm that God was creating the worlds that preceded ours. This world is only one moment in a cycle of worlds that is, he implies, as eternal as any Platonist could wish. The belief that there have been many worlds has affinities with the Stoic doctrine of continually repeating world cycles. Origen rejected, however, the Stoic belief that these worlds must be exactly the same on the basis of his belief in human freedom and an argument from mathematical probability.

Origen's denial that matter exists as an independent principle seems, at first, a characteristically Christian denial of the Platonic doctrine. It is worth noting that although belief that God had created the universe out of nothing had already become, as it would remain, a matter of Christian dogma, Origen could only find scriptural warrant for it in two books he considered marginal to the canon, 2 Maccabees and the *Shepherd of Hermas*. Why did Origen insist strenuously on a doctrine not at all prominent in the Bible and at odds with the Platonic mainstream? We may conjecture that, given his belief that the end of the world will be like its beginning, the doctrine of creation *ex nihilo* appealed to him as a position more consistent with the ultimate disappearance of all corporeality in the divine unity at the end of time than the creation of the world out of an already existing unformed matter. If so, his doctrine of creation out of nothing ultimately provides for an eschatology more consistent with Platonism than the new heaven and new earth of the Bible.

God's providence and the free will of rational creatures shape Origen's understanding of the world. God leaves souls free but in the creation of the material world sets conditions for them which will ultimately lead them to return to God willingly. This makes necessary the wearying succession of worlds Origen's system calls for. Souls must undergo bodily existence once in each successive world until they grow so tired of their sinful separation from God that they freely turn to God. All the seeming imperfections of the world, which the Gnostics ascribed to the incompetence or ill will of its Creator, are the means whereby God, as a loving Father, coaxes children home. If we can see no correspondence between the character of given individuals and their earthly happiness, that is because we cannot view the world and human existence in it from God's perspective. Could we do so, we should see that God treats each individual with perfect justice and never-failing benevolence. It is a vision of extraordinary moral grandeur and perhaps as satisfactory a solution, from the perspective of faith, to the problem of theodicy as has ever been suggested.[31]

But is this cycle of worlds an endless one? Is there any real hope that God eventually will be all in all? The dilemma these questions pose arises from the very fact that Origen made free will one of the mainsprings of his system. As he expressed it:

> This power [free will] is granted to [rational beings] by God lest, if they held their position for ever irremovably, they might forget that they had been placed in that final state of blessedness by the grace of God and not by their own goodness. These movements would again undoubtedly be followed by a variety and diversity of bodies, out of which a world is always composed; for it could never exist except as a result of variety and diversity, and this can in no way be produced apart from bodily matter.[32]

Origen's detractors made much of statements like this, saying that they showed that Origen considered it possible, nay, inevitable, that even the greatest saints, once they had ascended to the bliss of divine contemplation, would descend once more to the depths of moral depravity and undergo the eons-long purification all over again to return to God and then to fall once more. The wretched state in which *On First Principles* has come down to us makes it impossible to deny that Origen actually taught such a pessimistic doctrine. However, even if they are a logical consequence of his assumptions, unending cycles are scarcely consistent with the ardent optimism that characterizes so much of Origen's work. It seems more reasonable to think, and there are indications of it, that Origen believed that rational creatures would indeed by virtue of their experience be far more secure in their final adherence to God than in their first.

The ultimate status of materiality is another area of uncertainty in Origen's teaching. In his discussion of the last things, Origen set forth three alternative possibilities for the ultimate state of things. The first possibility is that there is a ninth heaven above the sphere of the fixed stars, a physical universe far better than ours, which will be the reward of the blessed. There they shall resume their physical bodies at the final resurrection. The second possibility is that the bodily substance that now clothes our souls will be changed into an ethereal substance whose fineness and splendor, marvelous in any event, will vary according to the merits of the individual. The third possibility is that materiality will cease to be altogether and that all things will return to the divine unity from which they proceeded. Origen did not indicate which of these alternative possibilities he considered most likely, but he must have preferred one.

The first possibility is the closest of the three to the understanding that most Christians in Origen's time and since have had of the afterlife, a glorified version of earthly existence in a realm beyond the sky. Nevertheless, it seems scarcely credible that Origen could have taken it seriously, and his inclusion of it in his list strongly suggests that he was not really impartial about the three possibilities. Elsewhere in his writings, Origen mocked crudely literalistic expectations of the resurrection which he seemed to present seriously here, and he nowhere suggested that life in the ninth heaven was the original status of rational creatures toward which we should expect them to return. At best the ninth heaven could be a stage in the ascent to God, not its goal.

The second possibility avoids the crudity of the first, but if the end is truly to be like the beginning, the third possibility—that material, bodily existence will cease when God is all in all—must be his preference. As it is, Rufinus would have had good reason to tone down Origen's views on the ultimate status of materiality; the inconsistency between his view and the church's teaching on the resurrection of the body was one of the first things which Origen's opponents noticed, and Rufinus did not want to present Origen in such a way as to give offense. Jerome, Rufinus' contemporary, and Justinian, both of whom had the access we lack to the Greek text Origen wrote, found there statements that materiality would cease to exist, as their comments, included in Butterworth's translation of *On First Principles*, attest. We are not under any obligation to take the word of Origen's enemies, but their agreement with what Origen said elsewhere about the limitations of corporeality[33] makes the testimony of Jerome and Justinian plausible. Furthermore, return to complete union with God is perhaps the only possible solution to the difficulty that bedeviled Origen with regard to the necessity for continual cycles of worlds. As long as rational creatures are separate from God, the possibility exists for them to fall repeatedly, but their reabsorption in God would obviate this danger. Origen's views on the end of the world, therefore, were, in all probability, far more radical in their modification of traditional Christian teachings than they might at first appear.

In his attitude toward bodily existence, Origen was a Platonist at heart, but not a conventional Platonist. If he agreed with Plato that matter limits the possibilities of the soul and that salvation is separation from it, he denied that this limitation is eternally given in the nature of things. The church, which taught Origen that sin caused the world's limitations, led him to ascribe matter to God's merciful provision for fallen rational creatures. Thus he could account more easily, within his system, for the soul's initial involvement in bodily existence than could Plotinus, for whom this is something of a mystery. Origen could also hold out the possibility that the achievement of union with God is the ultimate expectation, not just of a few souls trained in philosophy, but of the entire universe. We may thus describe his presentation of the world's origin and destiny as a genuine synthesis of Platonism and Christianity.

Whether or not the soul's ultimate state is to be the abandonment of bodily existence in union with God, Origen held that after death the soul would obtain a spiritual body not at all like the earthly body it has here as a remedial punishment for its sin. This view seemed to conflict with the church's teaching, which proclaimed in its interpretation of the resurrection of the body that the Christian hope is the resumption of the same bodies we once had on earth in a new world without sin or imperfections of any kind. In his discussion of the resurrection of the body as a special issue in *On First Principles*, Origen sought to reconcile his view with the church's teaching. Origen cited as warrant for his view Paul's statement in 1 Corinthians 15: 44, "It is sown a physical body, it is raised a spiritual body. If there is a physical body, there is also a spiritual body." In this text Paul sharply distinguished between the sort of body we now have and the sort of body we can expect to have at the time of the resurrection. Origen believed that Paul meant by "spiritual body" a body such as angels have, one fitted for dwelling in the heavens. (This is not to be confused with the bodily guise under which angels appear to people as radiant human beings.) In that life, of course, we will have no need for the organs of alimentation and locomotion suited to our earthly existence. Origen found Paul's language of sowing congenial because it suggested to him a philosophical explanation for the link between the physical and spiritual bodies which Christian doctrine proclaimed. This was the Stoic concept of the seminal principle, the seed, as it were, that determines that our bodies will develop as they do. It is the seminal principle which will persist from the physical to the spiritual body, producing, of course, a very different body in new conditions of existence.

Origen insisted that his teaching on the resurrection of the body upheld the church's teaching against heretics who denied the resurrection altogether and against simple Christians whose grossly materialistic interpretation exposed the church to ridicule by propagating ideas unworthy of God. He went into slightly more detail in a work written at Alexandria shortly before *On First Principles,* a fragment of which Jerome preserved.[34] There Origen pointed out to the simple the absurd consequences of their literalistic interpretation of the resurrection of the body and contrasted it to his own view. Those Christians who took literally the prophecies about eating and drinking in the coming kingdom should expect to evacuate there as well, and perhaps they intended to have hairdressers in heaven since the nutrition would cause their hair to grow. The narratives of Christ's appearance after the resurrection prove, Origen argued, how utterly different the spiritual body is from the one we know. Although Christ assumed the appearance of a physical body in order to convince doubters of the truth of the resurrection, his ability to pass through walls and disappear before people's eyes demonstrates that Christ did not have flesh at all like ours. The spiritual body will be composed of ether, the element Aristotle considered proper to the heavens, rather than out of the four earthly elements.

If literal-minded Christians took umbrage at Origen's doctrine of the resurrection, they found his teaching on the punishment of the wicked even less appealing. Tertullian's treatise *On Spectacles,* where heaven's best feature is its superb view of the damned frying in hell, illustrates the relish which some of Origen's contemporaries took in the traditional understanding of the fate of the wicked. Origen found such a view utterly abhorrent. It is a fundamental principle of his thought that all punishments, in this world and succeeding ones, are remedial; they belong to God's providential plan for bringing all erring rational creatures back to God. Origen, therefore, interpreted the fires of hell as purgative. They are the torments of conscience which the wicked suffer on account of their sins, torments which will, eventually, bring them to repentance. Similarly, the outer darkness with which Christ threatened the wicked is deep ignorance of spiritual reality and may refer to a return to corporeality. Origen's speculations along these lines continue the tradition of Clement and were a major source for the doctrine of purgatory.[35] Origen, however, like Clement, considered such purgation after death the destiny of all sinners, not just those fortunate enough to be baptized Christians.

If the wicked have to expect a painful purgation in the afterlife that will eventually prepare them to return to God, what is the hope of the righteous? In the chapter in which Origen described it, it sounds a great deal like an institute for advanced research. He, of course, rejected a literalistic reading of such works as the book of Revelation which would make heaven out as a place of sensual delights. The food and drink promised there are not physical but spiritual, that is, intellectual. In a fervent passage that anticipates Dante's *Paradiso*, Origen described the ascent of the soul from an earthly paradise through the various heavenly spheres, at each of which it will obtain a deeper understanding of the world. Along with a comprehension of the secrets of nature, the soul will achieve a comprehensive understanding of the Bible, an understanding that will resolve such issues as the spiritual meaning of the ritual legislation in Leviticus. Thus heaven will continue the philosphically informed study of the Bible of Origen's own school, and those who have begun such study on earth will be the best prepared for it. As so often in his work, Origen's sheer exhilaration about the joys of the life of the mind is astonishing.

## Free Will

The first chapter of book three of *On First Principles*, which takes up over half of that book, brings us to the heart of Origen's theology, the doctrine of free will. We are fortunate that, except for one paragraph, the full Greek text survives. The chapter falls into three unequal parts. The first part is a discussion, in philosophical terms, of the question. The brief second part cites biblical texts that uphold the doctrine of free will. The third and longest part discusses in detail passages from the Bible that seem, on what Origen insisted to be a superficial reading, to deny free will.

In the philosophical argument of the first part of the chapter, Origen made our status as rational beings the basis of his argument for free will. He distinguished between created things on the basis of their movement. Portable things, like stones, only move from outside themselves. Other things move from within themselves. Of these, some like spiders and bees act instinctually on the basis of sensory impressions, so that their actions, though proceeding from within themselves, are entirely determined by their inherent nature and the external situation. Rational creatures, on the other hand, have the privilege of being able to move from within themselves on the basis of a reasoned choice between courses of action in response to external situations. Since we have this ability, we are responsible for its use; we can never claim that things external to us have determined our response to them and moved us as if we were stocks and stones. When temptations come to act irresponsibly, we can never claim that we lack power to resist them. Discipline, it is true, assists our will to resist temptation, but it is well within our power to acquire discipline. The power of education, in fact, confirms the error of those who claim that we are naturally good or bad and cannot be held responsible for our actions. How many times, Origen says, has education not made the licentious chaste and the savage gentle? Moral lassitude, similarly, can gradually ruin even persons who seem naturally steady and respectable.

Origen's terminology and his argument place him squarely in the Middle Platonist tradition. The terminology of the different sorts of movement comes from Plato, as does the suggestion that the soul's ability to move from within itself is the basis of moral responsibility.[36] Plotinus, likewise, made practically the same points as Origen and concluded that, while the soul's ability to move itself makes evil possible, God's providence, nonetheless, makes that evil work toward a larger good.[37] The idea that the soul's ability to choose between sense im-

pressions is at the basis of free will, and moral responsibility is one of
those things which Platonists borrowed from the Stoics. We find it most
eloquently expressed in Epictetus, whose passionate feeling for the dignity that free will confers on us comes very close to Origen:

> But what says Zeus? "Epictetus, had it been possible I should have
> made both this paltry body and this small estate of thine free and unham-
> pered. But as it is—let it not escape thee—this body is not thine own,
> but only clay cunningly compounded. Yet since I could not give thee
> this, we have given thee a certain portion of ourself, this faculty of
> choice and refusal, of desire and aversion, or, in a word, the faculty
> which makes use of external impressions: if thou care for this and place
> all that thou hast therein, thou shalt never be thwarted, never hampered,
> shalt not groan, shalt not blame, shalt not flatter any man."[38]

Origen did not want to give the impression that he was forcing the Bible
into a philosophically determined straitjacket, so he cited, in the second
part of the chapter, a great many biblical texts that support the doctrine
of free will. These texts do not, of course, deal theoretically with free
will as the philosophers did, but since they affirm moral responsibility
they presume that we have within ourselves the power to do the good
and to shun evil. Origen cited twelve such texts, including Deuteronomy 30:15,19: "See, I have set before you this day life and good, death
and evil . . . choose life, that you and your descendants may live." He
may not have exaggerated when he boasted that he could have cited ten
thousand more texts along the same lines. What sense could such exhortations have, Origen argued, unless we had the power to choose freely
to obey them? He could not believe that God would reward or punish
actions which we have no choice about doing.

The whole tenor of the Bible, Old Testament and New Testament,
proclaims that our will is free; only a few passages seem to imply the
opposite. In the third part of the chapter he sought to deprive heretics
who deny free will the specious comfort such passages provided them.
Most of the passages which seem to deny free will come from the
epistles of Paul, and it was with Paul that Origen found it most necessary to wrestle. Origen, however, declared that his argument was not
with the great Apostle, but with Marcion, whose false interpretation of
Paul led him to deny the goodness of the God of the Old Testament, and
with Valentinus, whose doctrine of presdestination denied human free-

dom to choose the good. The first text Origen treated, perhaps the most difficult text in the Bible for him, was the reference to the hardening of Pharaoh's heart, itself an allusion to Exodus 9:12 in Romans 9:18. Origen devoted a long exposition to this problem later in his life when he commented on the book of Exodus, and that passage from his commentary has survived. Hardening the heart, he argued, is simply a figurative way of describing the effect of God's grace on a soul already inured to wickedness. God could scarcely need to harden the heart of the wicked to damn them; that would be superfluous since their own obstinate pursuit of evil already condemns them. Rather, God in mercy allows already hardened sinners like Pharaoh to reach the full extent of their wickedness in order that they may all the sooner turn from that wickedness and live. God knows that some, if allowed to repent too soon and too easily, would despise that mercy and, in the long run, be worse off than if God allowed them to become utterly satiated with evil-doing and its consequences and desperate to alter their condition. The relatively short period human souls have to live here on earth is not sufficient, in most cases, to complete this process of divine healing, but that should not cause us to doubt the efficacy of God's designs. It may take eons for a soul utterly hardened and debased to repent, but God has that much time:"for God deals with souls not in view of the fifty years, so to speak, of our life here, but in view of the endless world."[39] Thus it follows that Pharaoh was not destroyed when he drowned in the Red Sea; his soul went on toward the further purgation that God in mercy was preparing for him so that he might eventually be saved. Images of healing and of teaching mingle in Origen's description, for if Christ appears as a teacher to those spiritually advanced, Christ appears as a physician to those still afflicted with sin. The idea that God, as a wise physician, may at times allow the disease to reach a crisis before alleviating it enabled Origen to dispose of other texts that seemed to imply that God forced people to sin or denied them the grace to repent.

If the passage about the hardening of Pharaoh's heart seemed to imply that God actually makes people sin, other texts in the Bible seemed to imply that only God can make them do good, so that their own efforts play no part in it. One of these is Ezekiel 11:19–20: "I will take the stony heart out of their flesh and give them a heart of flesh, that they may walk in my statutes and keep my ordinances and obey them."

Origen argued that while God as the passage states must heal us of the stony heart, the disposition that keeps us from following God's commandments, the need for divine healing does not impair our free will or detract from our moral responsibility. The ignorant need a teacher to cure their ignorance, but the fact that they cannot cure it on their own does not make them any less free or responsible to seek the help they need. Similarly, we can and must present our hearts to God for the healing Ezekiel promised.

In his interpretation of another problem text, Romans 9:16, "So it depends not upon man's will or exertion, but upon God's mercy," Origen again stressed that our efforts to do the good and God's gracious assistance to us are complementary rather than mutually exclusive. Paul, Origen argued, only intended to say that God's work in our salvation far exceeds ours. Paul, in phrasing the text as he did, is like a sailor who, at the end of a safe voyage, ascribes all the credit to God. The sailor is quite aware of the indispensable role skill in navigation played in bringing the ship to port, but the sailor is far more impressed, and rightly so, with the overwhelmingly greater part of God's role in providing a strong favorable wind, hospitable weather, and the shining of the stars as a guide. Origen's argument is always that God's grace is necessary if our efforts to do the good are to come to fruition, but those efforts must begin with us. Moreover, there could be no question in Origen's mind but that if we do what is in our power to act well, God in benevolence will always assist us.

When also in Romans 9 Paul spoke of God's making one vessel for honor and one for dishonor, Origen refused to accept that this could imply unmerited election on God's part. Such an interpretation, he insisted, flew in the face of the sense of moral responsibility Paul inculcated everywhere in his epistles. Rather, if God made Jacob a vessel of honor and Esau a vessel of dishonor, certain older causes, namely, their souls' conduct before they were conceived, must account for God's apparent favoritism. Nowhere is the difference between Origen's piety and Paul's more evident than in his comment on the exclamation that precedes Paul's discussion of the vessels of honor and dishonor: "But who are you, a man, to answer back to God?" (Rom. 9:20). Paul clearly meant to close off discussion of the justice of God's ways, but Origen simply could not fathom such a response to divine mysteries.

Citing the example of Moses, who certainly did question God's purposes, Origen reassured readers that no one who questions God with the clear conscience that comes from a faithful and good life will ever hear this rebuke. There is nothing impertinent, Origen firmly believed, in intellectual curiosity or serious theological perplexity.

To reinforce his message on free will, Origen appended a brief chapter, not preserved in Greek, proving that the devil's temptations no more deprive us of free will than do God's gracious favors. The whole treatment of the subject, including this pendant, constitutes the first serious analysis of the issue of free will in the Christian tradition. The texts which Origen chose to deal with became the standard ones in discussions of the topic for more than a thousand years. Although in Western Christianity Augustine's very different interpretation of Paul, more faithful but less humane, has always dominated the discussion, Origen's treatment still deserves serious attention.

## Interpretation of the Bible

The other large fragment of *On First Principles* that survives in Greek is the discussion of biblical interpretation in the first three chapters of book four. Since this topic does not directly concern God's dealings with the created world, the theme that occupies the rest of the treatise, Origen presented it as a digression. It is, however, a necessary digression because of his claim that the Bible, interpreted allegorically, is the basis of his entire endeavor. Origen's attempt to prove that the Bible, so interpreted, is the ultimate source of truth, proceeds in two steps. The first step, occupying the first chapter of book four, is the demonstration that the Bible is divinely inspired. The second step, occupying chapters two and three, is the demonstration that we must penetrate beneath the letter of the Bible to the spiritual sense that its status as a divinely inspired book implies.

Origen's argument that the Bible is divinely inspired is that the widespread and unique appeal of Judaism and Christianity as opposed to other religious cults and to Greek philosophy proves that the book these two faiths revere is of divine origin. Except for Moses and Jesus, "we have no record of a lawgiver who has succeeded in implanting an enthusiasm for the acceptance of his teachings among nations other than his own." As for the philosophers, whose aims are admittedly laudable, "none of them has succeeded in implanting what he regarded as the truth among different nations or even among any number of persons worth mentioning in a single nation."[40] Origen noted that Jesus' appeal extends to all social classes and levels of education and that neither social opprobrium nor actual persecution have caused it to slacken. There is no other way, he argued, to explain this empirically verifiable appeal except by granting that Jesus spoke by divine authority. This empirical fact certifies the accuracy of the prophets who predicted, long before the event, that Christ would convert the nations. The fact that the prophets also described his life and death in circumstantial detail makes their achievement all the more remarkable. Nothing but divine inspiration can account for the accuracy of the biblical prophecies, and this accuracy proves the inspiration of the entire Bible. Furthermore, Origen argued, the Bible in spite of its humble style immediately impresses the mind of the reverent reader with its divine origin.

Origen's understanding of biblical inspiration was entirely consistent with a rigorously critical approach to the text. If the Bible is inspired by God but appears in places to be irrelevant to our condition, unworthy of God, or simply banal, we may take it for granted that we have failed to grasp its inner sense. If no spiritual significance is apparent on the surface, we must conclude that this surface meaning, which may or may not be factual, is intended symbolically. Allegory is the method of interpretation that claims to yield the hidden, symbolic meaning, and it was Origen who, more than anyone else, made allegory the dominant method of biblical interpretation down to the end of the Middle Ages.

Allegory is, like so many aspects of Origen's thought, a legacy of Greece. We have already seen how the need to defend the *Iliad* and the *Odyssey* from charges of impiety and immorality was a major impetus toward its development. Stoic authors like Heraclitus, the author of the *Homeric Problems*, employed allegory in this way and made it a recognized method of interpretation. Their works, however, were often shallow as well as artificial. Only pedants could delight in an *Iliad* that was nothing more than a handbook of commonplace physical phenomena hidden behind a cryptic style. It took no genius to recognize that such allegory was a desperate effort to avoid the plain meaning of the text, and that, indeed, is how Origen viewed it. At times similar motives actuated Origen, for example, when he sought to reinterpret the blood-

thirsty war for the conquest of Canaan as Christ's conquest of the fallen
human soul. Stoic allegory, however, though it provided the method,
provided neither the content nor the inspiration for Origen's allegory.

In order to appreciate Origen's passionate devotion to allegory, in
fact his conviction that allegory could lead to the very knowledge of
God, we need to look again, as so often, at Plato and the Platonic
tradition. It is the Platonists who provided, in their understanding of
myth and symbol, a religiously satisfying explanation of allegory. It
was the Platonists who argued for the necessity of myths and symbols to
convey philosophical truths otherwise inaccessible. Plato, indeed, rejected allegory as a means of justifying Homer, though not because it
was invalid, but he keenly appreciated the role of myths. Plato even
invented his own myths, such as the magnificent myth of Er that closes
the *Republic*. A passage in the *Phaedrus* illustrates how deliberate Plato
was in his use of myth. After making a tightly argued case for the
immortality of the soul, Socrates, the narrator in the dialogue, says:

> As to soul's immortality then we have said enough, but as to its
> nature there is this that must be said. What manner of thing it is would
> be a long tale to tell, and most assuredly a god alone could tell it, but
> what it resembles, that a man might tell in briefer compass.[41]

There follows the myth of the soul's loss of its wings.

Although Plato preferred to create his own myths because he believed that the traditional myths created false ideas about the gods, later
Platonists were not so scrupulous. Maximus of Tyre, a second-century
rhetorician with a strong interest in Platonism, actually expressed a sort
of nostalgia for the mythological imagination that had characterized
more primitive times. Plotinus shared Plato's understanding of myth
and frequently resorted either to Plato's myths or to traditional ones in
his teaching. *Ennead* 3.5, "Love," is, in fact, a sustained allegorical
interpretation of Plato's two myths of the origin of love, those in the
*Phaedrus* and in the *Symposium*, in the light of the traditional mythology. Plotinus recognized the limitations of myths but considered them
no greater than the limitations of logical discourse:

> Myths, if they are to serve their purpose, must necessarily import time-
> distinctions into their subject and will often present as separate, Powers
> which exist in unity but differ in rank and faculty; and does not

philosophy itself relate the births of the unbegotten and discriminate where all is one substance? The truth is conveyed in the only manner possible; it is left to our good sense to bring all together again.[42]

Plotinus, no doubt wisely, did not try to present his philosophy in the guise of an interpretation of Homer, but he occasionally drew from the *Odyssey* for symbols to illustrate his ideas. For example, he used the scene where Odysseus finds Heracles' shade in the Underworld, even though Heracles himself, having become a god, feasts eternally on Olympus, to illustrate his doctrine of the soul.[43] Numenius, the Platonist whose allegorical interpretations of the Old and New Testaments so appealed to Origen, applied the same treatment to Homer, as we learn from Porphyry's *On the Cave of the Nymphs*, a Platonic interpretation of *Odyssey* 13.102–112, which describes the cave where Odysseus stashed his gifts from the Phaeacians after he returned to Ithaca. Porphyry himself transformed the cave of the nymphs into a profound religious symbol for the world, connecting it with Plato's metaphor of the cave in the seventh book of the *Republic* and the use of caves as places of worship by Cretans, Mithras-worshipers, and others. Although such an allegory apparently bears no genuine relation to the actual meaning of the text as the poet wrote it, its inspired transformation of that text into a luminous religious symbol more than justifies it. Such a respect and appreciation for symbolism, and an ability to exploit it, is what Origen brought to his interpretation of the Bible.[44]

The appreciation of symbols and myths as a means of conveying profound religious and philosophical truths, which was one of his legacies from Platonism, reinforced Origen's conviction that the Bible contained the oracles of God. Allegory was not just a code language, it was an awesome, powerful means of conveying the truth, well adapted to pique the curiosity of the learned and to compel the respect of the simple. Origen was also heir to a reasonably long tradition of allegorical interpretation of the Bible, which further disposed him to adopt it himself. This tradition began with Jews at Alexandria who were convinced that the faith of their fathers was more consistent with the highest aspirations of Hellenism than the polytheistic and morally unstrenuous religion of the Greeks. These Jews, however, found that the passionate God of their Bible bore little resemblance to the Platonic One, and that the patriarchs often acted in ways that would not have met with approval in polite Alexandrian society. Their response was to interpret the Bible in such a way as to demonstrate that its content was identical with the most enlightened Greek philosophy, though, of course, older and more authoritative. This was the movement which reached its fulfillment in Philo, whose philosophical learning and stylistic elegance were unsurpassed in his time. His work fell out of favor among the Jews, but it survived long enough to be transmitted to Christians who accepted it enthusiastically. Origen probably came to know Philo's works through Clement, and he thoroughly approved of them.

The circumstances in which Christianity developed into a religious tradition independent of Judaism gave allegory from the very first a strong appeal to Christians. Christians retained the Old Testament, which for some time was their only Bible, as their sacred Scriptures, but they quickly found it appropriate to cease demanding literal observance of the commandments of the Torah. Allegory enabled Christians to justify their abandonment of the ceremonial law. Paul, for example, in Galatians 5 interpreted allegorically the two wives of Abraham, Sarah and Hagar, and the two mountains, Zion and Sinai. Similarly the anonymous author of the *Epistle of Barnabas* argued that the Torah was never intended to be followed literally. Allegory also provided a way to transform, for Christian purposes, parts of the Torah which, once they were no longer taken literally, had no obvious religious function. We find such a use of allegory in the interpretation of Jewish ritual in the Epistle to the Hebrews, the one book in the New Testament with decided Platonic overtones. The author of Hebrews may have been influenced by Philo, and it is possible that Apollos, the Alexandrian Jewish convert to Christianity whose interpretation of the Bible Paul admired, practiced Philonic allegory. Clement of Alexandria continued this tradition, extending his allegorical interpretation to the New Testament as well as the Old.

Allegory, however, had opponents inside and outside the Christian community. Jews rejected Christian claims to possess a more profound interpretation of the Bible and loudly insisted that God intended the Torah to be followed literally. Many philosophical pagans, while they might allow allegorical interpretation of Homer, considered it simply an attempt to whitewash the barbarities of the Bible. Marcion rejected allegory for the same reason these pagans did. He believed that the Old Testament was a barbaric book conveying a religious consciousness totally at odds with that of the New and not, in fact, proclaiming the same God. Within the church, many people believed that allegory, by making interpretation subjective, opened the way to heresy. Presumably such people objected to Origen's interpretation of Genesis and led him to counter their objections by writing *On First Principles*.

At the beginning of the second chapter of the fourth book of *On First Principles*, Origen chronicled the errors that stem from ill-advised literalism in the interpretation of the Bible. The Jews, by being overly literalistic in their interpretation of the Old Testament messianic prophecies, failed to recognize the Messiah when Christ came and demanded his crucifixion instead. In their obtuseness, they demanded that the Messiah literally cut off the chariots from Ephraim, as prophesied in Zechariah 9:10, before they could accept him, and asked where, at his coming, an actual wolf was feeding harmlessly with an actual lamb, as prophesised in Isaiah 11:6. Similarly, the Gnostics interpreted the characteristics of God so literally in the Old Testament that they could not see that Yahweh was the same God as the loving Father of Jesus Christ in the New. The implication is that the rejection of allegory, not its abuse, is the great danger to the Christian faith. The reader will thus sympathize when Origen states that even among genuine believers the more simple run the risk of falling into grave error by refusing to accept this form of interpretation. The simple "believe such things about [God] as would not be believed of the most savage and unjust of men."[45]

Origen, as the champion of traditional orthodoxy, answered the critics of allegory that we must according to the rule of the church, seek allegorically the spiritual sense of the Bible. It makes no difference that allegory is a method partially borrowed from non-Christians; even his enemies the Pharisees, Christ said, possessed the key of knowledge to unlock the secrets of Scripture, though they condemned themselves by not using it.[46] The Bible, Origen argued, contains three levels of meaning, corresponding to the three-fold Pauline (and Platonic) division of a person into body, soul, and spirit. The bodily level of Scripture, the bare letter, is normally helpful as it stands to meet the needs of the more simple. The psychic level, corresponding to the soul, is for those making progress in perfection. It is hard to say what Origen understood this level of meaning to be. Some scholars have taken the psychic level to be what later interpreters of the Bible called the "moral" level of interpretation, the level at which the text provides guidance for conduct, but there is no good reason to think that Origen thought of it in that way. The actual example Origen gave of psychic interpretation—Paul's interpretation of "You shall not muzzle an ox when it is treading out the grain" (1 Cor. 9:9) as a justification for the support of itinerant Apostles—only indicates that Origen considered the psychic level a non-mystical level of allegory.[47]

It was, of course, with the third level of meaning, the spiritual, that Origen was chiefly concerned. Spiritual interpretation deals with "unspeakable mysteries" so as to make humanity a "partaker of all the doctrines of the Spirit's counsel."[48] It thus differs from psychic interpretation, not in terms of method, but in terms of content. And what are the unspeakable mysteries with which spiritual interpretation deals?

> When we speak of the needs of souls, who cannot otherwise reach perfection except through the rich and wise truth about God, we attach of necessity pre-eminent importance to the doctrines concerning God and His only-begotten Son; of what nature the Son is, and in what manner he can be the Son of God, and what are the causes of his descending to the level of human flesh and completely assuming humanity; and what, also, is the nature of his activity, and towards whom and at what times it is exercised. It was necessary, too, that the doctrines concerning beings akin to man and the rest of the rational creatures, both those that are nearer the divine and those that have fallen from blessedness, and the causes of the fall of these latter, should be included in the accounts of the divine teaching; and the question of the differences between souls and how these differences arose, and what the world is and why it exists, and further, how it comes about that evil is so widespread and so terrible on earth, and whether it is not only to be found on earth but also in other places—all this it was necessary that we should learn.[49]

They are precisely the matters Origen dealt with in *On First Principles*. He went on to explain that it is these doctrines which are concealed in the first five chapters of Genesis, the work he was commenting on when he interrupted his work to justify his procedure in *On First Principles*. The first five chapters of Genesis provide, on the surface, an edifying account of the creation of the visible world and the creation and subsequent multiplication of the human race. As such they can be read with profit by those who have not the slightest inkling of the profound truths they contain. This, Origen believed, is the case in most of the Bible. The Spirit has so contrived it that it presents accounts of deep mysteries to those capable of penetrating to the spiritual sense, but, at the same time, provides moralistic stories and ethical advice for the more simple. Origen did not question the truth of most of the stories in the Bible; it was better that they be historically true since that enhanced their value as morals. The Spirit, at the same time, purposefully included in the Bible a number of passages that are either false historically or ethically unworthy of God on the literal level. The adequacy, on the whole, of the literal level assures that the more spiritual will not neglect the Bible as unworthy of God. The inadequacy of particular passages, on the other hand, assures that they will find it necessary to abandon the letter and seek the diviner sense beneath it.

In this account of the nature of the Bible, Origen exhibited his uncanny knack for having it both ways in an argument. On the one hand, by allowing that the Bible, read literally, contains errors, he disarmed the criticisms of pagans and Gnostics. On the other hand, by defending the Bible as divinely inspired throughout, he ingratiated himself with orthodox Christians. This explanation also laid the groundwork for his own method of interpretation, in which the discovery of errors, loose threads that enable one to unravel the whole, is the first step in seeking the spiritual meaning beneath the letter.

Origen, in the third chapter of book four, expanded on the themes of the first by providing examples of spiritual interpretation. The early chapters of Genesis, to begin with, disclose a number of impossibilities to more discerning readers. These include the evening and morning on the first day, which somehow alternate before the sun exists, and God's "planting" the Garden of Eden and, even more outrageous, "walking" there in the cool of the day as if God had feet. There are also many impossibilities in the Jewish ritual legislation of the Torah, at least as Origen read it in the Septuagint. How could God possibly have intended people to take seriously the prohibition of eating the vulture, which no one would ever consider eating, or the griffin, which is mythical? The same applies to God's allowing the consumption of the nonexistent goat-stag. The sheer impossibility of keeping the Sabbath legislation to the letter also indicates that it is meant spiritually. Such impossibilities occur in the New Testament as well. Think carefully about the command to turn the other cheek in the Sermon on the Mount. It says that if anyone strikes on the right cheek, we should turn him the left as well (Matt. 5:39). But who, Origen asks, ever gets struck first on the right cheek? Anyone who is going to strike leads with his right, so that it is the left cheek that takes the first blow. (We may presume that Origen was right-handed.) Well aware that some Christians would find such criticisms subversive to the historical reliability upon which, as far as they were concerned, the moral authority of the Bible rests, Origen insisted that there are relatively few actual impossibilities in the Bible. Fear of being overcritical, however, should not deter the serious scholar. Our Lord commanded us to search the Scriptures, a command that makes it imperative for us to apply our critical powers to their fullest extent.

The rest of the chapter provides further examples of spiritual interpretation. Origen sought to present the spiritual significance of the various nations named in the Bible as part of what appears to be an overall scheme for interpreting the historical parts of the Old Testament. Unfortunately, the end of the chapter does not survive in full in the Greek, and Rufinus seems to have garbled Origen's text. In both cases this is almost certainly because Origen's interpretation was too bold to be left untampered with. Apparently Origen closed his discussion with an interpretation of the "eternal gospel" of Revelation 14:6 as being as far greater than the New Testament as the New Testament is greater than the Old.

## A Spiritual Vision

The final chapter of *On First Principles* recapitulates Origen's conclusions and ties up a few loose ends. The treatise provided the best defense Origen knew how to write of the church's tradition. Against the Gnostics, it demonstrated that the church's doctrine had an inner coherence fully as strong as that of their own systems and that it did not promote the worship of a God who was a petty tyrant. Against pagan despisers, it demonstrated the depth and profundity of Christian doctrine and its harmony with their own highest ideals. But Origen did more than that. *On First Principles* is a spiritual vision as well as a theological treatise. In the process of explaining the origin and destiny of rational creatures, Origen established how and why we can expect to have communion with God. How? By separating ourselves intellectually and morally from purely sensual concerns and attachments. Why? Because, as rational creatures, we share something of God's nature and are the objects of God's concern. As Origen put it:

> We see, therefore, that men have a kind of blood-relationship with God; and since God knows all things and not a single intellectual truth can escape his notice—for God the Father, with his only-begotten Son and the Holy Spirit, stands alone in his knowledge not only of the things he has created but also of himself—it is possible that a rational mind also, by advancing from a knowledge of small to a knowledge of greater things and from things visible to things invisible, may attain to an increasingly perfect understanding. For it has been placed in a body and of necessity advances from things of sense, which are bodily, to things beyond sense perception, which are incorporeal and intellectual.[50]

# VI
# Controversy
(230–34)

## Tension with Bishop Demetrius

Eusebius' account of Origen's life states that some time after he returned from visiting the governor of Arabia, "no small warfare broke out again in the city, and leaving Alexandria secretly he went to Palestine and abode in Caesarea." Until recently, scholars have assumed that this statement refers to the so-called "fury of Caracalla." In 215 Septimius Severus' son, the Emperor Caracalla cleverly contrived a massacre of Alexandrian citizens after they jestingly referred to his murdered brother Geta. But it is not reasonable to think that this massacre involved a persecution of Christians. Furthermore, if Origen was simply lying low to avoid political trouble, there is no way to explain the fact that Demetrius would send a special embassy to persuade him to return. It seems more likely, therefore, that it was "the fury of Demetrius," not the "fury of Caracalla," that drove Origen away.[1]

Any number of issues might have led to this first, fateful break with Demetrius. Ultimately it was a conflict between an organizer and an intellectual. Demetrius, the first great bishop of Alexandria, considered the aggrandizement of the power of its bishop crucial to the strength of the Alexandrian church, so that he could in good conscience bend all his efforts toward that end. This involved cultivating ties with other bishops, particularly the prestigious bishop of Rome. Perhaps it was under Demetrius that the legend got started that ascribed a Roman foundation to the church at Alexandria in the person of Peter's protégé, the evangelist Mark. Increasing the power of the Alexandrian episcopate involved establishing its ascendancy over the church in the rest of Egypt. It involved gathering into the hands of the bishop of Alexandria the power

to ordain presbyteis and deacons, to excommunicate refractory members of the church, and to reconcile penitent sinners. Furthermore, it
involved repudiating the Alexandrian church's former toleration for
Gnosticism and limiting what would be considered theologically acceptable to a more and more narrowly defined adherence to the emerging
Christian consensus embodied in the rule of faith. At the very least, all
this meant gaining control over the preaching at the service of instruction that preceded the eucharist. Demetrius therefore insisted that only
presbyters, whom he could appoint and discipline, should preach. He
thus silenced lay teachers, whose only qualifications were their acknowledged gifts of exposition. Demetrius may have impelled one such
teacher, Clement of Alexandria, to quit Alexandria for the more congenial atmosphere of Bishop Alexander's Jerusalem.

The institutional structure that Demetrius built was not, to borrow a
phrase from the Apostle Paul, of wood, hay, and stubble—it endured.
During the third century Christianity gained the adherence of Egypt's
Coptic peasants, who were the mainstay of the church's resistance to the
Great Persecution. The bishops of Alexandria maintained until a fateful
breach in the fifth century their special relationship with Rome. They
had a powerful effect on the norms of Christian doctrine and on the
furtherance of monasticism, thus exercising a permanent influence on
Christianity.

Having given Demetrius credit for building an enduring structure,
we may observe that it was not, however, of gold, silver, and precious
stones. Demetrius all too easily identified the strength of the church as a
whole with the strength of the Alexandrian church, the strength of the
Alexandrian church with the power of the bishop, and the power of its
bishop with his own personal power and respect. His successors frequently did the same thing, sometimes with terrible consequences. In
particular, Demetrius could not appreciate the contribution of Origen, a
man whose legacy, though different in kind, was at least as valuable as
his. Like so many institutionalizers, he looked upon the church's best
friends as its worst enemies. Origen was loyal to the institution and to
the rule of faith for which it stood. Nonetheless, he recognized, as
Demetrius and many others did not, that simple acceptance of this rule
of faith did not go very far toward meeting the intellectual and spiritual
needs of his time. That rule of faith, in order to meet those needs, would

have to be explained in terms of a larger world view; otherwise it would remain for the learned an irrelevant formula. Origen, in the process of making the rule of faith comprehensible, had to admit that certain parts of it could not be accepted at face value. The resurrection of the body, for example, symbolized a spiritual rather than a corporeal transformation, and the eternal damnation of sinners was only a way of expressing the enormous ethical seriousness of human decisions. Demetrius could not understand this. His power rested on the standardization of doctrine according to the rule of faith, and these attempts to buttress and explain that rule seemed to him more like direct challenges to it. Origen's loyalty seemed like a subterfuge so that he might wreak havoc all the more effectively from within.

We do not know exactly what touched off the first estrangement between Demetrius and Origen. Perhaps Origen took offense when Demetrius pointedly slighted him by ordaining his rival, Heraclas, to the presbyterate. Perhaps Demetrius got access to Origen's *Commentary on Genesis* or his *On First Principles* and was shocked by Origen's departures from Christian doctrine as he, Demetrius, understood it. Perhaps Demetrius was simply trying to exercise more and more control over Origen's private teaching. It is easy to see how Origen's powerful patronage and ever-increasing fame, along with his inquiring disposition, could have made Demetrius more and more uneasy. No doubt the visit to the governor of Arabia galled Demetrius because it clearly showed that, within the highest circles of power and social status in the empire, Origen commanded a respect Demetrius could never hope to obtain. He might also have resented and suspected Origen's free and open relationship with the pagan intellectual community, another circle of respect closed to him. Perhaps it simply bothered him that, while Origen had no position as an official representative of the faith, many Alexandrian Christians, among them Ambrosius, who must have been the most eminent man in the community, clearly took Origen much more seriously than they did him or any of his chosen presbyters. As an old man—and he must have been close to eighty by this time—the obvious eminence of a much younger man could have been threatening.

Whatever the cause of Origen's estrangement from Demetrius and his consequent feeling that he could not remain in Alexandria, Origen, in 230 it seems, followed in Clement's footsteps and went to Palestine.

He took up residence, however, not in Bishop Alexander's Jerusalem, but in Caesarea, where Alexander's colleague Theoctistus was bishop.

The situation of Caesarea in the third century makes it easy to understand why Origen would have preferred that city to Jerusalem.[2] Caesarea lacked Jerusalem's historic associations. Herod the Great founded it as a city on the site of an insignificant port named Strato's Tower. Herod, who named it Caesarea out of respect for Emperor Caesar Augustus, intended the new city to be a bastion of Greco-Roman civilization. He therefore provided it lavishly with the cultural amenities of a Greek city: gymnasia, theaters, and so on. He also created a magnificent artificial port which, together with the city's excellent location for trade—it was near the outlet of the valley of Esdraelon, the principle east-west route across Palestine—laid the foundation for the city's prosperity. When the Romans took over Palestine, they made Caesarea, with its easy communications and congenial, Hellenized population, the capital of the province instead of the forbiddingly Jewish city of Jerusalem. It remained the Roman capital in Origen's time. Caesarea was thus the city in Palestine most like Alexandria, even if it was provincial by comparison. Like Alexandria, it was a predominately Greek city with flourishing intellectual institutions, the administrative center of a province, a busy commercial center dealing in the Far Eastern trade, a manufacturing center specializing in glass and textiles, the center of a rich agricultural region, and a cosmopolitan city with large Christian and Jewish minorities.

Caesarea may also have appealed to Origen because it, unlike Jerusalem, was a major center of Jewish learning. We have seen already how, under the influence of a converted Jew, Origen had at Alexandria developed a keen interest in the Hebrew language and in the Jewish exegetical tradition. The Jewish wars of the first and second centuries, which had sadly reduced the Jewish community in Alexandria, all but eliminated Jews from Jerusalem. In 70 A.D., the Roman general Titus, soon to be emperor, plundered and destroyed the Temple in Jerusalem and turned Jerusalem into a ruin. About fifty years later his successor Hadrian, a great builder and a fervent pagan, decided to rebuild the city. He refounded it as a Hellenistic city, Aelia Capitolina. "Aelia" referred to Hadrian's family name, Capitolina to Jupiter Capitolinus, the chief god of Rome, whose cult Hadrian established on the site of the ancient

Temple of Solomon. Hadrian's desecration of the sacred spot led to the tragic Bar-Cochba rebellion which came to an end in 135. After putting down this rebellion, Hadrian strictly forbade Jews to reside at Aelia; his only concession was to allow them to enter the city on one day of the year to weep at the Wailing Wall. His regulations were still in force in Origen's day. Even if some Jews circumvented them, Jerusalem was obviously not a place where Jewish culture could flourish.

Following these calamities, the social and intellectual center of Judaism moved to northern Palestine, and the increasingly tolerant policies of the Severan dynasty encouraged Jews to settle in Caesarea, where they had never lived in large numbers before. Thus it came about that a large Jewish community with its own rabbinic academy existed there. Moreover the Jewish population there, as at Alexandria, was largely Hellenized. Although Jews carried out their studies in Hebrew, they spoke Greek—one rabbi even encouraged girls to learn Greek—and many of them were accustomed to mingling with non-Jews. Thus the accessibility of Jewish learning would have made Caesarea highly attractive to Origen, and we find that he took full advantage of it.[3]

Caesarea was a backwater as a Greek intellectual center even if it probably did have a respectable school of rhetoric. Thus Origen could not have hoped for the stimulating intellectual atmosphere of Alexandria; that would have been available only in Rome or Athens. Nonetheless, while there must have been few if any Christians in Caesarea as refined as Ambrosius and Tatiana, Origen must have been grateful for Theoctistus, who was a sympathetic bishop.

One can imagine that, viewed purely from the point of view of his own aggrandizement, Theoctistus' attitude toward Origen would have been different from Demetrius'. To Demetrius, Origen was a dangerous young rival to his power and prestige and a person whose theological opinions could only cause disunity. To Theoctistus, at least at first, Origen was a great ornament to his church. The greatest living Christian theologian embarrassed the bishop of Alexandria by his presence there, but he gave Caesarea considerable prestige. In addition, Origen's relationship to Theoctistus must have differed subtly from his relationship to Demetrius. At Alexandria, Origen was his own man; as the son of a martyr and the founder of his own school of Christian philosophy, he owed nothing to Demetrius. At Caesarea he was, at least, under an obligation; as a refugee from Demetrius, he depended on Theoctistus' good offices to maintain his position in the church. This new relationship was established during Origen's first, relatively brief, stay in Caesarea in 230. Theoctistus, with Alexander present and concurring, invited Origen to do what he had never been allowed to do in Alexandria, to expound the Scriptures in the service of public instruction which preceded the eucharist.

Demetrius took Theoctistus' action as an assault on his own judgment, as indeed it was. He fired off an angry letter charging that for a layperson to preach in the presence of bishops was a breach with ecclesiastical discipline. Demetrius' memory was probably failing him in his old age since the same thing had almost certainly occurred at Alexandria, at least before he became bishop there. Alexander and Theoctistus responded with a joint letter in which they defended their action, citing a number of precedents.

It would have seemed, after this exchange of letters, that Demetrius had become Origen's implacable enemy, and that Origen could not hope to return to Alexandria during Demetrius' lifetime. But Demetrius inexplicably changed his tune. Perhaps the evident appreciation Alexander and Theoctistus had shown for Origen convinced Demetrius that he was valuable. Perhaps Ambrosius was able to exercise that special influence which wealthy laypeople often have. At any rate, Demetrius sent two deacons to Caesarea to solicit Origen's return. This extraordinary embassy, a tribute to Origen's importance, persuaded him to return.

Once Origen was back in Alexandria, he abandoned his *Commentary on Genesis*. Perhaps Ambrosius advised him that, for the time being, it would be wiser not to venture any farther along the speculative lines which the early chapters on creation and fall suggested to him. Origen's new project was a *Commentary on John*, intended to refute the commentary which the Gnostic heretic Heracleon had composed seventy or so years earlier. Again Origen was lecturing to his stenographers, proofreading rough copies, and producing books.

Origen had only finished four books, and still had much of the first chapter of the Gospel yet to comment on when he again left Alexandria. In the autumn of 231, Julia Mammaea, the powerful dowager empress officially known as "mother of the emperor, the armies, the senate, the country, and the entire human race,'' was wintering with her son, the young Emperor Alexander Severus, at Antioch. The two of them were preparing for a campaign against the Persians in the following year. Antioch, now in extreme southern Turkey, was another Hellenistic city, which stood in relation to Syria roughly as Alexandria did to Egypt. Unlike Alexandria, Antioch had played a very important role in earliest Christianity; it was the place where Christians first came to be called by that name.[4] Julia was herself a Syrian, a native of the inland city of Emesa, and she, like the rest of her family, took a keen interest in religious matters in general and Christianity in particular. Hippolytus dedicated to her a now lost treatise on the resurrection. Indeed, her nephew Elagabalus—who became emperor (218–22) by claiming, falsely, that he was an illegitimate son of the assassinated Emperor Caracalla—took religion far too seriously for his own good. Before becoming emperor, Elagabalus had been priest of the local Baal of Emesa. For a few years he shocked the empire by presiding as emperor over the orgiastic rites of his native religion, whose deity came to Rome in the form of a large rock, probably a meteorite. Julia Mammaea contrived to have him assassinated in 222; she kept his job in the family by making her thirteen-year-old son Alexander emperor. An unreliable history credits Alexander with more conventional, if eclectic, religious tastes. It is said that he erected statues of Abraham and Christ, along with two Hellenistic heroes, Orpheus and Alexander of Tyana, in his *lararium* or private chapel.

Julia, having heard of Origen, requested that he meet her in Antioch that same autumn and sent a military bodyguard to see him safely there. We do not know what Origen discussed with Mammaea, and, at any rate, within four years, the army, tired of having a mama's boy for emperor, assassinated her and her son and brought the checkered Severan dynasty to an end. The visit, however, coming as it did, after his triumphs in Arabia and Palestine, must have made Origen all the more loath to return to the shadow of Demetrius. He probably stayed in Antioch until shipping began again the following spring. While there he wrote, at Ambrosius' insistence, a fifth book of his *Commentary on John*, pushing up through verse 1:18. A large gift from the empress, customary in such situations, probably gave Origen the resources to leave Alexandria soon after returning there from Antioch.

Origen may have decided while he was in Antioch to leave Alexandria permanently. On his return he did not stay long enough to complete the sixth book of his commentary on John but set out for Greece almost immediately. Rather than sail, he took the land route up the eastern coast of the Mediterranean and through Asia Minor. This enabled him to pass through Caesarea on the way. There an event occurred which permanently settled Origen's relationship with Demetrius; Bishop Theoctistus ordained him to the presbyterate. Theoctistus must have done so with the clear understanding that Origen no longer considered himself a member of Demetrius' church.

With this new dignity, Origen continued toward Greece, and it seems likely that he meant to establish himself there, though it is possible that he intended to return to Caesarea. The reason he later gave for his journey to Greece, "the urgent needs of church business," sounds intentionally vague. He would presumably have mentioned just what business it was, had he not simply been scouting out the land. On his way overland toward Greece, Origen accepted the hospitality of churches in the cities through which he passed and preached at the church in the large city of Caesarea Mazaca in Cappadocia, now Kayseri in central Turkey, where Firmillian was bishop.

Greece, for Origen, almost certainly meant Athens, the third great intellectual center of the empire, and the one he had not yet visited. Athens, in Origen's time, was politically and economically insignificant but retained its eminence as an intellectual and cultural center. The city had changed very little in the eighty years since Pausanias described it in great detail.[5] It resembled nothing so much as a great open-air museum in which the splendid artistic and architectural monuments of the Periclean age, augmented by later benefactions, survived largely intact. The city's sheer profusion of shrines to the gods, lovingly preserved as relics of a glorious antiquity, gave the Athenians a reputation as the world's most superstitious people. Origen would scarcely have gone to Athens, as many cultured pagans did, as a tourist, but he would have found the city's reputation as an intellectual center highly attractive. Since the time of Socrates, Athens had never ceased to be an important center for philosophical study. Hadrian's construction of a library there in 132 and Marcus Aurelius' endowment of teachers in each of the four major philosophical schools—Platonism, Aristotelianism, Stoicism, and Epicureanism—in 176 fostered the continuation of philosophical learning. It is uncertain if, in Origen's time, an institution claiming to be Plato's Academy existed in Athens, but it was certainly a center for the teaching of Platonism.

Origen remained in Greece for a year or two. Presumably he worshiped with the Christian community at Athens and availed himself of the city's intellectual resources. We do not hear, though, that he either preached or composed any books. In the spring of 233 he found himself embroiled in a very serious controversy.

## The Break with Demetrius

During these years in Athens, Origen probably did not know just what was happening at Alexandria, but he might have guessed. It seems that his ordination had made Demetrius furious, and that Demetrius, a consummate ecclesiastical politician, had laid plans to strike at Origen and his Palestinian supporters. Apparently in 232 Demetrius, learning of Origen's ordination, wrote a letter lining up the support of his ally, Bishop Pontian of Rome. Demetrius presented, it seems, two principal grievances against Origen. The first was that the bishops of Palestine had committed a major breach of ecclesiastical discipline by ordaining to the presbyterate a member of his congregation and, what is more, a eunuch. The second was that, still worse, they were harboring a heretic. Demetrius, it appears, quoted a damaging passage from Origen's *Dialogue with Candidus* which implied that the devil would be saved. He could also point to Origen's known relations with Gnostic and pagan philosophers. By the end of the year, it appears, Demetrius had received some form of backing from Pontian. He had also lined up the support of the rest of the bishops of Egypt, who excommunicated Origen and deposed him from his office as presbyter. At this point Demetrius could attack Origen through his supporters. He probably intended to engineer a council in Palestine which would depose Alexander and Theoctistus and condemn Origen. On hearing of Demetrius' machinations, Alexander found himself under considerable pressure, and the evidence implicating Origen as a heretic may have seriously disturbed him, but he did not simply throw Origen to the wolves. Instead, in the spring of 233, Alexander seems to have written to Origen requesting that he answer Demetrius' charges.

This communication may have been Origen's first intimation of the storm that his ordination had raised. He responded with a letter which probably saved his career in the church.[6] Origen provided Alexander with a correct copy of his *Dialogue with Candidus*, which made it clear that he claimed no more than that the devil *could* be saved—not that the devil *would* be. This must have satisfied Alexander, though Demetrius probably would have considered it quibbling. To the charges that he had kept suspiciously close contact with Gnostics, he responded that his poverty as the orphan of a martyr had forced him to take lodging in the same household with the Gnostic Paul, but that he had carefully abstained from compromising his principles in his relations with him. Besides, he had converted to orthodoxy the eminent Ambrosius. He admitted to frequenting philosophical schools but insisted that he had done so in the interests of the church. He, at any rate, had not had his head turned by them as had his erstwhile colleague Heraclas, now a presbyter in the Alexandrian church, who had gone about in a philosopher's cloak. Origen, furthermore, explained as best he could the reasons for his journeys away from Alexandria. A copy of this letter to Alexander in the church archives at Caesarea was apparently Eusebius' principal source for his account of Origen's life in the *Ecclesiastical History*.

The letter was effective. Alexander wrote to Pontian of Rome defending Origen. He also wrote a warm letter to Origen, recalling their mutual teacher, Clement, and addressing Origen, a much younger man, as "best in all things, my master and brother." About the same time as he received Alexander's support, Origen probably learned that Demetrius had died and that Heraclas had succeeded him as bishop of Alexandria. While Heraclas, Origen's rival, scarcely meant him well, the death of Demetrius probably averted a major crisis. Soon Origen was on his way back toward Caesarea, where he established his residence in 234.

The events just described did not weaken Origen's loyalty to the church, but they did put him in a cruelly awkward position. Demetrius' efforts were bent on forcing Origen to choose between being expelled from the fellowship of the church or renouncing his own deepest insights. Demetrius' death spared Origen this choice, but the crisis left him hurt and embittered. The first thing he wrote, once he was settled in Caesarea, was the preface to the sixth book of his continuing *Commentary on John*. He had partially written this book after returning to Alexandria from Antioch, but he had lost the manuscript in the haste of his departure and had to begin it afresh. It is scarcely surprising, given what he had been through, that Origen gave vent to his bitterness in a preface in which he explained how his work had been interrupted. There he spoke of his departure from Alexandria in biblical imagery as a "deliverance from Egypt," and one can scarcely doubt whom he had in mind as Pharaoh.[7] Nor was Origen's hurt entirely psychological; Demetrius' actions were to have lasting consequences. Origen's position in the church at Caesarea was secure, and he was shortly to obtain a degree of influence and respect he had never possessed at Alexandria. Nevertheless, having been accused of heresy, he lived under a cloud. Furthermore, he could not return to Alexandria since the church there still considered him a heretic and would continue to. Demetrius' successor, Heraclas, was to prove just as implacable an enemy as Demetrius himself had been.

## Views on Ecclesiastical Leadership

These events forced Origen to consider the nature of leadership in the church, ultimately the basic issue in his conflict with Demetrius. Origen and Demetrius, in fact, represent two conflicting understandings of authority—one could call them charismatic and hierarchical—which have always existed uneasily together in the church. As an institution builder, Demetrius relied heavily on the hierarchial understanding of authority. Demetrius claimed the right to direct the church at Alexandria and to distinguish true doctrine from false on the basis on his position as bishop. He might accept fraternal correction from his fellow bishops, he might seek counsel from his presbyters, but he did not need to be answerable to the laity. The second century had seen the spread of this hierarchical understanding of authority within the Christian church. Already in the first decade of the century, Bishop Ignatius of Antioch had written to the churches on his path to martyrdom at Rome admonishing them to revere their bishops as if they were Christ himself. Even earlier Clement, a Roman presbyter, wrote on behalf of his church to Corinth, advising the Corinthian Christians that they had acted improperly in replacing the presbyters who constituted the established authority in their church. Demetrius, more than anyone else, assured that this hierarchical understanding would prevail at Alexandria.[8]

In Origen's charismatic understanding of authority, unmediated divine inspiration, not human ordination, is the legitimating factor. Charismatic authority does not demand obedience because it has a quasi-legal right to it; rather, it commands and evokes obedience because it mediates God's word.[9] A close look at Origen's understanding of religious authority makes it clear why Origen frequently found himself at odds with the church's official leaders. In examining this aspect of Origen's thought, it will be useful to take into consideration works that he wrote in the later part of his life after he had settled in Caesarea, but their consistency with the views set out in *On First Principles* and the early books of the *Commentary on John*, works which Origen wrote while he was still at Alexandria, shows that his understanding of religious authority was already well formed by the time he settled at Caesarea. Origen never wrote a work addressed specifically to the issue of religious authority, but we find the issue treated incidentally throughout his works. In his interpretation of the Bible, Origen presented priests and Apostles, the typical religious leaders of, respectively, the Old and New Testament, as the models for religious leaders in the church of his own time. In choosing these figures as models, Origen was scarcely original; where he radically challenged the hierarchical conception of religious authority was in the meaning he gave them. For Origen, priests and Apostles were persons whose advance in moral perfection and intellectual understanding gave them access to the deeper mysteries of the Bible. Their position as religious authorities stemmed, not from any official position they might have, but from the privileged access to God which their insights into Scripture provided them. As persons with such insights, they naturally possessed charismatic authority as mediators of God's word to the larger community, which had no such access to God.

Origen followed Clement[10] in identifying priests in general and the high priest in particular as symbols of the inspired exegete. Their privileged ritual access to the divine presence and their responsibility in the sacrificial cultus to mediate between God and the people as a whole symbolized the spiritual exegete's special access to the deeper meaning of the Bible and responsibility to mediate that awareness through teaching. In his *Homilies on Leviticus* at Caesarea Origen interpreted the ritual legislation of the Old Testament along these lines. Thus, the priest's vestments symbolized moral and intellectual qualifications.[11] Similarly, the details of the sacrificial ritual symbolized his teaching activity. Removing the skin of the sacrificial victim was the removing of the veil of the literal sense to reveal the mystical meaning of the Bible, while taking fine incense in the hand was making fine distinctions in the interpretation of difficult passages.[12] Unquestionably Origen did not identify priests with the existing officials of the church. The prime characteristic of priests, Origen stated in the first book of his *Commentary on John*, is that they "abandon everything to pursue a study of rational argument," a study which enables them to gain a direct apprehension of the truth of Christian doctrine which far excels mere reliance on the authority of tradition.[13] Origen did not identify any such priests, but he made it clear that he thought they still existed in the church.

As with priests, the prime qualification of the Apostles was their insight into the mysteries of the Bible. The "fields . . . white already to harvest" which Jesus called upon the Apostles to reap were the books of the Old Testament.[14] When he called upon them to cross the Sea of Galilee, this symbolized his call to pass from the literal to the spiritual sense of Scripture.[15] A prime characteristic of the Apostle's function as an interpreter and teacher of the Bible was the duty to exercise discretion. Paul, the greatest of the Apostles, provided Origen with an example of apostolic discretion. When among spiritual Christians, Paul boldly imparted "a secret and hidden wisdom of God" (1 Cor. 2:7), but among the simple he judged it expedient "to know nothing . . . except Jesus Christ and him crucified" (1 Cor. 2:2).[16] Origen was careful in the case of Apostles, as with priests, to remove any suggestions that those who fulfilled the apostolic function in the church could be identified as the holders of particular positions. Apostles are those who perform the works of an Apostle, works such as restoring to sight those blinded by false doctrine and raising to life those dead in their sins.[17] Apostleship is verified in its fruits, or as Paul said: "If to others I am not an apostle, at least I am to you; for you are the seal of my apostleship in the Lord" (1 Cor. 9:2).[18]

From this description of the priest and Apostle as biblical models of religious leadership, it should be obvious that Origen was himself a perfect exemplar. Origen did not explicitly claim such a dignity for himself, but we can be certain that he did consider himself as apostle and priest. Such a claim to religious authority is implicit in Origen's introduction to *On First Principles* and is, indeed, the theoretical justification for that work. There he claimed that the Apostles were highly reticent about the deep, spiritual truths they had learned from Jesus and contented themselves, in their writings, with setting forth only basic doctrines necessary for salvation, doctrines which they expected to be accepted on authority. The Apostles, however, fully expected that in the generations after them there would be persons who, by virtue of their diligent study, would merit the same spiritual insights they themselves had been privy to.[19] This claim to a deeper level of Christian truth is the foundation of Origen's effort in *On First Principles,* so that by the very undertaking of such a project he was implicitly claiming to have an insight into divine mysteries at least comparable to that of the Apostles. By setting forth such doctrines Origen was also implicitly claiming that the possession of such knowledge carried with it the spiritual discretion to know when and how to reveal it. We see the same principle operating in Origen's interpretation, later in his life, of the parable of the unmerciful steward in Matthew. Origen noted that the Apostle Matthew, the putative author of the Gospel, saw fit not to include the interpretation of the puzzling parable he must have heard from Jesus' lips. Origen belied his disclaimer that he could claim no such understanding as Matthew had by providing a spiritual interpretation of the parable. But what gave Origen the authority to reveal a secret Matthew had supposedly deliberately withheld? His response that God, who grants the interpreter the comprehension of the spiritual meaning, also grants along with it the discretion to judge how much should be said about it.[20]

Although Origen was careful to avoid identifying the priests and the Apostles of the Bible with any existing officials in the church, he believed, nonetheless, that the moral and intellectual elite that these biblical figures symbolized should, by all rights, be the actual authorities in the church. Ideally, bishops should combine irreproachable virtue with skill in argument and the ability to seek out the hidden truths in the Bible.[21] The selection of Joshua as Moses' successor, a selection based entirely on such spiritual qualities, was a model for the selection of a bishop.[22] Sadly enough, however, few bishops and presbyters actually met these high standards. In terms of biblical symbolism, their models are not the Jewish priests but the priests of Pharaoh, who symbolize those preoccupied with worldly concerns.[23] They do not imitate the Apostles, whom Jesus chose as his successors, but the high priests, scribes and Pharisees, whom he excoriated. This is especially true of bishops in the larger cities, who set themselves up as petty tyrants, inaccessible to the people they ought to serve.[24] Lacking ethical purity, such clergy, naturally enough, have no perception of the hidden meaning of Scripture. Still worse, they despise those who do have such perception, persons who "search even the depths of God."[25] They may even be purveyors of false doctrine. It is fortunate for many clergy that God no longer treats heretics as God did Korah, Dathan, and Abiram, whom the earth swallowed up alive![26]

Is it the case, then, that God has failed to provide the church with worthy leaders? Far from it. Such persons are available, but the church often fails to give them their rightful place of honor and responsibility. In fact, the members of the spiritual elite are, in reality, the true clergy of the church, as opposed to those who have the worldly honors but only seem to be presbyters and bishops.[27]

Penitential discipline makes clear the contrast between the genuine authority of this spiritual elite and the spurious claims of unworthy ecclesiastics. In the course of the second and third centuries, as we have seen, bishops increasingly inclined to claim the power to excommunicate sinners and to reconcile penitents to the church. Since to readmit persons still in sin would endanger the church's purity, readmission to fellowship was tantamount to a declaration of forgiveness. Bishops claimed this power as successors to the Apostles, to whom Jesus had given the keys to the kingdom of heaven with the words of Matthew 16:19: "Whatever you bind on earth shall be bound in heaven, and whatever you loose on earth shall be loosed in heaven."

Origen did not believe that bishops could claim this power of forgiveness simply by virtue of their official position. Only a genuine priest and Apostle could forgive sins because only such a person was inspired by the Holy Spirit with a spiritual insight into the sinner's condition. Because he rejected the spurious claim of ecclesiastics, Origen was inclined, for a long time, to support the rigorist position on penitential matters; he held that certain serious sins were incurable in this life and that persons who had committed them could never be reconciled to the church.[28] Later, Origen abandoned rigorism, but he continued to insist that an unworthy cleric had no legitimate authority. In his *Commentary on Matthew* he pointed out that Christ gave the power of the keys to Peter so that only "a Peter"—a person with Peter's virtue and intellectual insight—could exercise that power.[29]

Origen's denial of spurious authority to clergy who failed to meet his qualifications for religious leadership has little in common with the position that would be taken a generation after his death by the Donatist and Melitian schismatics. The Donatists in western North Africa and the Melitians in Egypt claimed that the sinfulness of clergy not only made their ministrations worthless but endangered the purity of the church so gravely as to compel true Christians to withdraw fellowship even from those who were in communion with them. Origen, for all his bitterness about the unworthiness of some clerics, displayed, by contrast, almost complete complacency about their presence. Insofar as the ministrations of unworthy clerics were invalid, they were simply meaningless external actions. Such actions simply had nothing to do with the genuine Christian's spiritual communion with God. A bishop could readmit sinners to the external fellowship of the church under the pretense that the bishop had forgiven their sins; nonetheless, as long as those persons remained sinners, they were excluded by their sin from the church's genuine, spiritual fellowship. Likewise, no unworthy bishop—not even Peter himself—could exclude righteous persons from that spiritual fellowship, even if he could, by unworthily excommunicating them, cut them off externally from the church.[30] Origen's understanding of religious leadership made him immune from Demetrius' fulminations, but it did not involve the church at Alexandria in Demetrius' unworthiness.

This understanding of religious leadership contrasts markedly with the hierarchical understanding that Demetrius exemplified and upheld. Origen's appropriation of priests and Apostles as models for the charismatic authority of inspired interpreters of the Bible was a direct challenge to the claims of the officially constituted clergy. In the course of the second century, bishops had increasingly come to look upon themselves as successors to the Apostles of New Testament times by virtue of their succession from them through a chain of legitimate ordinations. This claim provided an orthodox alternative to Gnostic claims to secret traditions mediated to them from various Apostles. In that context

Origen's claim that spiritual qualities alone are the basis of apostolic authority must have appeared to subvert good order. Similarly, it was in Origen's time that clergy were beginning to present themselves as the equivalent, under the new dispensation, of the Levitical priesthood of the Old Testament.[31] Origen's argument that priesthood is an utterly different matter and his protest against the usurpation of the priestly title by persons not worthy of it was almost certainly his reaction to this development.

The events of 231–34 do not actually account for Origen's understanding of religious authority. His mentor, Clement of Alexandria, had much the same ideas, and *On First Principles* exhibits an exalted sense of Origen's authority as a teacher. It is more likely that conflicting understandings of religious authority were one cause of Origen's conflict with Demetrius. Those events, nonetheless, brought a bitter, personal animus to an issue that had before been theoretical. The rift between Origen and Demetrius may have had to come. Demetrius, as an institution builder, could not tolerate insubordination. Origen, as an intellectual, could not accept external limitations on his freedom to pursue the truth. The rift with Demetrius thus illustrates the awkward position of an intellectual in a disciplined, ideologically motivated movement, a phenomenon with which our own time has become very familiar. The church needed Origen if it was to make its faith attractive and comprehensible to the larger Greco-Roman world. Origen needed the church as a place of fellowship and as an embodiment of his spiritual ideal. But Origen's brilliant, questioning mind could not help disturbing the church, and the church's manifest imperfections could not help disturbing Origen. The events of 231–34, the subsequent events in Origen's life, and the turbulent history of his posthumous reputation illustrate the tortured but fruitful relationship between the man and the institution.

# VII
# Exegesis and Prayer
(234–38)

In 233, having settled in Caesarea, Origen rejoiced that the tumults of the preceding years were over and that he once again had the peace he needed to undertake sustained work. His departure from Alexandria had not cost him Ambrosius' friendship and patronage, nor had a brief contretemps over Ambrosius' indiscreet handling of *On First Principles* marred their relationship. Soon after returning from Greece Origen set to work once more, with the aid of clerical assistants Ambrosius supplied, on the *Commentary on John*. Ambrosius was an enviable patron; he not only provided Origen with the means to publish but continually stimulated him intellectually and even collaborated with him. Origen referred to Ambrosius as his taskmaster and in a letter complained disingenuously that Ambrosius,

> supposing that I am a zealous worker and utterly athirst for the word of God, convicted me by his own zeal for work and passion for sacred studies. Wherefore so far has he surpassed me that I am in danger of refusing his demands; for neither when we are engaged in collating can we take our meals, nor, when we have taken them, walk and rest our bodies. Nay, even at the times set apart for these things we are constrained to discourse learnedly and to correct our manuscripts. Neither can we sleep at night for the good of our bodies, since our learned discourse extends far into the evening. I need not mention that our morning studies also are prolonged to the ninth, at times to the tenth, hour; for all who wish to work zealously consecrate that time to the investigation and reading of the divine oracles.[1]

In addition to the *Commentary on John*, other works which Origen wrote at Ambrosius' request in the years immediately after his move to Caesarea include a treatise *On Prayer*, the continuation of his *Commen-*

147

*tary on Genesis,* and books of disconnected notes on Exodus, Leviticus, and perhaps, Numbers and Deuteronomy. Origen also composed for Ambrosius' benefit his short *Exhortation to Martyrdom.* Of these works, only fragments of the commentaries survive, but the treatises survive intact and are among Origen's most valuable works. The fragments which survive of the Genesis commentary and of the notes on Exodus are minimal, but of the *Commentary on John,* nine of the thirty-two volumes are nearly intact.

## Commentary on John

Origen did not attempt to maintain at Caesarea the same scale that had characterized the Alexandrian portion of the *Commentary on John,* in which he had only managed to comment on seventeen verses of chapter one in the course of five volumes. Nevertheless it remained massive, too massive in fact, for Origen to complete it. Although he had made it to the thirteenth chapter, more than halfway through the Gospel, Origen was clearly running out of steam at the beginning of his thirty-second book, composed perhaps fifteen years after he had undertaken the project. There, in the preface, he told Ambrosius he expected he could not complete the commentary and would have to resume his study of John's Gospel in paradise. That volume and the commentary as a whole, ends abruptly at John 13:33. The work's forbidding scale stems from Origen's method of commenting on a text. He not only paid critical attention to the meaning of the words in the manner of Alexandrian scholarship, but compared each significant word or concept in the text at hand with that word or concept as it appears elsewhere in Scripture. Employed exhaustively, such a procedure can turn the commentary on only one word into a treatise in its own right, as in the first volume of the commentary, which deals only with two words, ''beginning'' and ''word,'' from John 1:1. Although Origen sought to rein in his tendency to digress, often postponing detailed treatment of complex issues or referring to his treatment of them elsewhere, his conviction that each word in the Bible was specifically inspired just as it was and could be the key to the mystical sense made expansiveness inevitable. Thus the seemingly casual mention that Jesus was teaching in the temple treasury in John 8:20 led Origen to ask where else the temple treasury appeared in Jesus' ministry, the answer being in the story of the widow's mite, recounted in slightly different versions by Mark and Luke. One word therefore led Origen to discuss in his commentary on John 8:20 the spiritual principle involved in the story of the widow's mite, that of serving God to the utmost of our ability.[2] But how could the sheer volume this procedure entailed be justified in the light of the saying in Ecclesiastes 12:12, "Of making many books there is no end"? Truth, Origen replied, is unitary, simple, and briefly stated, but error is multiple, and the defender of the church's teaching must reply in detail to the innumerable errors which Gnostics falsely so-called made in interpreting the gospel.[3]

The defense of orthodoxy was a major purpose of Origen's *Commentary on John*, as it was of his *Commentary on Genesis*. Both books of the Bible had contributed significantly to Gnostic systems, particularly those of the Valentinians. Although the Gospel of John, as we have it, is not a Gnostic book, its depiction of Jesus as a life-bringing divine emissary from heaven was much closer to Valentinus' concept of a savior than the earthy rabbi of the Synoptic Gospels. It is likely, in fact, that Ambrosius commissioned Origen's *Commentary on John* specifically to provide an orthodox alternative to the commentary on John by Valentinus' disciple, Heracleon. At any rate, Origen carefully refuted Heracleon's interpretation whenever he had the opportunity. Even when he was not specifically dealing with Heracleon, Origen took pains to uphold free will against the Valentinian doctrine of salvation by nature, and to refute the Marcionite doctrine that evil exists independently of God or the Sabellian doctrine that Christ is identical with God the Father.

Although the refutation of heresy was a valuable fruit of his commentary, its basic purpose was the exposition of the mystical sense of the Gospel. Origen considered the study of the Gospel of John particularly promising because that Gospel was, as he stated in the preface to the commentary, the book which most nearly approximated the eternal gospel of which the entire Bible is the earthly symbol. John not only leaned on Jesus' breast at the Last Supper, but Jesus made him, in effect, a second Christ, when he gave him Mary as his mother as they stood at the foot of the cross. Since John, its author, was the disciple closest to Jesus, his work contained the grandest and most perfect of

Jesus' sayings. But this should not lead us to expect John to the the easiest Gospel to interpret; it is, in fact, the most obscure precisely because it is the most profound. Those who believe things unworthy of God cannot possibly understand it, and even orthodox Christians can attain to the mystical sense only if God graciously aids their long and diligent study. In the story of the Samaritan woman at the well, John depicted allegorically the difficulty of arriving at the full meaning of his Gospel. The story reveals three possible approaches to Scripture: that of the heretics, which is utterly false; that of simple Christians, which is very limited; and that of spiritual Christians, which offers the possibility of mystical communion with God. The Samaritan woman, Origen believed, was a heretic whom Jesus redeemed from her error. Having found a preoccupation with earthly affairs and materialistic philosophy inadequate to her spiritual needs (this is the symbolism of her rejection of five husbands, the five senses), she had turned to the false doctrines of the heretics (the sixth man who is not really her husband). She draws from the well, which symbolizes the Bible, but because of her errors, the water she draws from it can satisfy her only temporarily. She arrives at interpretations of the Bible which are clever and initially plausible, like those of Heracleon, but they ultimately provoke doubts. Jacob and his beasts, who once drank at the well, symbolize the other two types of readers. Jacob, whose second name, Israel, means "he who sees God," is the spiritual person, who attains to the eternally satisfying mystical sense that Jesus himself offers. Jacob's beasts are simple Christians with meager powers of understanding whom the well satisfies at their own level.[4] While the literal sense is patent to all believing Christians, the mystical sense, the true meaning John intended, is open only to those who have been given the grace to receive it. For this reason, Origen prayed at the very outset of his commentary that God would assist him through Christ in the Holy Spirit to attain to the Gospel's mystical meaning.[5]

It is allegory in the Gospel of John as elsewhere in the Bible that makes the mystical sense accessible. Origen was as confident as any modern scholar relying on historical criticism that his method of interpretation was the best possible way to arrive at the meaning intended by the biblical author. There is not second guessing to it. All of the biblical writers knew, he repeatedly insisted, the full mystical meaning of their books and intentionally employed allegory to hide it. To assert the contrary would be to turn the biblical authors from genuine prophets into mere seers like Caiaphas and Balaam, wicked men who nonetheless uttered profound truths inadvertently or under constraint.[6] John, who conversed intimately with the Word made flesh, had come to know Christ's most profound teaching. He thus had more cause than any other biblical author to veil his message since, as a general principle, the more exalted the message, the more dangerous it is for the unworthy to know it. The Gospel of John itself, Origen believed, provided an object lesson in this principle. Origen considered it significant that Satan entered into Judas at the Last Supper causing him to go out and betray Jesus only after Judas had partaken of the sop which Jesus had presented to him. Since, as advanced Christians know, the eucharist which Jesus had just instituted symbolizes the Word of Truth, Judas' subsequent behavior demonstrates how dangerous it is to partake unworthily of profound doctrine.[7] We must, therefore, expect to find in the Gospel of John a veil of allegory yet more opaque than elsewhere in the Bible.

Critical analysis of the Gospel narrative, Origen thought, provided believers in the inspired character of the Gospels irrefutable proof that John employed allegory. Reading the Gospels literally, he held, necessarily involved the reader in discrepancies between the Gospel accounts and historical impossibilities within them. The second chapter of John contains examples of both. Verses 13–17 describe Jesus' ascent to Jerusalem at the time of the Passover. There he took a whip of cords and drove the moneychangers and merchants from the temple. This account is obviously inconsistent with those in the other three Gospels insofar as it occurs near the beginning of Jesus' ministry rather than in its final week. Desperate literalists might reply that Jesus cleansed the temple on two separate occasions, but a close critical analysis, noted Origen, makes it appear unlikely that a literal cleansing of the temple occurred at any point in Jesus' ministry. If Jesus did drive moneychangers and merchants from the temple, he had to have done so either by human or by divine power. If by human power, it is doubtful that he could have accomplished it. How could one person, and he to all appearances a carpenter's son, have created such a major public disturbance with impunity, must less have succeeded? If, on the other hand, Christ had intended to cleanse the temple by divine power, a single word would have sufficed; he would not have needed to go about undignifiedly overturning tables while swinging a whip of cords.[8]

The narrative of the triumphal entry into Jerusalem recounted in all four Gospels, and associated with the cleansing of the temple in the Synoptics, makes literalism even more improbable. Besides suspicious details—the branches strewed in Jesus' path, to cite one such, would have served better as an obstacle to his entry than as a manifestation of respect—there are irreconcilable inconsistencies between the Gospel narratives. For example, three of the Gospels mention only one animal on which Jesus rode, but Matthew mentions two. If we believe that all four evangelists were inspired to write just as they did, we must assume that their writings are true. When, however, they contradict each other on the literal level, we must assume that at least one is literally false but, of course, spiritually true. In this case, since Jesus assuredly would have needed only one animal for a journey of about two miles, Matthew is the one likely to be literally false. Such minor details, perceptible only to the attentive reader, point to the spiritual sense. In this case, the two animals of Matthew's account, one older and one younger, probably symbolize the Old and New Testaments, appropriately allegorized as beasts of burden because they bear the burden of the literal sense. This points to an overall interpretation of Jesus' entry into Jerusalem as an allegory of the entry of the Word of God into the soul of the believer, borne there by the study of the Bible. Such an interpretation of the entry into Jerusalem as a spiritual rather than a literal entry has the advantage of obviating one of the most common Jewish objections to the Christian interpretation of Old Testament prophecy. Jews frequently asked what gave Christians the right to consider Zechariah 9:9 a prophecy fulfilled in Jesus' entry into Jerusalem while ignoring the following verse, not fulfilled, which predicts that the Messiah will command peace to the nations and rule from the river to the ends of the earth. Considered spiritually, Origen argued, the prophecy was entirely fulfilled by Jesus' entry into the souls of Christian believers throughout the world.[9]

Simple Christians might understandably find such a devastating analysis of the historicity of the Gospel narratives a threat to their credibility as divinely inspired writings, but Origen claimed that his analysis was the best support for an informed belief in the Bible's authority:

> It must be demonstrated that the truth of the narratives is in intellectual
> matters, since many, being unable to resolve their contradictions, have
> renounced their belief in the gospels, taking them to be memoirs com-
> posed haphazardly rather than by the guidance of a diviner spirit.[10]

The Gospels are true spiritually in their entirety, but parts of them are
false literally.[11] Although Origen reserved most of his criticism for
heretics, he could spare some gall for obscurantist simple Christians
who refused to allow the legitimacy of allegory applied as widely as he
himself employed it. John 4:44, "a prophet has no honor in his own
country," called to his mind Jesus' scornful comments on the way the
scribes and Pharisees honored posthumously the prophets whom they
themselves would have killed as surely as their ancestors did. What
does it mean to honor the prophets by building tombs for them as Jesus
accused his adversaries of doing, Origen asked, if it is not to honor the
letter of the Bible that kills while ignoring the life-giving spiritual meaning that informs it?[12] Like Clement, Origen sharply distinguished his
own use of the allegorical method from the false and arbitrary interpretations of the Gnostics. Unlike the Gnostics, whom he accused of selec-
tively choosing snippets of the Bible which seemed to fit their fantastic
hypotheses, Origen claimed to arrive at the genuine spiritual sense by
interpreting the Bible as a connected whole. God indeed commanded
this when God demanded that the people of Israel wholly consume the
lamb of the Passover, which symbolized the Bible.[13]

Today Origen's allegorical interpretations of John often seem almost
as fantastic as those of the Gnostics he refuted. His understanding of the
Bible as an utterly unitary book shadowing forth the timeless vertities of
an unchanging ideal world enabled him to defend third-century orthodoxy while discouraging any but the most rudimentary notion of historical criticism. Yet Origen was not just a Platonizing allegorizer; he was
also a trained teacher of literature in the tradition of the great Alexandrian literary scholars. He was, in fact, one of the greatest interpreters
of the Bible on the literal level in the early church. This, given Origen's
presuppositions, is not as paradoxical as it might at first seem; we must
go beyond the letter, but we also have to start there. The *Commentary
on John*, like Origen's *Hexapla*, therefore, is the work of a student and
teacher of grammar.

This was quite natural. The Bible presented Origen with problems similar to those that faced an interpreter of Greek literature, problems that went far beyond establishing a reliable text. The Bible was a text to some extent alien to Greco-Roman readers in Origen's time, like the already classical works of Greek literature. More time had elapsed between Origen and Homer than between us and Chaucer, and the changes in language and culture were comparable. Just as the teacher of the *Iliad* had to explain that a *phasganon* was a sword and that Thebe, the home of Hector's wife Andromache, was a town in Phrygia not far from Troy, the teacher of the Bible had to make comprehensible the often opaque Hebraisms of the Septuagint (sometimes adopted by New Testament authors to give their work a scriptural ring) and tell his students where the Sea of Galilee and Jericho were. One word in the Lord's Prayer, as we shall see, had already become incomprehensible by Origen's time. Also, in an age before such conveniences as quotation marks or the distinction between capital and lowercase letters, it took some effort simply to make sense of a dialogue or a complex sentence.

Origen used the techniques he learned from Alexandrian literary study to refute heretical interpretations, to demonstrate to the simple the need for seeking a deeper meaning, and to provide the clues needed to reach the spiritual sense. In his interpretation of John 1:16 it was important to Origen to show that the phrase "from his fullness have we all received" belonged to the speech given to John the Baptist rather than, as Heracleon held, to the Evangelist. If John the Baptist had said it, it would imply that the grace of God was manifested before the coming of Christ and hence that the coming of Christ was not, as Heracleon belived, the irruption of a savior sent by a God unfamiliar to the Jews. Origen, as a professor of grammar, pointed out that assigning the passage to the Evangelist makes the Baptist's speech end abruptly and without notice.[14] (Many modern commentators think, nonetheless, that the author of the Gospel did just that.) In his interpretation of John 1:25–27, Origen also employed grammatical criteria of dramatic appropriateness. There John the Baptist responds to the question "Then why are you baptizing, if you are neither the Christ, nor Elijah, nor the prophet?" with the answer, "I baptize with water; but among you stands one whom you do not know, even he who comes after me, the thong of whose sandal I am not worthy to untie." Heracleon apparently considered this a *non sequitur*. Origen demonstrated the pertinence of the answer according to the enigmatically terse logic of the Gospel: John has a right and duty to baptize even though he is not the promised Messiah because his humble baptism in water is a necessary preparation for the spiritual baptism of the Messiah who is to come.[15]

Origen's tour de force in demonstrating the impossibility, on the literal level, of the narratives of the triumphal entry into Jerusalem and the cleansing of the temple were basically exercises in the techniques of Alexandrian grammar. The Alexandrian grammarians distinguished between history, fiction, and myth. History did take place; fiction could have taken place, but did not; and myth could not have taken place. The discrepancies between the Gospel accounts demonstrate that some of them, at least, cannot be historical. The inappropriateness of the actions recounted in them demonstrates that we should understand them entirely as myth.[16]

One aspect of grammar particularly useful, in Origen's opinion, for determining the spiritual sense was etymology. One reason Origen probably wished to learn Hebrew was to become more proficient at finding the roots of Hebrew names. Origen shared the belief, common in his time, that the root meaning of a word remained somehow associated with it even when the word itself had come to mean something else entirely and that knowledge of this original meaning could be a very useful clue to the meaning of the text. As a result, scarcely a Hebrew name goes by in the Gospel of John without Origen's presenting its supposed etymology as a clue to the deeper meaning of the text. Origen's concern for etymology contrasts grotesquely, in one of its applications, with a laudable concern for geography. He proposed reading "Bethabara" instead of "Bethany" in John 1:28, arguing that he had been to both places and that Bethabara was the only one appropriate to the text, which gives the name of the place near the Jordan where John baptized. Besides being close to the Jordan, Bethabara was superior to Bethany as the place where John baptized because it means, in Hebrew, "place of preparation." Thus there could be no more fitting place for John the Baptist to prepare the way for the Messiah.[17]

Lexicography, the study of definitions, was a branch of Alexandrian scholarship that Origen brought to bear in the *Commentary on John* in a more fruitful way. The entire first volume of Origen's commentary is, in fact, a study of the definitions of "beginning" and "word." Origen's treatment of definition shows a sophisticated grasp of semantics. Relying on the distinction Greek literary scholarship made between words as names and the actual notions they express, he demonstrated that a single word may have a wealth of denotations, only some of which may be appropriate in any given context.[18] Although Origen's presuppositions frequently vitiate, at least from our perspective, the usefulness of his conclusions, his training in the methods of Alexandrian literary scholarship, methods still fundamental to the interpretation of texts, is evident throughout his work. Although it is his use of allegory that places Origen in continuity with a great tradition of biblical interpretation stretching down to the end of the Middle Ages and beyond, it is his use of grammar that gives his work a genuine kinship, unusual among early Christian exegetes, with modern biblical interpretation.

The books of Origen's *Commentary on Genesis* composed at the same time he was completing his *Commentary on John*, have disappeared almost entirely, and only traces remain of another exegetical work composed roughly contemporaneously, Origen's *Notes* on other books of the Pentateuch. These notes were apparently not *scholia*—that is, marginal notes—but treatises in the style of Origen's commentaries that, instead of taking the book verse by verse, dealt only with disconnected passages. Origen probably intended them to cover the important issues in a given book of the Bible where a full-scale commentary would be impractical. Four well-attested fragments survive from Origen's *Notes on Exodus*. They display the same style as Origen's commentaries and deal with similar issues. All, in fact, deal with the familiar problem of the hardening of Pharaoh's heart and display the same concern we find in *On First Principles* to argue against the Marcionites that this text does not imply any lack in God's goodness as well as a concern to deprive the Valentinians of a text which might imply a limitation of human free will.

### On Prayer

In 233 or 234 Ambrosius asked Origen to resolve some philosophical paradoxes concerning prayer that had troubled him and Tatiana, a cultivated lady of his acquaintance. What need is there, Ambrosius and

Tatiana asked, for us to pray to God if God knows what we need before we ask and, as a loving parent, provides for us more appropriately than we could even know how to ask? Furthermore, if God not only knows but determines the future, why should we pray that anything might come about? Either our prayer is superfluous because God has already determined to grant our request, or it is vain because God has determined not to grant it. This line of reasoning even calls into question prayer for the good of our souls. Either God has predestined us to salvation, in which case it is unnecessary to pray for salvation or to receive the Holy Spirit, or God has predestined us for damnation, in which case such prayer is futile. Whether or not Ambrosius and Tatiana were entirely candid about their request—and it is hard to see how an avid reader of Origen's work could doubt his opinion on predestination—they evidently desired a philosophically sophisticated treatise on prayer. Origen's response is one of the very few works of his that we are privileged to have intact in Greek.

Though short enough to fit into a single codex, *On Prayer* is an extraordinarily broad treatment of its subject and perhaps the most representative of Origen's works. Here we see Origen as a grammarian, an allegorist, a philosophical theologian in the Platonic tradition, an opponent of heresy, and a Christian of fervent piety. At the outset Origen announced his intention in a prayer for the divine aid that alone could enable him to write a "clear, exact, and appropriate account of the whole matter of prayer." [19] Going well beyond the philosophical issues Ambrosius and Tatiana brought to his attention, Origen dealt with every conceivable issue connected with prayer, beginning with the most mundane matters: how often we should pray, at what times of the day, in what place, with what posture, with what order of topics? Because of this breadth of concern, Origen's *On Prayer* provides us with a number of insights, unusual in his work, into the conventional religious practices of Christians in his day. As well as being a splendid example of Origen at his best, *On Prayer* marks an important step in the development of Christian piety. It is the first clear and thoroughgoing exposition, within the Christian tradition, of prayer as the contemplation of God rather than as a means of achieving material benefits. As such, *On Prayer* stands at the head of a body of literature dealing with Christian spiritual life as an end in itself that extends through such figures as Bernard of Clairvaux and Teresa of Avila down to Thomas Merton and Henri Nouwen in our own time.

Although reasonably concise and clear, Origen's treatise is not perfectly well organized, and it will not do to present the contents in quite the order in which they arise in his work. Although Origen considered a virtuous life one unbroken prayer, he recommended specifically praying to God at least three times a day: in the morning, at noon, and in the evening. It is best, he wrote, to pray in a place consecrated to that purpose since this helps to put the mind in the right disposition for prayer. At any rate, one should avoid praying near the marital bed since it is inappropriate to pray in a place where even legitimate sexual intercourse occurs. One should kneel when one is accusing oneself of one's sins before God; otherwise one should stand, facing east, with arms outstretched and eyes uplifted. One should begin and end one's prayer glorifying God; in between one should in turn give thanks for God's blessings, confess one's sins, and request spiritual blessings. Origen recommended no fixed forms of prayer but in providing examples relied heavily on the language of the Psalms. In all of these matters Origen's advice probably reflects the conventional practices of pious Christians in his day.

Origen departed, however, from the conventional piety of his day or any other in his advice on the contents of prayer. He summed up his views on what Christians should pray for in his interpretation of two supposed sayings of Jesus: "Ask for the great things, and the little things will be added unto you," and "Ask for the heavenly things, and the earthly things will be given unto you." The "great" and "heavenly" things, Origen argued, are entirely spiritual blessings for ourselves and others; God does not intend for us to ask at all for material blessings. With this presupposition, Origen radically allegorized Hannah's prayer for a child; Hezekiah's prayer for health; the prayers of Mordecai and Esther (in the Septuagint version) for the salvation of their people; Judith's prayer for victory; the prayers of Shadrach, Meshach, and Abednego for deliverance from the fiery furnace; Daniel's prayer for deliverance from the lions' den; and Jonah's prayer for deliverance from the belly of the whale. Hannah's, for example, symbolizes the prayer of those who find that their reason has become barren and their minds sterile and long to give birth to words of truth. Hezekiah's is a prayer for the health of the soul, that the sickness of sin may not bring it to the spiritual death of alienation from God. Origen made no commitment one way or the other as to the historicity of the material benefits procured by these famous prayers in the Bible, but they were obviously insignificant as far as he was concerned.[20] What, then, of the request for bread in the Lord's Prayer? Here Origen the allegorist was not at a loss, and a peculiarity in the prayer's wording made the job all the easier for him. The adjective we plausibly translate "daily" in our versions of the Lord's Prayer is one which occurs no where else but in the two versions of the Lord's Prayer in Matthew and Luke. Origen took this word, *epiousios,* as cognate to *ousia,* the philo-sophical term for the substance of things, incorporeal in itself, that makes possible whatever attributes they have. The bread we request in the Lord's Prayer can thus be the bread of the Word of God, which is wisdom and truth.[21]

Throughout the treatise we have an emphasis on the genuine spirit-ual benefits prayer provides. In his reply to Ambrosius and Tatiana's questions, Origen stated that, quite apart from the efficacy of prayer itself, it is obvious that simply preparing ourselves to pray confers blessings on us. In order to be in the proper disposition to pray, we must call to mind our sins, forgive any grudges we have against others, and free ourselves of any disturbances of mind. Doing this alone three times a day improves our lives. Beyond this, by the very act of prayer, the soul becomes more spiritual. It separates itself from bodily concerns and turns entirely to spiritual things. Origen presented prayer thus, not as a duty we owe to God, but as an exercise conducive to the transfor-mation of the entire personality. One is reminded of Calvin's dictum that we pray not so much for God's sake, as for ours.[22] As such, there is no fundamental difference between the act of praying and all other acts the Christian performs in a life consecrated to God. A Christian's entire life is a prayer in which the exercise commonly called prayer is only a part.[23]

Such an understanding of prayer invalidates the question of how we can logically pray for earthly benefits which God already provides. It is obvious that we should pray because praying provides us with spiritual benefits we would not otherwise obtain. As to his friends' question concerning prayer for the spiritual benefits themselves, namely how prayer for such benefits can be squared with predestination of the elect, Origen simply replied along the line of *On First Principles* that our free choice to pray or not for spiritual benefits is entirely consistent with God's providence. Again, as in the earlier treatise, he used Carneades' argument that the very fact that we can move ourselves by the exercise of our own wills makes it impossible to uphold a strict determinism.

*On Prayer* is, by and large, singularly free of theological statements at odds with prevailing orthodoxy in Origen's time. The one exception is his assumption that there have been a succession of worlds prior to ours. One statement, though, while unexceptionable in Origen's time, subsequently gave the work the taint of heresy and is probably responsible for its not being translated into Latin. This was Origen's statement that, while we may pray to God through Christ, we must address our prayer to God the Father alone. At least, we must offer to God the Father alone that prayer that constitutes actual worship. Origen, turning a grammarian's eye to 1 Timothy 2:1, made a careful distinction between the "supplications, prayers, intercessions, and thanksgivings" mentioned there. We may, in fact, offer supplications, intercessions, and thanksgivings to our fellow Christians, and it is certainly appropriate to offer them to Christ. But Christ himself taught us to pray, not to him, but to God the Father. Origen believed that offering prayers indiscriminately to God the Father and to Christ implied the heresy that the Father and the Son are identical in substance, which the church condemned in Sabellius and his followers.[24] Later generations suspected that Origen's care to subordinate Christ to God the Father was the source of the heresy of Arius, who denied Christ's full divinity. Such a subordination is also implicit in Origen's refusal to allow any distinction between the type of prayer offered to Christ and the type offered to the saints.

The saints, for Origen, are all spiritual persons, living and dead. Such people have the power to intercede with God for us and to obtain for us the forgiveness of our sins. When Origen spoke of prayer to the saints, he usually meant requesting the prayers of fellow Christians, but he had no objection to prayers offered to the departed saints. In fact, the departed saints may be better able to intercede for us than our fellow Christians since they have obtained fullness of knowledge and are no longer hindered by bodily passions. Since the saints at rest are still members of the body of Christ, in which all members care for each other, we may safely presume that they take an interest in our needs.[25] The angels, like the saints, intercede for us and, more importantly, assist us in our prayers. It is in fact the angels, Origen believed, who actually bring our prayers to fruition. When we pray, God so arranges things through providence that angels will be present to fulfill our prayers. Although we do not offer our prayers to them, they, like good servants, are as quick to fulfill a legitimate request to their Master which they know God intends to grant as if God had told them to do so.[26] For this understanding of the role of the angels, Origen found a biblical warrant in the books of Tobit and 2 Maccabees. Although those books express popular Jewish ideas in the centuries immediately before Christ, the notion that a class of spiritual beings less than God actually mediates our relations with God is a prominent feature of Middle Platonism given considerable attention by Plutarch. His concern for angelology thus conveniently embodied Origen's synthesis between Platonism and the biblical tradition.

The Platonism of *On Prayer* is nowhere more apparent than in Origen's interpretation of the Lord's Prayer. The same is true of Origen's training as a grammarian. Before undertaking a line-by-line interpretation, Origen discussed the differences between the versions of the prayer in Matthew and Luke and expressed his intention to use the Matthaean version with constant reference to the Lucan. The choice of the version in Matthew then entails a consideration of the prayer in the context of that Gospel. Origen pointed out that Matthew 6:5–8, which discusses the way we should pray, forms a sort of preface. In those verses Jesus advises us not to pray on the street corners but to withdraw into an inner chamber to pray. What, Origen asked, does it mean to withdraw into an inner chamber but to shut the doors of the faculties of sense? Similarly, Jesus advises us not to use vain repetitions in our prayers. What, then, are vain repetitions but requests for material things, which by nature are divisible, rather than for spiritual things, which are incorporeal and indivisible?

This Platonizing spiritualization continues in Origen's actual discussion of the prayer. When we address God as "our Father," we express thereby our intention to be formed in God's image. We speak of God as "in heaven" to denote God's utter separation from all created things. Of course, God is not literally in heaven as in a place; Christ's ascension to the Father, which misleads the simple into believing that God lives somewhere above the sky, was an ascension of the mind rather than of the body.[27] The hallowing of God's name and the coming of God's kingdom refer to our gradual sanctification. We pray that God's name may be hallowed in our good works and that God's kingdom may come in our well-ordered life. There is not the slightest trace of apocalyptic eschatology, the notion that Christ will in fact reappear to establish God's reign on earth, in Origen's understanding of the kingdom of God, "the blessed state of the reason and the ordered condition of wise thoughts."[28] When we pray that God's will may be done "on earth as it is in heaven," we request that those whose lives are dominated by the vices (allegorically, "on earth") may become like those who live virtuously ("in heaven"). As mentioned earlier, we do not ask God for actual bread; to do so is inconsistent with God's dignity and Jesus' saying in John 6:27, "Do not labor for the food which perishes, but for the food which endures to eternal life." The debts we owe to God, as, in this case, modern interpreters agree, are the debts of loving service we owe to all people. In connection with the notion of forgiveness of debts, Origen criticized bishops who arrogated to themselves powers of forgiveness that properly belong only to genuinely spiritual persons.

"Deliver us from evil" Origen interpreted, as do some modern scholars, as a request for deliverance from Satan. The one verse in the Lord's Prayer Origen found genuinely problematical was "lead us not into temptation." How is it, Origen asked, that Christ bids us pray God not to lead us into temptation when the Bible everywhere proclaims that temptations are inevitable? Moreover, it teaches that there are times, as in the case of Job, where God specifically permits us to be tempted to sin in order to test us. Temptation is so all-pervasive that even the Bible itself is a source of temptation to vain readers like the heretics who draw the fatuous conclusion that the God of the Old Testament is not the same as the God of the New Testament. This line of thought led Origen again into the themes of the third book of *On First Principles*, in this case the argument that all the trials and temptations of our life are God's way of bringing us to perfection. He went on to apply this principle to the one case that obsessed him, the hardening of Pharaoh's heart. Temptations, if we are alert to them, are, in fact, advantageous to us spiritually:

The use of temptations is as follows. What our soul has received is unknown to all save God—is unknown even to ourselves; but it is manifested by means of temptations: so that it may be no longer unknown what kind of persons we are, but rather that we should also know ourselves and be aware, if we will, of our own faults and give thanks for the good results manifested to us of temptations.[29]

When, therefore, we pray that God may not lead us into temptation, this must really mean that we pray that God will enable us to overcome temptation when it comes and allow us to profit by the experience.

*On Prayer* makes apparent how effortlessly Origen combined a concern for the intellectual contemplation of ideal reality derived from the Platonic tradition with the ordinary piety of the Christian church. We should never make the mistake of considering Origen's spirituality in isolation from his philosophical and exegetical concerns; all are inseparable parts of a coherent whole.

## An Exhortation to Martyrdom

A treatise Origen wrote not long after *On Prayer*, his *Exhortation to Martyrdom*, gives even better testimony to his capacity to synthesize Platonism and conventional piety. In 235 Maximinus the Thracian, an uncultivated soldier from the mountains of the Balkan peninsula, overthrew the reigning emperor, Severus Alexander, and killed him and his mother, Julia Mammaea. Although there was, it seems, nothing like a full-scale persecution, Christians who had been associated with Alexander and his mother were exposed to danger. In Rome Hippolytus, who had dedicated a book to Julia Mammaea, was deported along with Bishop Pontian to the island of Sardinia. Closer to Origen, Ambrosius was taken into custody or feared arrest, as did Protoctetus, a presbyter who was a mutual friend. Origen himself, who had been received by Julia Mammaea, must have been apprehensive about his own situation. This occasion called forth a treatise to Ambrosius and Protoctetus which was meant to encourage them to stand fast in the faith. Unlike Clement of Alexandria, who denigrated martyrdom and made clear his preference for a life of moderate asceticism as the realization of the highest Christian ideal to the suffering of a heroic death, Origen completely shared in the exaltation of martyrdom so characteristic of the church of his time. The ultimate example of heroism was, for him as for countless other Christians of his time, the martyrdom of the seven Jewish brothers recounted in the book of 2 Maccabees. Such sentiments are by no means peculiar to the *Exhortation*, and we may assume that they closely parallel those of the letter which Origen, as a boy of seventeen, wrote to his father on a similar occasion.

At the same time, the *Exhortation* is a model of Christian Platonism. Martyrdom, for Origen, is the ultimate test of the Christian's willingness to prefer spiritual to corporeal realities:

> I think that they love God with all their soul who with a great desire to be in union with God withdraw and separate their soul not only from the earthly body but also from everything material. Such men accept the putting away of the body of humiliation without distress or emotion when the time come[s] for them to put off the body of death by what is commonly regarded as death.[30]

The reward of martyrdom is, as all Christians believed, unspeakable joy, but for Origen that joy was distinctly intellectual:

> Just as each of our members has some ability for which it is naturally fitted, the eyes to see visible things, and the ears to hear sounds, so the mind is for intelligible things and God who transcends them. Why, then, do we hesitate and doubt to put off the corruptible body that hinders us and weighs down the soul . . . ? For then we may enjoy with Christ Jesus the rest which accompanies blessedness and contemplate him in his wholeness, the living Word. Fed by him and comprehending the manifold wisdom in him, . . . we may have our minds enlightened by the true and unfailing light of knowledge. . . .[31]

Although there is little philosophy in the *Exhortation to Martyrdom*, it presumes the cosmology of *On First Principles*. In discussing the vanity of sacrifices to the pagan gods, Origen allows that the heavenly bodies are genuine spiritual beings. But, he says, that does not make it any more legitimate to sacrifice to them; the sun itself, subjected to the futility of bodily existence until it shall obtain liberty, would not wish to be worshiped. It has been fashionable for some time to present Platonism and the biblical heritage as radically incompatible, especially in their attitude toward the body. Given the all-pervasive asceticism of early Christianity, Origen would have found such a position absurd. This point bears emphasis today. It would have seemed obvious to Origen and his fellow Christians and Platonists that asceticism does not imply hostility to the body. On the contrary, it is the natural outcome of a quite positive view of the body, properly disciplined, as a fitting vehicle during our life on earth for our ascent to God. This acceptance of the body and the sense of wholeness that it provided is precisely what separated Christians and Platonists from the Gnostics.

As it turned out, Origen's exhortation to Ambrosius and Protoctetus to stand firm in the face of death was not itself put to the test. Maximinus fell from power as he had risen to it, in a mutiny in 238. His successors for more than a decade had no interest in persecuting Christians. Ambrosius and Protoctetus, if they had in fact been arrested, were soon at liberty. One lasting legacy of this brief period of tension was a better acquaintance with Firmillian, the bishop of the Cappodocian metropolis, Caesarea Mazaca. Firmillian fled to Caesarea in Palestine to avoid a local persecution in his home province, where the governor had humored local pagans who held Christians responsible for recent earthquakes. Although his early years at Caesarea had been tranquil and productive, Origen was about to enter an even more productive period, one during which he would enter into his own, for the first and only time in his life, as a prominent leader in the church.

# VIII
# Teaching and Preaching

## (238–44)

The years from 238 to 244 were, to all indications, the most satisfying of Origen's life. They were, at the same time, a terribly unsettled time for the Roman Empire. The Roman Senate never liked Maximinus the Thracian, the barbarian soldier who overthrew Alexander Severus, and in 238 they encouraged Gordian, the Roman proconsul of Africa, to contest the throne. Gordian appointed his son as coemperor, but within twenty-three days the two of them, known to history as Gordian I and II, were dead; they had not counted on the loyalty of Maximinus' commander in Africa. In the meantime, Maximinus was marching on Rome to settle scores with the Senate. He never arrived. His army murdered him as he was besieging the city of Aquileia, the key to Italy, and acclaimed as emperors Balbinus and Pupienus, two men with the support of the Senate. Within a year, however, the elite Praetorian guard at Rome assassinated Balbinus and Pupienus and replaced them with the thirteen-year-old grandson of Gordian I, who reigned as Gordian III. The commander of the Praetorians, Timesitheus, soon pushed aside the boy's mother and assumed effective power. In 242 Timesitheus, with Gordian III in tow, invaded Persia, an invasion Plotinus accompanied in the vain hope of getting to India to discuss philosophy with the Brahmins. Timesitheus died in the course of the ill-conceived expedition, and, in the confusion, the general who replaced him, Philip the Arab, assassinated Gordian III and assumed the purple himself. Thus in 244 another barbarian soldier ruled the Roman world.

From 238 to 244 Origen continued to be a teacher of Christian philosophy but also emerged as a respected spokesman for the church. We know about his ideas and methods as a teacher from the *Speech of*

*Appreciation*, ascribed to Gregory Thaumaturgus, which describes his activities along that line during these years. In addition to teaching and composing numerous commentaries, Origen preached regularly for a time at the church in Caesarea and acted as a consultant in doctrinal disputes. During this period also, in all probablility, he wrote the recently discovered *On the Passover*, a treatise intimately concerned with the church's worship. It seems appropriate, therefore, in connection with these churchly activities, to discuss Origen's views on the sacraments and on ecclesiastical discipline.

## A Student's Testimonial

The *Speech of Appreciation* was probably delivered in 245 and described a seven-year-long course of instruction. There is reason to believe that Gregory Thaumaturgus (the "wonder-worker," c. 213–c. 270) did not write it. Gregory, the founder of the Christian church in the Roman province of Pontus, now a part of northeastern Turkey, is venerated as a great saint by the Eastern Church. Early evidence, however, identifies the author of the *Speech of Appreciation* positively as the work of a man named Theodore. While it is possible that Theodore may have been Gregory since the name "Gregory" could have been a baptismal name assumed by Theodore, it is more probable that the attribution is confused and Gregory Thaumaturgus did not write the speech or, in all probability, know Origen at all.[1] At any rate, the identity of its author has no bearing on the value of the *Speech of Appreciation* as a historical source; whoever wrote it was a student of Origen. Unlike Origen's writings, the *Speech of Appreciation* is a polished piece of rhetoric. It hews closely to the prescribed pattern of a panegyric, a speech of praise, and employs an ornate style sprinkled with allusions to Plato. Theodore, as the author will be referred to here, only departs from the conventional pattern by leaving out the usual references to the subject's noble ancestry and glorious deeds. Instead he tactfully avows ignorance of the circumstances that brought Origen to Caesarea.[2] Although the speech alludes several times to the Bible, it largely avoids specifically Christian terminology. Jesus Christ is "the Logos," a good philosophical term, and Christian doctrine is "the barbarian philosophy"—barbarian, of course, because not originally Greek. No doubt Theodore wished to avoid the jarring effect such nonclassical terminology would create in such a highly formalized discourse. Clement of Alexandria displayed similar reticence in his *Exhortation* and *Pedagogue*.

Because of the artificiality of the form, the *Speech of Appreciation* strikes us as fulsome, but it probably expressed genuine gratitude and fondness. The conventional exordium and peroration frame two major sections. The first section describes how the Logos brought Theodore to study with Origen. The second, and more valuable, section describes how Origen educated Theodore. This is our only first-hand testimony to Origen's teaching methods. The entire speech also provides us, incidentally, with a picture of Origen's characteristic concerns as reflected in an intelligent student.

According to the custom of the time, Theodore actually lived in Origen's household. He testifies to Origen's preoccupation with the Bible—all of Origen's household dreamed about the Bible at night for having studied it so intensively during the day—but his own education was in philosophy. Origen, like Clement, regarded philosophy as the proper preparation for the intelligent study of the Bible.[3] Most likely, Theodore's training differed little from the education Origen received under Ammonius Saccas. Theodore already had the necessary prerequisites—grammar and general education—which he had supplemented with study in rhetoric and Latin, the latter intended to prepare him to study Roman law at Beirut. The course Origen taught embraced, in succession, each of the conventional areas of philosophy: dialectic (or logic), physics, and ethics. Origen, however, included in his "physics" only that part of the discipline that dealt with the natural world. The part of physics that dealt with God he considered a fourth discipline, which he referred to as "mystics," the science of mystical contemplation, and Theodore called "theology." As the goal of philosophical training and the highest discipline, theology was the last to be treated, all the other branches serving as preparation for it. Theodore's description of how Origen instructed him in these disciplines is invaluable, but we should not assume that the philosophical education Origen provided Theodore was characteristic of his teaching activity. Theology, which Theodore did not apparently stay around to study, was really the focus of Origen's concerns, and it is to the *On First Principles* rather than to the *Speech of Appreciation* that we should turn if we want to know how Origen handled that subject.

In Theodore's case, as must have been true with most who undertook the study of philosophy as teenagers, the achievement of a measure
of self-discipline was a necessary preparation for his actual studies.
Origen, he says, cleansed him "in a very Socratic fashion" from those
defects of character that would otherwise have hindered him.[4] The
*Discourses* of Epictetus and Clement of Alexandria's *Who Is the Rich
Man Who Is to Be Saved?* describe this preparation for the philosophical
life.

Theodore's study of philosophy proper began with logic or dialectic, the discipline of critical reasoning. Following a procedure he probably learned from Ammonius, Origen sought to enable Theodore to reason for himself. He presented what he considered specious arguments
with all seriousness and what he considered sound ones with great diffi-
dence so that Theodore would not simply accept those ideas he could
see that his teacher approved but would learn to accept or reject ideas
only after serious reflection and logical examination. He was particularly concerned to overcome the prejudices, inculcated in rhetorical
education, against inelegantly expressed ideas and in favor of elegantly
expressed ones. This formation of the intellect prepared Theodore to
pass to the substantive branches of philosophy.[5]

Of these, the first was physics. Origen supplemented this by instruction in geometry and astronomy, subjects perhaps inadequately covered
in Theodore's general education. We have already seen how Origen was
well acquainted with the natural science of his time and looked forward
to a better understanding of the mysteries of nature as one of the blessings of life after death. According to Theodore, it was under Origen's
guidance that he passed from a dumb wonder at the craftmanship of the
universe to a rational admiration of it.[6] Astronomy, in particular, which
provided those aware of it with access to the ordered beauties of an
uncorrupted heavenly realm, served as a step in the way toward still
more exalted heavenly mysteries.[7]

Origen's course in ethics centered on the four cardinal virtues as
defined by Plato: prudence, temperance, justice, and courage. By cultivating these virtues the philosopher acquired character like God, happy
and free from the domination of the emotions. These virtues, however,
are not the virtues of God, nor does the blessedness their cultivation
brings compare to the blessedness of God.[8] Prudence, as Origen taught
it, was the knowledge of self, which Platonists interpreted as the mean-

ing of the popular Delphic maxim, "Know thyself." Temperance, closely linked to prudence, involved discernment, on the basis of such self-knowledge, of which external things are good, harmful, or indifferent to the soul. Justice, the third cardinal virtue, is the capacity to give each thing its due. For Origen this meant subordinating all of the soul's activity to its true purpose in life, attaining knowledge of God, the alternative to which was the soul's dissipation in the affairs of the material world. Courage, the fourth of the cardinal virtues, is strength of character, the virtue that preserved all the others and made them operative. Origen, following a Platonic tradition that he may have learned from Ammonius, taught piety as a fifth virtue to crown all the others.[9] Origen characteristically taught one specifically Christian virtue as an aspect of courage. This is "endurance," the virtue of the Christian martyrs. Theodore stressed that, in contrast to other philosophers, Origen did not simply teach ethical theory, but exemplified his ethics in his behavior. In saying so, Theodore spoke as a student of Origen, whose principal objection to pagan philosophy was its failure to put its fine ethical theories into practice.

In his presentation of theology, Origen was careful, according to Theodore, to deal simultaneously with all the major philosophical systems, pointing out the weaknesses of each and the contradictions between them.[10] He did not want his student to become a dogmatic adherent of the first philosophical school he came across.[11] Ultimately, of course, the true source of theology was in the Bible, or, as Theodore referred to it at one point, "the sacred laws, hymns, odes, and mystic words."[12] Although Origen, like Clement, professed eclecticism in his theology, in fact, both were no more and no less eclectic than other Platonists like Plotinus. Open adherence to one school, however, evidently did not appeal to them since Christianity necessarily transcended all the sects of philosophy. Just as dialectic, physics, and ethics were preparatory disciplines for theology, so the theology of the pagan philosophers was but a preparatory discipline for the study of the true theology of the Christian Scriptures. The obscurity of the Scriptures, however, makes such a preparation absolutely necessary. Perhaps, Theodore mused, the Bible is in fact absolutely clear, and it is only the fact that our souls have so long been separated from God that they no longer know how to hear him that makes it seem obscure, or perhaps it is deliberately obscure to prevent the unworthy from comprehending it. In any event the comprehension of the Bible entails the soul's purification in philosophy from its attachment to this world and in addition the gift of the Holy Spirit.[13]

The two chapters of *On First Principles* that have survived in Greek—those on free will and on the interpretation of Scripture—are the ones with the themes where Theodore most clearly reflects his teacher. The first major section of Theodore's speech, which describes how he came to study with Origen at Caesarea, is filled with an appreciation of the divine providence, which brought together all of the circumstances of his life in such a way as to have him fall under Origen's supervision. At the same time, he insists, in characteristically Origenist fashion, on the actual freedom of the soul. In discussing the relationship thus providentially effected between himself and Origen, Theodore alludes to 1 Samuel 18:1 (in the Septuagint), "the soul of Jonathan was knit to David." Like Origen, he stresses, with the grammarian's interest in a single word, that it is the soul, the highest faculty of Jonathan, that was knit to David, and that since the soul cannot be constrained against its will, this explains how Jonathan could be knit to David even when they, to all appearances, were separated.[14]

Origen struck Theodore as precisely the ideal spiritual person whom Origen himself had described, the inspired exegete with charismatic authority.[15] Origen had "surpassed the human condition in his ascent toward the divine."[16] Since he had risen above earthly concerns, the Bible was clear to him.[17] Theodore thought it likely that Origen was privileged to have, as his spiritual confrere, not simply an angel of high rank, but "the Angel of great counsel," the Logos.[18] Plotinus' students felt similarly. On one occasion, supposedly, Plotinus was prevailed upon to attend a séance at which the participants were to be put in touch with their guardian spirits. It was there discovered, to the amazement of the other participants, that the philosopher's guardian was not a daemon, corresponding to a Christian angel, but a being from the divine realm.[19]

## The Letter to Gregory

Theodore of the *Speech of Appreciation* may have been associated with Gregory Thaumaturgus because of a letter Origen wrote to a young man named Gregory, a student of law and philosophy.[20] In it Origen argued that Christians should employ philosophy as an aid to the study of the Bible much as philosophers employed disciplines like geometry as an aid to the study of their discipline. This advice, whether given to the same person or not, corresponds to the educational method described in the *Speech of Appreciation*. Origen, always an allegorist, justified this use of philosophy with a biblical image. Christians who employed Greek philosophy for their own purposes were, he wrote, like the Israelites under Moses who employed the gold and precious stones which they had taken from the Egyptians for the worship of God as adornments in the tabernacle. Origen, however, cautioned that an uncritical appropriation of philosophy could lead to heresy. This letter survived only because the editors of the *Philocalia* included it, along with the fourth book of *On First Principles*, in their anthology of works dealing with biblical interpretation. The spoliation of the Egyptians was an effective image. It presented what could otherwise be criticized as a passive acceptance of non-Christian ideas from philosophy as an aggressive act of appropriation. As such, it was popular with later Christian theologians down through the Middle Ages when it justified the study of Muslim and Jewish as well as pagan philosophy. An image casually mentioned in a letter thus served, in a significant way, to justify the continued intellectual openness of the Christian tradition.

## Commentaries on Paul and the Prophets

Only fragments remain of Origen's most serious works during the years when Theodore was with him: commentaries on most, if not all, of the epistles of Paul and on the books of Isaiah and Ezekiel. The best preserved is his *Commentary on Romans*, which exists in an abridged Latin translation by Rufinus and in extensive Greek fragments. The commentaries on Isaiah and Ezekiel have all but vanished. The loss of Origen's commentaries on Paul is regrettable. Paul brought out Origen's full sensitivity to language and theological acumen but relatively little of his allegorical imagination. In a fragment of his *Commentary on Romans* preserved intact in the *Philocalia*, he showed great acuity in handling Paul's use of the word "law," ultimately distinguishing six different usages of the word. Origen suggested that the presence or absence of the article can be helpful in distinguishing Paul's two most important usages of "law," the use of it to mean the law of Moses and the use of it to mean natural law. Here, and in several other cases, Origen still provides a helpful commentary on Paul's notoriously obscure use of language.

Origen's enthusiasm for Paul may appear curious in light of the issues that have dominated Western Christian interpretations of Paul. The problem of law and grace interested him only mildly, and Paul's actual views on predestination were anathema to him. We have already seen how the ninth chapter of Romans, where Paul used the hardening of Pharaoh's heart and his preference for Jacob over Esau, haunted Origen. We should remember that the same Paul who wrote Romans, the book in the forefront of our understanding of him, also wrote 1 Corinthians. In the latter book Paul appears as a person much like Origen: an allegorist who understands the secrets of the Bible and expounds them discreetly, a stern ascetic who counsels celibacy and the expulsion of a sinner from the church, a charismatic leader who relies on the self-authenticating power of the Spirit, a spiritualist who seeks to correct a fleshly understanding of the resurrection, and a visionary who expects a cosmic redemption which will culminate when God is all in all. Origen also relied heavily on Paul's Christological ideas and on his understanding of providence. Origen's idea of redemption rejects predestination without regard for merit but affirms that God orders all events to serve God's purposes.

Origen's treatment of the relation between faith and works in Paul, which Maurice Wiles has reconstructed, illustrates his sensitivity.[21] Origen, like Clement before him, ordinarily compared faith, understood as a blind reliance on authority, unfavorably with knowledge. Nonetheless, he could appreciate Paul's understanding of faith as an attitude of radical trust in God. Paul, Origen argued, understood faith in Christ as subjection to and life in Christ, not simply as holding a belief about Christ. What then does it mean to be "in Christ" by faith? It means to be "in" all the virtues, such as wisdom, righteousness, and truth, that are aspects of Christ. These aspects are not simply attributes of Christ, he *is* all of them. Therefore we cannot be in Christ without having these virtues ourselves. This means that, to the extent one has faith in Christ in Paul's sense, one possesses all the virtues. It is thus logically impossible to suggest that such faith could be unaccompanied by the good works in which the virtues must issue, and Paul is reasonable to reject as contemptible the suggestion that reliance on faith gives people a license to sin.

## Combating Heresy

Origen, however, did not spend all this period of his life expounding Paul and the prophets to a small coterie of disciples. As he taught Theodore and prepared his commentaries, he was a leader and spokesman for the church, assisting in synods concerned with the establishment of correct doctrine and preaching to the church at Caesarea.

The most important of the synods Origen participated in was one called to deal with the alleged errors of Beryllus, a Christian author and bishop of Bostra, the principal city of Arabia. Beryllus rejected the Logos theology. Specifically, he denied that Christ existed before his earthly life and that Christ had a divinity of his own apart from the divinity of God the Father. His views recall those which had exercised Christians at Rome over a generation earlier. It seems likely that Alexander of Jerusalem and Theoctistus of Caesarea brought Origen into the investigation of Beryllus. As bishops of the oldest church in Christendom and of the seat of administration in the neighboring province of Palestine, they would be the obvious leaders of a synod called to investigate a man of Beryllus' eminence. Evidently they took Origen with them to Bostra, where the synod would have been held, because they thought he could be of assistance. If our record is true, they were right; Origen persuaded Beryllus to renounce his views, and the synod ended amicably with a subscription to a common statement of faith.[22] Beryllus' rejection of the Logos Christology is consistent with traditions, strong in Arabia, of Jewish Christianity. Jewish Christians, spiritual descendants of the church at Jerusalem in apostolic times, considered Jesus the Messiah but were unwilling to conceive of him as a second God. The other bishops whose trials for similar heresies Origen was involved in were probably from Arabia also. Origen thus helped bring the teachings of the church in that province on the fringe of the Roman Empire into line with the theological consensus that had arisen in the church elsewhere. This shows definitively how orthodox he was by the standards of his time in his position on a central issue of Christian doctrine.

A transcript that was made of the synod held to investigate Beryllus has not survived. What has survived, at least in part, is a transcript of the proceedings of another synod in which Origen was involved, this one investigating the Christology of a bishop named Heraclides. The work in question, known as *The Dialogue of Origen with Heraclides and the Bishops with Him Concerning the Father, the Son and the Soul*[23] has an interesting history. It was discovered in 1941 in a cave used as an ancient Egyptian quarry at Tura, near Cairo, as workers were clearing out the quarry for use by the British as an ammunition dump. It was part of a small cache of works by Origen and by Didymus the Blind, a fourth-century follower of his, which monks of a neighboring monastery probably stashed there when the second council of Constantinople in 553 condemned both men and decreed the destruction of their writings. Because the scribe responsible for our copy of the proceedings was apparently interested only in Origen's views, we are missing the early part of the proceedings, which would make it clearer than it is with what errors Heraclides was charged. Their similarity to Beryllus' views is evident from Origen's insistence that Heraclides confess "two Gods," God the Father and God the Son, and agree that God the Father and Christ had existed separately and distinctly before the Incarnation. Origen realized that there was a danger of scandalizing simple believers with the formula "two Gods," but he considered it essential to the integrity of the church's teaching. Of course he was quick to say that God the Father and Christ were also, by virtue of a transcendent unity, one God.

Heraclides dropped out of the debate after making the required concessions, and Origen threw the floor open to questions. The participants in the ensuing discussion were all bishops, but they treated Origen deferentially and, one senses, with a little suspicion. A question, politely phrased as a point of information, concerned the meaning of Jesus' last words on the cross, as recorded in Luke 23:46: "Father, into thy hands I commend my spirit." How could Jesus' spirit be commended into the Father's hands if his soul went down to Hades? The issue of theological anthropology, which this question raised, dominated the rest of the discussion. Origen expounded and gave a moralistic twist to the Pauline (and Platonic) view of human nature as consisting of body, soul, and spirit. The next question, "Is the soul the blood?" may have astonished him. Here the contrast between Jewish Christian and Hellenic Christian presuppositions emerges dramatically. Apparently most of the assembled bishops believed that the soul, somehow associated with the blood, shared the mortality of the body and only a special act of God would confer immortality on it, along with the body, in the general resurrection at the last day. Origen, of course, taught that the soul is a rational creature of a spiritual nature that preexists the body and continues to exist after the body's dissolution. His attempt to demonstrate this from the Bible to the bishops illustrates the brilliance and the weakness of Origen's allegorical interpretation. As a matter of fact, modern biblical scholars would say that the bishops were more nearly correct in their understanding of the Bible on this point than Origen was. Origen did not challenge openly the validity of the biblical passages that identify the soul with the blood or speak of the finality of death. Instead, he sought to show that such passages had a deeper meaning consistent with his own views. He showed how the Bible frequently uses parts of the body in a figurative sense to refer to spiritual realities and refers symbolically to sin as a death. This was the case, he argued, with the passages about the blood and about death that the Arabians were mistakenly taking literally. Although Origen's logic was scarcely flawless, none present chose to dispute him, and he brought the proceedings to a close.

## The Homilies

Origen acted more regularly as a spokesman of the church when he preached at Caesarea. Stenographers took down his sermons, and more than two hundred of them have survived more or less intact, though they are only a fraction of the total that he preached. Practically all of these sermons belong to series that provide a more or less continuous commentary on particular books of the Bible. Unfortunately, only one such series, and that incomplete, survives in Greek, Origen's homilies on Jeremiah. There also exists in Greek one of Origen's homilies on 1 Samuel. The rest survive in Latin translations, the work of Rufinus and Jerome in the fourth century. These include homilies on Genesis, Exodus, Leviticus, Numbers, Joshua, Judges, 1 Samuel, the Psalms, the Song of Songs, Isaiah, Jeremiah, Ezekiel, and Luke. Jerome and Rufinus transmitted the basic content of Origen's homilies, but not their style; they did not hesitate to condense passages they found tedious and to embellish those they considered too plain.

The sheer quantity of Origen's surviving homilies, a major portion of his extant work, has given the impression that preaching must have been his principal activity during most of his years at Caesarea, but this was probably not the case. Pierre Nautin's painstaking reconstruction of the chronology of Origen's works has demonstrated convincingly that Origen preached practically all his sermons during a three-year period beginning in 239 or 240.[24] Apparently Origen preached his sermons on the daily lessons in a three-year cycle of readings covering the entire Bible that was already current in the Caesarean church. Such a cycle would enable catechumens to hear the entire Bible interpreted during the three years they would ordinarily take to prepare for baptism. Origen, in his writings, referred to daily worship services with preaching and to eucharistic services on Sundays and on the two fast days, Wednesdays and Fridays. The daily service, which probably took place in the early morning before the participants had to work, included prayers, the reading of an extensive passage from the Old Testament, a preacher's exposition of that passage, more prayers, and the kiss of peace. The eucharistic service, which replaced it on three days, included a reading and exposition of the Old Testament along with a selection from the epistles or Acts and from a Gospel, each of which would also be expounded in a sermon. The passages read from the New Testament were considerably shorter than those read daily from the Old Testament. Origen's homilies on Luke, his only New Testament homilies that survive, are brief and cover much shorter passages than those from the Old Testament. This is what we should expect for the third of three sermons. The cycle apparently involved reading through each of the three sections in the traditional sequence of the books. Origen took over responsibility for all the teaching during one cycle, an obligation involving prodigious labor (some of the sermons lasted over an hour) but certainly no more time than he was accustomed to spend composing his commentaries. He began preaching about half-way through one cycle and then began the cycle that followed, although he did not quite take the second cycle to the point where he had taken up the first.

Origen's sermons help us to avoid the all-to-common tendency to idealize the life of the church during the pre-Constantinian period; if we are to believe him, the church in Caesarea was in sorry shape. He complained in the course of his preaching that relatively few Christians bothered to attend any but the Sunday services. Some only came then in order to relax and enjoy the company of their friends and were chatting in the back of the room during the sermon.[25] People did not convert to Christianity in Origen's time for worldly reasons, as they would once Constantine made Christianity the preferred religion of the empire, but many belonged to Christian families and continued in the church out of habit and training rather than out of zeal. There had been no persecutions for a generation, so that the winnowing of adversity had not occurred. Origen found himself looking back wistfully to the heroic days of persecution in his youth:

> Then there were believers, when there were noble martyrdoms. As soon as we returned from conveying the martyrs to the cemetery, we gathered together in assembly. The whole church was there, not the least bit anguished, and the catechumens were instructed in the midst of the confessors, and in the midst of the dead who had confessed the truth unto death, nor were they anxious or perturbed, because they believed in the living God. Then we saw great and marvellous signs. Then there were few believers, but they really did believe, and they travelled the strait and narrow way that leads to life. But now we have become numerous . . . and there are few indeed among the many who profess Christian piety who will actually attain divine election and blessedness.[26]

Origen did not mince words. The brief persecution under Decius, which would leave him a broken man, showed he was correct about the relative shallowness of many Christians' commitment.

Origen the speculative theologian does not appear in the homilies, but Origen the grammarian does.[27] Formally, Origen's sermons are the lectures of a teacher of literature, not public orations. Origen only employed the simplest rhetorical devices and rarely strayed (as in the case quoted above) from a straightforward exposition of the text at hand. He eschewed the complicated structure and phraseology, the literary allusions, and the vivid imagery that were the stock and trade of public speakers. After a brief preface introducing the topic, a nicety he occasionally omitted, Origen proceeded, in units of a sentence or so at a time, to explain the text that the lector had just read. Such speaking techniques as he employed were pedagogical. He frequently asked rhetorical questions or engaged in a debate with a hypothetical adversary. As he brought the exposition of one unit to a close, he would summarize what he had said before proceeding to the next unit. Origen, as in the commentaries, which examined such matters in greater detail, was acutely aware of grammatical concerns such as the order and choice of terms or the particular voice speaking in a given verse. As in the commentaries also, he freely associated the text he was expounding with others throughout the Bible that shared similar ideas. He expressed himself quite naturally in biblical phraseology, even when he was explicitly comparing one text with another. The quotation above, not at all unusual in style, contains seven brief allusions to six different books of the Bible. Origen customarily concluded his sermons with a moral exhortation that modulated into the doxology of 1 Peter 4:11, as in the following example:

> Therefore, now that these things are said, let us gather together the words of the Bible, in so far as we can, and deposit them in our hearts, and let us conform our lives to them so that we can become pure before we depart this life, so that, having prepared our works in view of that departure, we may be received once we do depart among the righteous who are saved in Jesus Christ, to whom belong glory and dominion, world without end. Amen.[28]

The central theme in Origen's homilies, the soul's attainment of unity with God, is the same as that of his more learned works, and the method that enabled him to expound that theme in the interpretation of every book of the Bible is also the same, the massive use of allegory. With such a theme and such a method, Origen often had little use for what we would consider the actual content of the books he interpreted. Although he did not hesitate to do so when he found them absurd or unworthy of God, Origen did not ordinarily deny that the events described in the history of Israel actually occurred or that the laws of Moses were intended as positive legislation. Nonetheless, he frequently paid no attention to the literal meaning of the Bible even when he accepted it. Origen always assumed that any purely historical information was irrelevant. In his first homily on Jeremiah, Origen dealt with the second and third verses of the first chapter, in which the ancient Hebrew editor of the book dated the prophecies of Jeremiah in terms of the last kings of Judah and the Babylonian captivity. He asks: "What do these things teach us if we pay attention to the reading?" They teach us that we, in our personal lives, can find ourselves in a position comparable to that of the Jewish people in Jeremiah's time:

> If we sin, we are also going to become captives, since "to deliver such a one to Satan" does not differ at all from delivering the inhabitants of Jerusalem to Nebuchadnezzar. Just as, in that case, they were delivered into captivity on account of their sins, so we are delivered to Satan, since that is who Nebuchadnezzar is, on account of our sins.[29]

This disdain for history appears even more obviously in Origen's comments as he prepared to preach on the passage which narrates the battle of Ai in the book of Joshua:

> On hearing this passage, listeners will certainly say: "What does this have to do with me? Why should I care to learn that the inhabitants of Ai were defeated? Have there not always been wars like that, and more significant ones? Are there not still? What did the Holy Spirit intend? Why did he leave so many mighty and glorious cities out of the Bible and include in it an account of this city of Ai?"[30]

Origen must have considered the objections decisive because he proceeded to allegorize the passage. The Holy Spirit described psychology rather than history in the book of Joshua; the various peoples whom the Israelites displaced from the promised land are the vices that disturb the human soul:

> The Canaanites are within us. The Perizzites are within us. The Jebusites are right here. How strenuously must we travail, how vigilantly must we watch, how long must we persevere, if we are to exterminate within us so many races of vices, so that "our land may have respite from wars."[31]

Even the overtly moralistic story of Joseph disappears in a fog of allegory. If Joseph had succumbed to the blandishments of Potiphar's wife, he would have died spiritually by sinning, and his brothers could not have later reported to his father that he was alive. Moreover, Joseph's dominion over Pharaoh's grain-stores symbolized his dominion over his own emotions.[32] In the same way, the ritual observances of the Jews are entirely symbolic in Origen's homilies on Leviticus. Cosmology dissolves into moralistic psychology in Origen's homiletic interpretation of the early chapters of Genesis. For example, the creeping things God created symbolize impure thoughts (God could still call them "good" at the end of the day, since God brings good out of evil).[33]

Little but the naturalness of the symbolism links Origen's interpretation of the books on which he preached to what we would consider those books' actual content. Thus Ezekiel's prophecies of judgment at the time of the Babylonian captivity elicited from Origen a concern for the ultimately salvific purpose of God's chastisement; the laws about ritual and purity in Leviticus led him to discuss the church's worship and the nature of sin and its remedy; and the stages of the people of Israel's wanderings in the wilderness in the book of Numbers suggested to him the stages of the soul's ascent to God. Most notably, perhaps, the gradual conquest of Canaan under Joshua's leadership gave rise to an account of the soul's gradual conquest of its emotions under the leadership of Joshua's namesake, Jesus Christ.

Origen, with his concern for the spiritual life of the individual Christian, was always moralizing, as he regularly insisted on ethical rigorism and on the glories of asceticism and martyrdom, but he was scarcely a moralist in the ordinary sense of the term. His fulminations are against sin in general rather than against particular sins. His homilies contain none of the circumstantial detail that characterize the sermons of the great preachers of the fourth century or, for that matter, Clement of Alexandria's *Pedagogue*. Origen's homilies are therefore a poor source of information on Christian life at Caesarea. Zealous as he was to inspire his congregation toward seeking holiness, Origen remained a scholar.

A number of subthemes appear in Origen's homilies in addition to the major theme, the soul's achievement of unity with God. These are not, to be sure, the topics that concerned him in *On First Principles:* the doctrine of God, Christology, cosmology, eschatology, the nature of the soul, and free will. Origen had not lost interest in those issues, but to speak of them in anything other than a superficial manner before an ordinary congregation would be to cast pearls before swine.[34] He chose to limit himself to topics his congregation needed to understand in order to avoid sin and error, but within that limitation he employed his full powers as a scholar to assist them. Concerning the doctrine of God, Origen contented himself with warning his hearers against taking literally passages in the Old Testament that seem to ascribe human characteristics or emotions to God or to detract from God's perfect beneficence and justice. Concerning Christology, he simply reaffirmed the church's insistence that Christ was not identical with God the Father and that Christ was fully God and fully human. Nonetheless, although

Origen said little about the doctrine of Christ, his sermons were thoroughly Christocentric. Figures as diverse as Joshua, Jeremiah, and the bridegroom of the Song of Songs appear as symbols of Christ's salvific activity. We have seen how Origen substituted moralizing allegory for cosmology in his homilies on Genesis, where he covered in one sermon passages to which he had devoted volumes of commentary. Origen was just as vague about his views on eschatology although he did feel compelled to dissent from prevailing views about divine punishment in the afterlife. As to the soul and its free will, Origen upheld conventional views without going into controversial issues like the soul's preexistence. One area where Origen did, as in *On First Principles*, have a good deal to say was that of angelology and demonology. Origen frequently interpreted the Bible as a source of information, conveyed through symbols, of the unseen powers active in our lives. Here, however, Origen was neither original nor speculative.

We have seen, in chapter VI, how Origen spoke a great deal in his homilies about church leadership and the role of the preacher. This topic was prominent in his homilies on Leviticus, where he interpreted the Levitical priesthood as a symbol of Christian leadership and the sacrificial cultus as a symbol of preaching. Origen stressed the skill and learning required of preachers and their responsibility to speak the truth before their congregations even if doing so should provoke hostility. Evidently he felt such hostility himself because he identified the Christian preacher's situation with that of the beleaguered prophet:

> Prophets *and teachers* endure from those who do not wish to be healed of their sin the same things that physicians endure from patients unwilling to accept harsh medical treatment. . . . Such undisciplined patients flee their physicians or injure and insult them, treating them as if they were their enemies.[35]

Origen was willing to face this risk and took very seriously what he considered a preacher's obligations.

To be saved, Origen believed, one needed a holy life and knowledge of the truth. Although he stressed personal holiness, he did not neglect to caution his congregation against error. A large part of Origen's preaching is therefore concerned with defending the church's teaching against the claims of its rivals. Judging from his sermons Origen considered those rivals to be Judaism, Gnosticism, and materialistic philosophy. The state-supported paganism was a threat only insofar as it might compel weaker Christians to apostasize under duress. Origen did not even bother to mention the mystery religions. He apparently did not consider it at all likely that anyone who might be inclined to take Christ seriously would also be attracted to Isis or Mithras.

Judaism was by far the most serious threat. It is easy enough to see how it posed an intellectual challenge to a person of Origen's perspicacity. Jews declined, with few exceptions, to accept Jesus as their promised Messiah, and they did not hesitate to explain why. They also rejected, once Christians confronted them with the issue, the notion of a plurality of hypostases in the Godhead. More tellingly, they called into question the Christian appropriation of the Old Testament, pointing out that the book itself taught clearly the eternal election of Israel and the lasting validity of the Torah, positions intolerable to gentile Christianity. We shall see how a pagan enemy of the church turned these Jewish disagreements with Christianity to his advantage. Judaism's very existence confronted Origen with these issues, but as a preacher Origen had to face a more than simply intellectual challenge. Jews and Christians actively competed for the allegiance of pagans and for each other's adherents as well, and, in Palestine at least, the Jews did very well at it.

Historians have only recently become aware of how vital and aggressive a missionary religion Judaism was in Origen's time. It was the steady, restrictive policy of the Christian emperors of the fourth and fifth centuries, not the disasters that culminated in the quelling of the Bar-Cochba revolt of 132, that effectively ended the proselytizing spirit of Judaism.[36] Jews, in the wake of the destruction of the temple, the massacre of much of their population, and their expulsion from Jerusalem, did not turn in on themselves but continued, with few exceptions, to present themselves as a light to the nations. Some rabbis, though not a majority, even urged the relaxation of demands that gentiles be circumcised, recommending that baptism suffice for full membership in the synagogue. Although they strenuously upheld the authority of the Hebrew text of the Old Testament, Jews continued to worship and read the Bible in Greek in areas like Caesarea where that was the dominant language. As a result, gentiles found the synagogue accessible as well as welcoming.

Jews had several advantages over Christians. In the first place, they had Hebrew learning, learning of which Christians like Origen freely availed themselves. Jewish rabbis were only too willing to point out Christian ignorance of the Old Testament, and Origen was sensitive on that score. There seem to have been debates between Jewish and Christian scholars. Origen himself spoke of a formal debate with rabbis over the interpretation of the suffering servant figure in Isaiah. Two literary works—Justin Martyr's *Dialogue with Trypho* and the now lost *Dialogue of Jason and Papiscus*—also testify to such interaction.[37] In the second place, Jews had a rich and varied liturgical calendar, beside which Christian worship seemed quite dull. In the third place, Jews had a reputation for spiritual powers, whether magical or not. Church leaders throughout the empire were embarrassed that ordinary Christians would tend to turn to a rabbi when they desired a really effective blessing on their crops or exorcism of their demons. Origen's homilies show that a number of gentile Christians succumbed to the attractions of Judaism to the extent of attending the synagogue on high holy days and practicing some ritual observances.[38] These were gentile Christians, not Christians of Jewish descent, many of whom continued to observe the Torah while accepting Jesus as the Messiah.

Origen responded in a number of ways to the Jewish challenge. His method of interpreting the Old Testament was, by itself, a refutation of Jewish claims. If, as he taught, the Old Testament spoke on every page of Christ and the individual soul, the Jews were missing the whole point of its message. Origen's homilies on Leviticus boldly attempt to appropriate for Christians the very heart of the Torah. His allegorical interpretation involved, at least to some extent, a rejection of any literal sense. This is clear in his discussion of the laws concerning clean and unclean animals:

> If, following this allegorical interpretation, we say that the supreme God has promulgated laws for me, then I think that the legislation will seem worthy of the divine majesty. But if, on the contrary, we tie ourselves to the letter and accept, following the advice of Jews and unlearned Christians, the law just as it is written, then I blush to proclaim or to admit that God gave such laws. Human laws—those, for example, of the Romans, Athenians, and Lacedemonians—appear to be more elegant and rational than these. But surely, if we accept the law of God in

accordance with the allegorical interpretation, which the church teaches, then it manifestly surpasses all human laws and we may really believe it to be the law of God.[39]

History also provided Origen with anti-Jewish arguments. He argued that since the temple was destroyed, the law can no longer be fulfilled literally. God could not, therefore, have intended it to be lastingly valid. In addition, the expulsion of the Jews from Jerusalem definitely proved to him that God no longer regarded them as the elect. Origen, for example, did not hesitate to charge the Jews with guilt for the murder of Christ, explaining it characteristically as a result of their failure to interpret the Bible allegorically:

> If he who is commonly called a Jew murdered the Lord Jesus and is still today responsible for that murder, it is because he has not understood the law and the prophets in a hidden manner.[40]

Although such remarks have today the ring of anti-Semitism, we must bear in mind that they were uttered in the midst of an intense rivalry between groups on an equal footing and that Jews gave as well as they got. Intriguingly, Origen on at least one occasion relied on a more subtle strategy to compete with the Jews: imitation. David J. Halperin has shown that in his homily on the first chapter of Ezekiel, a favorite text for Jewish mystical speculation, Origen borrowed specific motifs of a highly visionary character from Jewish preaching for the feast of Pentecost and transposed them from Moses to Christ.[41] His ability to do so, and to borrow in other ways from Jewish scholars, demonstrates that he felt no qualms about close relations with the Jewish community, even if he thought the synagogue could corrupt simple Christians.

By contrast with his arguments against Judaism, which clearly evidence active competition, Origen's arguments against Gnosticism lack urgency. He simply repeated arguments he developed at Alexandria against the same trio of heretics—Basilides, Valentinus, and Marcion— with no indication that his congregation was actively threatened. Origen's homilies do not exhibit the logical argumentation against Gnosticism of *On First Principles* or the *Commentary on John* but seek by less direct means to cut the nerve of Gnosticism's appeal to thoughtful Christians. This meant demonstrating that the God of the Old Testament, the Creator of the world and giver of the law, was a God of love and mercy as well as of judgment. As in his controversy with the Jews, allegory was Origen's first line of defense. He ridiculed ritual laws that struck him as irrational and denied that God could have commanded the massacres recounted in the book of Joshua. One doctrine commonly taught in the church seemed to conflict with the picture of God as completely benevolent that he sought to present, the doctrine that unrepentant sinners would suffer eternal torment. We have seen how Origen posited an ultimately universal salvation in *On First Principles*. While he did not go so far as to affirm this explicitly in the homilies, he insisted unceasingly that God's punishments are never simply retributive but seek to benefit the sinner. This principle left no room for the Gnostics to present God as a merciless tyrant.

Origen recognized the need for delicacy in presenting this view. Some simpler Christians would object that when Christ warned of "eternal" fire (Matt. 18:8), he really meant it, and that the church had always taught that the wicked would be damned forever. Origen had the burden of proving that a literal reading of such a phrase was unworthy of God, yet he had to admit a certain efficacy in the view of the simpler Christians. Fear of eternal damnation promoted a lively and healthy fear in those incapable of being motivated to abstain from sin in any higher way. Would such persons, if they knew that they would ultimately be saved, feel any urgent need to amend their lives? That "ultimately" would include much unnecessary grief if they failed to take advantage of the opportunity God gave them to turn from sin during their earthly life. He therefore sought to inoculate the more sensitive against Gnostic claims while keeping the dull majority anxious about their salvation. While he affirmed God's good intentions toward even the most obdurate sinners, for example Pharaoh and his army,[42] he warned his flock to flee the wrath to come and taught them that their God was a consuming fire. We have already seen how, in a complaint about his congregation's tepidity, he called their salvation into question.

Origen's polemic against materialistic philosophy is not as pervasive but, if anything, even more severe. Epicureanism offended him, not simply because it was materialistic, but because it made pleasure the highest goal. For Origen the leprosy of the head in Leviticus 13 symbolized Epicurean philosophy. That leprosy mars the beard, the symbol of spiritual maturity, and the Epicureans, who teach that pleasure is life's highest goal, are like children, easily seduced by sin.[43] Origen was even more extravagantly harsh in his homilies on Judges. The woman Jael killed Sisera, the defeated general of the Canaanites, by driving a tent-peg through his head. This symbolizes the defeat of materialism since Sisera's head symbolizes the doctrine that pleasure is the highest good, and the tent-peg is the cross, which pierces through such falsehood and reveals the strait and narrow path of salvation.[44]

Although unrelentingly critical of Epicureanism, Origen preached the potential value, when properly assimilated, of Greek philosophy in general. In his homilies on Leviticus he created an image for the critical assimilation of Greek philosophy which, like spoiling the Egyptians in his letter to Gregory, caught the imagination of medieval exegetes. In Deuteronomy 21 the law prescribes that an Israelite warrior, if he captures a beautiful woman in a war against the enemies of Israel, may keep her as his wife if he follows rituals which include having her cut her hair and pare her nails. Origen did not accept the literal sense of the text; he objected, captiously, that the law could not apply if the woman happened to have cut her hair and pared her nails immediately before she was captured. The real meaning of the passage concerned "anything we find expressed well or reasonably among the writings of our adversaries," that is, the good parts in the writings of the pagan philosophers. Cutting the hair and paring the nails symbolizes the critical appropriation of pagan ideas. Christians must first cut and pare away whatever is vain or dead in such writings. Having done so, they can be confident of excluding heretical doctrines.[45] Origen's attitude toward philosophy in the homilies is thus what we find elsewhere: Epicureanism is totally worthless, but the doctrines of other schools contain many useful ideas.

There is no record of Origen's preaching on any of the historical books after 2 Samuel, and it seems as if Origen delivered his last sermons at Jerusalem rather than at Caesarea. There is also evidence in Origen's homilies that he was meeting opposition. We know from them that some members of Origen's congregation considered his allegorization far too extreme and resented his willingness to substitute the readings in more recent Jewish translations for the church's received Septuagint text of the Old Testament. Origen's sensitivity about presenting his views on the eventual salvation of the wicked also indicates that he met opposition on that score. Origen's scathing denunciations of the Caesarean clergy and people must also have alienated many who would have been well disposed to him otherwise. Pierre Nautin has inferred from these indications that Theoctistus relieved Origen of his duties as a preacher at Caesarea before the three-year cycle was complete. If, in fact, Theoctistus bowed to pressure from Origen's detractors and forbade him to preach, that may account for Origen's second journey to Greece and for his unrelieved bitterness toward ecclesiastical officials, both of which bespeak a strain in their relationship during the later years of Origen's life.

## On the Passover

The cache of manuscripts at Tura included, along with the *Dialogue with Heraclides*, a work entitled, in Greek, *Peri tou Pascha*, which has much in common with the homilies Origen preached and probably comes from the same period of his life. We can translate the title either as *On Easter* or *On the Passover*. Since it is a commentary on the twelfth chapter of Exodus, which recounts the origin of the Passover festival, the latter translation is better. Although ancient lists of Origen's works mention Easter homilies, the work's modern editors convincingly make the case that the work is a previously unknown treatise.[46] At any rate, *On the Passover* shows every sign of authenticity.

The relation between the Christian Easter and the Jewish Passover was at issue in a major controversy during the later second century. Many churches in Asia Minor, relying on an ancient tradition allegedly from the Apostle John, celebrated Easter on the same day as the Jewish Passover, the fourteenth of the lunar month of Nisan, which could fall on any day of the week. Most likely the Passover the first Christians celebrated as Jews imperceptibly became a feast celebrating Christ's sacrifice. This ran counter to the practice of Christians elsewhere, who took care to celebrate Easter on a Sunday and to see to it that it did not coincide with Passover. Bishop Victor of Rome, whose church celebrated Easter on Sunday, led a movement to force all churches to follow the Roman usage. Leaders of the church in Asia Minor resisted. They were probably right about the greater antiquity of their tradition, but they found themselves isolated as Quartodeciman (''Fourteenther,'' from the fourteenth of Nisan) heretics. The Quartodeciman controversy was spent by Origen's time, and he did not allude to it, but he dealt with issues it raised.

As he did with Leviticus in his homilies, Origen transformed the ritual instructions of Exodus 12 into a visionary account of Christian spiritual life. In this case, Origen built his interpretation on a crucial grammatical point, the etymology of *pascha*, the name of the feast. Melito of Sardis, a staunchly Quartodeciman bishop of Sardis in Asia Minor (d. c. 190) had established the generally accepted etymology. He derived *pascha* from *paschein*, the Greek verb "to suffer," which further linked it to *pathos*, "suffering," the word for the passion of Christ that culminated in his crucifixion. This etymology suited Melito's purposes since, by connecting *pascha* with the suffering of Christ rather than with Christ's resurrection, it provided an argument against those who would celebrate Easter on Sunday, the day of the resurrection. Melito's views on the date of Easter lost out, but his seemingly self-evident etymology continued to enjoy the favor of most Christians. Only Clement of Alexandria, who learned of it by reading Philo, knew the correct etymology from a Hebrew word that means "passage." Origen knew this and complained that the incorrect etymology gave Jews an opportunity to ridicule Christians.[47]

Origen buttressed this grammatical point, which severs any connection between the Passover and the passion of Christ by a general principle of interpretation we have seen in the homilies: the Bible is always directly relevant to our present situation. If the Passover were a prefiguration of the passion of Christ, its interest for us would be entirely historical, and for Origen historical interest was of no interest whatsoever. As it is, the Passover, correctly understood as "passage," symbolizes our soul's passage, here and now, from sin and ignorance to the knowledge of God.[48]

In his interpretation of Exodus 12, Origen, although he did not explicitly mention it, described this passage on two levels, the worship of the church and the spiritual experience of the individual Christian. As always he insisted that his reading of Exodus 12 fully accorded with the intentions of its author. Moses, by virtue of a divine science, knew the reality which he set forth figuratively and intended every detail to con-

vey a spiritual meaning.[49] The interpreter's task was to discover and
expound that meaning. Why did Moses stipulate that the Passover lamb
be acquired on the tenth day of the month although it was not destined to
be slaughtered until the fourteenth? In terms of the church's worship,
this five-day interval symbolized the catechumenate, the time when the
candidate for baptism prepared to pass from a life of sin to the life of
righteousness. In terms of the individuals's spiritual experience, the five
days symbolized the five spiritual senses that enable him to perceive
divine realities.[50]

On the liturgical side, Origen linked the Passover with both Christian mysteries, baptism and the eucharist. Baptism, which normally
took place on Easter, was an obvious rite of passage even if Origen
stated that it was only a genuine passage from sin to righteousness when
Christians took their baptismal obligations seriously. The Passover
lamb was also a symbol of the eucharist. Origen, however made the
eucharist itself a symbol for another aspect of the church's worship,
preaching. Feeding on Christ's body is the mystical feeding on the word
of God that occurs when the preacher presents that word in a way that
the hearers can assimilate. Moses spoke allegorically of preaching the
word when he commanded that the lamb be eaten roasted with fire
rather than raw or boiled in water. To eat the lamb roasted with fire
means to feed upon God's word once the preacher has interpreted it with
the assistance of the fire par excellence, the Holy Spirit. To eat the lamb
raw means attempting to feed on the word when it has been presented
with the inadequate literal interpretation of the Jews. To eat the lamb
boiled in water means attempting to feed on the word when it has been
misinterpreted by heretics, who contaminate the word with their own
nonbiblical doctrines, much as boiled meat is mixed with water, a substance foreign to it.[51]

The church's worship is significant only insofar as it facilitates the
moral and intellectual transformation which, at its deeper level, the
Passover symbolizes. Moses' instruction to leave none of the lamb for
the morrow indicates the transitory character of the church's life. On the
morrow, that is, in the life to come, the direct vision of God will make
the eucharist and the Bible, which mediate the vision of God to us on
earth, unnecessary.[52] As in his other writings, Origen depicted this
interior passage transcending the church's worship as a gradual process,

occurring in discrete stages. At all stages it is the grace of God through Christ that enables the soul to progress, but Christ appears in different aspects to Christians at different stages of achievement. When Moses commanded that the Passover lamb be taken from among the sheep and the goats, he symbolized two aspects of Christ. Christ appears as a goat to those still entrapped in sin since it is the goat which the law prescribes as an offering to remove sin, but Christ appears as a sheep to those who have obtained a measure of freedom from sin because Christ is the lamb of God who takes away the sin of the world.[53] Elsewhere, these aspects of Christ appear as the various organs of the lamb to be consumed, the highest being the head, which symbolizes the rational understanding of Christ that appears to those farthest advanced in perfection.[54]

Origen's *On the Passover* thus provides, in a short and self-contained form, a fine example of Origen's allegorical genius and a significant insight into his understanding of the church's worship. Although the modern scholar is bound to find his interpretation of Exodus 12 artificial, it achieves, in its own terms, remarkable persuasiveness and consistency.

## Views on Sacraments

*On the Passover*'s devaluation of the church's worship in favor of the individual's spiritual experience is typical. The external aspects of the church's worship have, in fact, much the same role in Origen's thought as the letter of the Bible: they symbolize deeper, spiritual realities. Nevertheless, they have on the surface level a genuine validity. Just as the church's official leaders validly maintain order whether or not they are genuinely leaders before God, the sacraments validly provide the simple an introduction to the Christian life and sustain them in it.

Baptism, at its deepest level, symbolizes the Logos' purification of the soul so that it may obtain the knowledge of God. The actual rite of immersing in water, on a far more superficial level, makes Christians members of the church and provides them a powerful motive not to sin. The Christian tradition, as it came to Origen, taught that baptism instantaneously forgave sins as it empowered and obligated the Christian to sin no more. Origen echoed this teaching when he preached on the miraculous healing of the Syrian officer Naaman, who found himself cured of leprosy when he obeyed Elijah's command to bathe in the Jordan. Just as Naaman's formerly scabby skin became instantaneously as smooth as a baby's, so the newly baptized Christian is as innocent of sin as a newborn child.[55] The scapegoat in Leviticus 16 gave him an opportunity to preach to his congregation on the danger of sinning after baptism. Since the goat is a clean animal, fit for God's altar, it must symbolize a baptized Christian. Yet the people expel the goat into the desert, bearing away sins. It must therefore represent the Christian who has sinned after baptism and, in consequence, suffers expulsion from the church. Caesarean Christians had better not yield to licentious temptations, or they will suffer the scapegoat's fate.[56] Origen recognized that some leaders in the church considered such sentiments too rigorous to be practical, but he warned them not to provide people pretexts for sinning under cover of a seemingly reasonable recognition of human weakness.[57] While the moral level of the church by no means satisfied him, he was confident that Christians did at least meet minimal standards. Since Christians do not steal, break oaths, or abuse deposits, Moses' laws on those topics must be interpreted allegorically.[58]

Such statements give the impression that Origen simply restated the church's traditional teaching, but other statements belie that impression. In fact, Origen ascribed baptismal holiness, not to the rite itself, but to the discipline prospective Christians undergo as catechumens. He warns catechumens not to expect the Holy Spirit to remove their sins unless they have removed them first.[59] The fact that catechumens frequently put baptized Christians to shame shows that baptism is not essential for holiness. The Bible itself demonstrates this in the contrasting figures of Cornelius and Simon Magus from the book of Acts. Cornelius was worthy of the Holy Spirit even before he was baptized; Simon Magus was shamefully unworthy of the Spirit after having been baptized.[60] Even pagans can achieve a level of holiness that contrasts with the lassitude of most baptized Christians. Origen rebuked those who wished to suppress the literal meaning of Jesus' advice to the rich young man to sell all that he had and give it to the poor in order to be perfect—did he have Clement in mind?—by pointing to the example of Crates, the Theban Cynic philosopher. Saying ''today may Crates liberate Crates,'' he gave away all his possessions and obtained the freedom of his soul.[61]

Baptism, in such a context, is simply one stage, albeit a very important one, in the gradual process of obtaining liberation from sin. It gives the power or shows the way for the Christian to become like Christ, but that process requires time, just as it takes time for must to turn into wine.[62] In his homilies on Joshua, Origen interpreted the crossing of the Jordan as a symbol of baptism with the full awareness that this implied that baptism was only a stage in a gradual process; the wilderness had been crossed, but the conquest of Canaan was still to come.[63] Occasional lapses may even benefit the soul since they teach it how to recognize the temptation to sin and prevent it from getting overconfident.[64] Baptized Christians must continually nourish their spirits by attending church regularly, listening attentively to the sermon, reading the Bible, and praying. Otherwise they will not have the strength to resist temptation.[65]

The New Testament provided Origen the opportunity to suggest deeper levels of baptism by referring to the baptisms of fire and of the Holy Spirit. In his *Homilies on Jeremiah* Origen contrasted these two further baptisms:

> Jesus baptizes . . . with the Holy Spirit and with fire; not that he baptizes the same person with the Holy Spirit and with fire, but that he baptizes the holy person with the Holy Spirit, but the person who, having once believed and been found worthy of the Holy Spirit, has sinned again he washes with fire. . . . Therefore he is blessed who is baptized with the Holy Spirit and does not need the baptism of fire, and he is three-times wretched who needs to be baptized with fire.[66]

The church's rite therefore anticipates one of two further baptisms which God administers directly. The baptism of fire is the remedial chastisement that must befall all who fail to make the best use of their opportunity to attain holiness this side of death. The baptism of the Holy Spirit is a further stage of blessedness only a select few obtain.

In other contexts Origen asserted that the baptism of the Spirit is an experience living Christians may obtain and is, in fact, the experience that distinguishes spiritual Christians from their simpler friends. Jesus' act of footwashing at the Last Supper was one biblical symbol for this higher baptism. This is a rite the Logos administers to those who, even if they are not absolutely sinless, a condition impossible for mortal humans, are as sinless as possible. This is why Christ only washed the disciples' feet, the lowliest part of the body since they are farthest from the head.[67] By contrast with this higher baptism, the baptism of water is largely hortatory, turning souls from evil. It is the beginning and source of divine gifts rather than their fulfillment. Unlike the first baptism, which makes use of the corporeal medium of water, the baptism of the Spirit is incorporeal. Origen did not understand it as a second rite Christians undergo but as an act of the Spirit signifying the Christian's entry into a more perfect life.[68] Origen did not intentionally devalue the church's rite of baptism. He claimed to accept and teach all of the church's traditional baptismal doctrine, but by placing that doctrine in a new context, he radically altered its meaning. Baptism is no longer a single act that constitutes a person a Christian. It is only a stage marking the achievement of an acceptable level of morality during the catechumenate and obligating the Christian to maintain that level and, if possible, advance beyond it. The incorporeal spiritual baptism of the Christian elite replaces the corporeal baptism of the mass of Christians as the focus of Origen's attention, and the latter becomes only a pale foreshadowing of the former.

Origen held the material bread and wine of the eucharist in the same disdain we have seen him display toward the material water of baptism as a vehicle of God's grace. The eucharist, which the church at Caesarea celebrated three times a week, including at its principal gathering on Sunday, was the central act of Christian worship. Christians agreed on the need for saints alone to participate in the eucharist; unbaptized persons could not even be present during the rite, and every attempt was made to exclude persons who had committed sins grave enough to compromise their baptismal purity. Christians also agreed that the eucharist provided spiritual nourishment in the body and blood of Christ. They did not see any need to agree on precisely how that nourishment came about. Most Christians took literally the words which Jesus was recorded to have pronounced as he held bread and wine at the Last Supper, "This is my body" and "This is my blood." They taught that the bread and wine consecrated in the eucharist actually became the body and blood of Christ. Modern historians of doctrine call this the realist position on the eucharist. Others held that the eucharistic bread and wine symbolized Christ's body and blood, the position modern historians know as symbolist. The evidence of Origen's works shows that both understandings were current in Caesarea. Origen himself, as we should expect, strongly upheld the symbolist position, but he testified that the majority of those he considered more simple believed that the eucharistic bread and wine actually became Christ's body and blood and acted ritually on the basis of that belief, being scrupulous not to lose a crumb of the eucharistic bread.[69]

Origen, on the other hand, referred to John 6:53, "unless you eat the flesh of the Son of man and drink his blood, you have no life in you," as a good example of a letter that kills in the New Testament.[70] When Jesus pronounced his well-known words over bread and wine at the Last Supper, he did not intend to imply that he was actually holding his own body and blood in his hands.[71] What Origen considered the naively realistic eucharistic realism of the more simple was dangerous because it undermined Christian moral earnestness. The simple, who believe that the eucharistic bread actually is the body of Christ, assume that it will automatically sanctify whoever receives it. Origen, by contrast, stated that eating the bread, in and of itself, provides us with nothing good, and not eating it deprives us of nothing good. The eucharist, that is, benefits only those who approach it already with a good conscience. Matthew 15:17, in his opinion, demonstrates the folly of a realistic view of the eucharist:

> If "whatever goes into the mouth passes into the stomach, and so passes on," even the food sanctified through the word of God and prayer, because it is material, enters into the stomach and so passes on. But the prayer that has come upon it turns it, according to the proportion of faith, into a benefit and a means of clear vision for the mind that beholds what is beneficial. It is not the matter of bread but the word pronounced upon it which is beneficial to him who does not eat it unworthily of the Lord.[72]

Origen's respect for human responsibility to avoid sin thus joined with his contempt for matter to dictate for him a symbolist position on the eucharist. The customary term, realism, for a belief in the actual transformation of the bread and wine into Christ's body and blood can be misleading when it comes to Origen. For him as a Platonist, the eucharist was incomparably more real as a symbol than it could be if there were a material transformation since the intelligible world is far more real than the material. He was therefore as keen on the need not to abuse the symbol of Christ's presence as more simple Christians were on the need not to abuse the actual body and blood. Origen, accordingly, took pains to warn his congregation of the dangers of partaking of the eucharist unworthily, reminding them that Paul had told the Corinthians that such laxness was responsible for the sickness and death among them.[73]

Bread sustains us and enables us to work. The eucharistic bread therefore symbolizes Christ as the Word of righteousness, manifested in action. Wine gladdens the heart, which in the Bible is the seat of the intellect. The eucharistic wine therefore symbolizes Christ as the Word of truth, manifested in contemplation.[74] It is not, however, the consumption of the eucharistic bread and wine that actually makes accessible to Christians the word of God that enables them to do good works and attain the knowledge of God. That comes, rather, from hearing the word preached, the activity of which the eucharist is a ritual symbol. In his interpretation of the feeding of the five thousand in Matthew 14, Origen used the bread the disciples distributed to the assembled crowd as a symbol of inspired preaching. The crowd was hungry spiritually because, once John the Baptist had been put to death, the age of prophecy had come to an end, and they no longer had their customary access to the word of God. The five loaves of bread that miraculously multiplied to feed them represent the sensible words of the Bible, which the disciples, empowered by Jesus, transformed into genuine spiritual nourishment.[75] Origen chided his congregation for scrupulously eating every crumb of the eucharistic bread without realizing that they were committing a sacrilege against the word of God when they failed to pay as scrupulous attention to every word of the sermon.[76] He also reminded them that they drank Christ's blood, not only when they drank the eucharistic wine but when they heard God's word.[77] The eucharist, therefore, was significant to Origen largely insofar as it pointed beyond itself to rational appropriation of the word which is at the heart of his understanding of Christian growth.

## Views on Ecclesiastical Discipline

Origen spiritualized ecclesiastical discipline similarly. He readily accepted the right of church leaders to exclude notorious sinners from the eucharist, and he thought that they were betraying their pastoral responsibility if they failed to exercise that power. His concern was not that the presence of sinners would, in some mysterious way, impair the church's standing before God but that they would set a bad example. The toleration of known sinners, he thought, demoralizes a congregation, since the simple think, when they see a Christian sin and remain in the church, that they ought to be able to sin with impunity themselves. A good pastor therefore removes the mangy sheep from the flock, since otherwise its mange will inevitably spread to others.[78] Even so, the church's leaders should use their authority discreetly. It is best to see if exhortation and admonishment will cure sinners before excluding them from fellowship.[79]

Origen did not share the concern other Christians of his time had for the spiritual, as opposed to moral, contagion of sinners in the church because he did not believe that a sinner really belonged to the church. When one committed a particularly grave sin, one automatically excluded oneself from the fellowship. For the sinner's own good and for the good of the community, the bishop should excommunicate such a person should the sin become known, but this official exclusion is only a ratification of the spiritual exclusion that had already occurred.[80] Origen, in fact, assumed rather complacently toward the end of his life that the majority of ostensible Christians, including many of the clergy, were not genuinely part of the church. "Many are called, but few are chosen."[81] At the same time, an unjustified excommunication does not really sever the person excommunicated from the spiritual fellowship of the church.[82] Since Origen believed that the Christian was deprived of nothing by not partaking of the eucharist, such exclusion did no harm.

The church could readmit to its fellowship the excommunicated Christian who exhibited genuine repentance and a firm resolve not to sin again. Demonstrating such moral reformation was a serious process. According to Origen, it normally took longer than the period of preparation for baptism (itself probably three years) and had to be permanent or the sinner would be excluded again with no hope of return.[83] There was, in Origen's time and earlier, as we have seen, considerable debate over whether or not excommunicated sinners could even have one opportunity to return to the church. Although rigorists foresaw the wreck of the church's moral standards, most Christians, including Origen, eventually decided that the long period of probation gave the church ample opportunity to test the penitent's sincerity and was severe enough to discourage others from presuming on God's mercy.[84] The bishop, as the community's chief pastor, decided when and if the penitent sinner was to return to the church's fellowship and formally reconciled such a one to the church. The act of formal readmission to fellowship ultimately became routinized as the sacrament of penance, but that was after Origen's time. Nevertheless, bishops had, by Origen's time, come to see the act by which they reconciled the sinner to the community as an act of forgiveness, not simply as an official recognition that the sinner could rejoin the church. Origen found the notion of an official mediation of forgiveness intolerable and set forth his own alternative procedure for those who would like to be free from sin.

Origen objected to the notion that the bishop could forgive sins by an official act of reconciliation to the church not simply because he found it pretentious but far more significantly because he found it pointless. Forgiveness, for Origen, was meaningless apart from the reformation of character. The problem of sinners was not that they were liable to punitive chastisement on God's part from which the bishop, by virture of the power of the keys given to Peter, had the right to release them. Rather, sinners were victims of a psychological malady which prevented them from achieving the true purpose of life: service to others and attainment of the knowledge of God. The remission of penalties could not possibly do them any good. The only function of God's chastisement, after all, was to lead sinners to repent and to look to Christ for the healing of sin. The remission of those penalties, unaccompanied by a reformation of character, would leave sinners even worse off than they were before since it would postpone the day of reckoning with their sinfulness.

The exercise of ecclesiastical discipline could and should facilitate the genuine healing of sinners' maladies. The exclusion from fellowship would make them aware of the problem; the period of probation would enable them to come to terms with it; and the official reconciliation to the church would, like baptism, provide a powerful incentive to maintain the level of holiness achieved. Origen, however, put little reliance on the church's discipline as a way of attaining forgiveness. Not only was it frequently ill conceived, it was at best a procedure applicable only in cases of grave sins. He therefore advocated a much more private way to obtain healing from sin. In his homilies on Leviticus Origen

sought to disabuse his congregation of the idea that they were less
fortunate than the ancient Hebrews since they had only one way of
obtaining forgiveness, baptism, while the Jews of the Old Testament
had many sacrifices for sin. No, he said, Christians have seven equivalents for the Old Testament sacrifices for sin. In addition to baptism,
they have martyrdom, the second repentance allowed in ecclesiastical
discipline, almsgiving, forgiving the sins of others, turning others from
sin, and abounding love.[85] Elsewhere he spoke of hearing the sermon
attentively as a means, bitter at times, for obtaining deliverance from
sin.[86] But the best way to obtain forgiveness is through the pastoral
attentions of a spiritual person. Origen, like Clement in *Who Is the Rich
Man Who Is to Be Saved?*, advised sinners to seek such pastoral guidance but not to do so hastily. Before entrusting oneself to the care of a
spiritual adviser, one who is a sinner should first determine that the
person in question is capable of empathy. Having done so, though, one
should confess all sins and follow the advice given implicitly.[87] The
spiritual adviser will go about curing one of one's sins in the only really
effective way by exhortation, admonition, guidance, and example. We
have already seen how Origen considered such pastoral activity a central concern of a genuine church leader, and we have seen how Theodore, in the *Speech of Appreciation*, ascribed his own moral formation
to such activity on Origen's part.

Ecclesiology, the doctrine of the church, was not a major issue for
theologians in the Greek Christian tradition, least of all for Origen. We
should therefore beware of drawing too many conclusions from his
understanding of the church's leadership, the sacraments, and ecclesiastical discipline. By the standards of Latin-speaking Christians of his
own day, Origen's views on these subjects were dangerously, perhaps
even heretically, subjectivist: they made the soul's immediate relation
to God through the Logos, not that relation as mediated through the
church as an institution, the criterion of its spiritual status. The logical
consequence of such ideas might be to dispense with the church as an
earthly institution entirely, but this was not Origen's way; he sincerely
considered the church a unique vehicle of God's grace. The church and
the church alone made accessible to human beings the truth about God
and standards of morality that made it possible to advance toward personal knowledge of God. Pagans, Jews, heretics, and contumacious

sinners would be well advised to make their peace with the church and accept its authority. Yet the church as a spiritual fellowship was not identical either in its leadership or membership with the church as a social institution. Neither did its rites and teachings necessarily correspond with the rites and teachings of the institution. Origen, in his writings, left the relationship between the spiritual and the institutional church tenuous and ill-defined, but he did not divorce the two. Our own logic, reinforced by centuries of Christian tradition, might lead us to make Origen's views more specific, but it is best to leave them as vague as he did. Suffice it to say that Origen was a sincere and committed churchman, but one for whom the church's function as a vehicle of God's grace was always more important than its character as an institution.

# IX
# Standing Fast
## (244–c. 53)

During the last eight or so years of his life Origen managed to ride out a controversy that again seriously called into question his place in the church, and he died without quite attaining the one status that would have secured his reputation as a saint. Philip, the general who overthrew Gordian III in 244, favored the church—so much so that Christians in later generations considered him, without real justification, to have been a Christian himself. Ironically, it was Philip—an Arab who was perhaps the least Roman of all the emperors—who, on April 12, 248, presided over the celebrations that marked the thousandth anniversary of the founding of Rome. Philip's own glory was short-lived. Decius, a general from Illyria, overthrew and replaced him in 249. This coup dramatically altered Roman policy toward the church. Decius quickly shocked the church out of the complacency Origen complained of in his homilies and, unlike his predecessors, actually tried to extirpate Christianity. Fortunately, the Goths killed Decius in battle in 251 before he had killed very many Christians. His successor, the ineffective Gallus, who also reigned only two years, did not continue his policy. In 251 Origen, a broken man, effectively disappears from history and must have died within a few years.

## Athens and the *Commentary on the Song of Songs*

Origen had no reason to remain in Caesarea, given his estrangement from Theoctistus and the departure of his pupil Theodore. He therefore went to Athens, where he probably intended to settle permanently.[1] At least we know that he did not intend a brief visit because he resumed his writing. After completing a twenty-five book *Commentary on Ezekiel* that he had begun in Caesarea, Origen wrote five books of a *Commentary on the Song of Songs* and, perhaps at this time, a twenty-five book *Commentary on the Minor Prophets*. The Greek originals of all of these works have disappeared, but the prologue and the first three books of the *Commentary on the Song of Songs* survive in a Latin translation—perhaps adaptation would be a better word—by Rufinus.[2] This was a truly remarkable work and one that was to be highly influential. Jerome, in the preface to his translation of Origen's homilies on the Song of Songs, wrote that in his other works Origen surpassed all other writers, but in the *Commentary on the Song of Songs* he surpassed himself.

Origen set out in the prologue to his *Commentary on the Song of Songs* the major issue that confronted the interpreter. The first issue, for a person trained in literary criticism, was the work's genre. Origen identified this as an *epithalamium*, a wedding poem, in the form of a play celebrating the wedding of a groom (the Logos) and a bride (the soul or the church). They and their respective friends are the characters in the drama. It is the duty of the interpreter of the poem, as in the case of a Greek play or a dialogue by Plato, to identify to which character each line of the poem refers and by which each is meant to be spoken.[3] A more pressing issue is how to explain the poem's lush erotic imagery. Origen believed that the Song of Songs dealt with a heavenly rather than an earthly love, much like Plato's *Symposium*, but as with Plato's work it was possible for licentious persons to misunderstand it in a carnal way. He suggested that anyone who was still subject to fleshly urges not read the book, and he commended the Jewish tradition that kept the Song of Songs out of the hands of the immature.[4] This reserve was justifiable, not simply because the work could easily be misconstrued but because it dealt with the most profound and esoteric branch of philosophy, the science of mystical contemplation. The Song of Songs, he wrote, was one of three treatises Solomon wrote on the three branches of philosophy—ethics, physics, and "mystics"—which the Greeks derived from him. (Logic, the other traditional branch of philosophy, Origen identified as a method common to the three other disciplines.) The Bible depicts God as the ultimate source and subject of all three divisions of philosophy when it refers to "the God of Abraham, Isaac, and Jacob." Abraham symbolizes ethics because he lived a life of obedience; Isaac symbolizes physics because he dug deep wells, meaning that he delved profoundly into natural things; and Jacob symbolizes the mystical science because he had a vision of a ladder extending from heaven to earth.[5] Because this last is a division of philosophy which requires extensive preparation, most people have no reason ever to look at the book, which does not contain an edifying literal sense.

But how is it appropriate for erotic imagery to express such profound spiritual mysteries? To answer this, Origen posited a pervasive pattern of biblical symbolism, in which an inner, spiritual person corresponds to the outer, corporeal person.[6] He found this terminology set forth explicitly in Paul, but he traced it back to the first two chapters of Genesis where the two separate accounts of human creation represent these two realities, and it is, of course, the inner person who is created first. Just as the Bible uses this imagery to speak of spiritual perception, spiritual maturity, and spiritual nourishment, so it uses it to speak of spiritual love. It would, in fact, be inappropriate if there were not a spiritual equivalent of carnal love. It must be understood, though, that while spiritual love is higher than carnal, it is not necessarily good in and of itself. Just as a person may legitimately love his or her spouse carnally or illegitimately seek out prostitutes, so we can rightly love God spiritually, or we can, as the prophets said, go awhoring after strange gods.[7]

Like Plato in the *Symposium*, Origen identified love as the power that leads the soul from earth to heaven by enabling it to concentrate all its energies on the attainment of the beloved object. God the Creator, Origen argued, is love, and has made us kindred with God by implanting that love in us. It is, nevertheless, our duty to direct the love God has given us to its appropriate object. Such an object must be something of real value, something that will never disappoint us, hence something incorruptible. The common objects of human love—money, fame, and sexual enjoyment—all fail to meet this criterion and hence are delusory. The prime object of our love should be God, who is ever the same. Our neighbors are also appropriate objects of our love since insofar as they are rational creatures they also were created in incorruption. That is why Jesus summed up the entire law in the commandment to love God and to love our neighbor. We must not love earthly and corruptible things but use them to further our legitimate love. Love thus motivates ethics and mystical contemplation. Origen's application of erotic imagery to contemplation is particularly significant since it provided a way of speaking about the soul's union with God in a way particularly congenial to the Christian tradition. In nuptial mysticism the erotic imagery is able to express the ecstasy and the intimate union with God without calling into question the continuing personal identity of the mystic as some other ways of describing mystical union do.

Origen was ready for the objection that his concept of a heavenly erotic love was not really biblical. He knew and acknowledged that the Bible does not refer to love with the Greek word *erôs*, the ordinary word for sexual love, but with the word *agapê*, a relatively uncommon word that usually means disinterested affection. Origen believed that the authors or translators of the Bible did this in order to avoid the suggestive implications of *erôs*, but that *agapê* did not represent a fundamentally different concept. Origen took as evidence a number of cases in the Septuagint where *agapê* is used to refer very clearly to carnal love, most strikingly 2 Samuel 13, where it is used in connection with incestuous rape. He was also able to point out cases in Proverbs 4:6,8 and in Wisdom 8:2 where derivatives of *erôs* to refer to the love of Wisdom. In these cases since there could be no question of suggestiveness the Bible used the normal term for love. Moreover Ignatius, a revered martyr, had written "my *erôs*," meaning Christ, "has been crucified."[8] It is therefore fully appropriate for an erotic poem to be the vehicle for the profoundest doctrine in the Bible.

In the commentary, Origen interpreted the Song of Songs on three levels. On the literal level, which has no value in and of itself, the poem is a play about relations between the bride and bridegroom. In dealing with each unit of meaning, therefore, Origen explained its place in this drama. Following that he interpreted it on one or both of two allergorical levels, the ecclesiastical and the psychological, levels we have seen elsewhere in his exegesis. On the ecclesiastical level, the bride is the church. On the psychological level, she is the individual soul. In either case the bridegroom is the Logos. Thus, in verse 2:15, the little foxes that ruin the vines can be heresies on the ecclesiastical level or sins on the psychological level. Similarly, the approach of the bridegroom after a period of absence in 2:8 can refer either to Christ's consolation of the church in times of persecution or to his giving the Christian teacher a sudden inspiration when he is at a loss to explain a passage from the Bible.[9] In other cases Origen interpreted a passage on one allegorical level only. Thus 1:17, "the beams of our houses are cedars, our rafters of cypresses," refers to the good order of the church. Presbyters are the beams and bishops are the rafters. The rafters are cypress because it is strong and aromatic, symbolizing the need for bishops to be sound in good works and fragrant with the grace of teaching.[10] Origen also interpreted the Song of Songs in such a way as to discuss the gentile origin of the church and its relation to Israel as well as its cleansing from sin and error.

The psychological level, however, is the one that tends to predominate in Origen's allegory. Origen, on this level, compared the bride—the soul prepared to receive the direct attentions of the Logos—with her friends, who symbolize simpler Christians who must depend on the teaching of others for their access to the Word.[11] This access comes, of course, through the study of the Bible, and the *Commentary on the Song of Songs* has, like so many of his works, the interpretation of the Bible as its major theme. This lends a rather incongruous intellectualism to Origen's use of erotic imagery, yet it is quite consistent with the highly intellectual character of his own piety. The second verse of the poem, "O that you would kiss me with the kisses of your mouth!" is the soul's prayer to God for understanding of obscure passages in the Bible, insights into which are kisses of the Logos.[12] The bridegroom, similarly, praises his bride, the soul, for having dove's eyes, that is a spiritual (since at his baptism the Holy Spirit appeared to Jesus in the form of a dove) perception (through the inner eyes) of the meaning of the Bible.[13] The privacy implicit in erotic imagery suits Origen's esotericism very well. The bridal chamber thus refers to the secret, spiritual interpretation reserved for those advanced in holiness and knowledge.[14] This use of imagery extends, as always, throughout the Bible. The bridegroom's breast, which is praised in the poem, symbolizes the hidden meaning of the Bible. Thus, when, at the Last Supper, the Apostle John leaned upon Jesus' breast, this symbolized his ability to repose among the esoteric meanings of Jesus' teaching.[15] Although Origen's *Commentary on the Song of Songs* was widely imitated, this peculiarly intellectual tone retains a quality all its own.

## Further Controversy

We do not know how the Athenian Christians reacted to Origen's commentaries, but, in any event, he decided again not to settle permanently in Greece. During this sojourn there he went to Nicopolis, where he found the anonymous translation of the Old Testament that made a fifth column to his *Hexapla*. Nicopolis, in Epirus on the western coast of Greece, is far from Athens and not a place a third-century scholar would ordinarily go. Perhaps Origen went there with the intention of taking passage to Italy for another visit to Rome but thought better of it. At any rate, in 246 or 247, after spending one or two years in Athens, Origen returned to Caesarea. On the way an incident occurred that was to cause him trouble. At Ephesus, where after crossing the Aegean he picked up the land road for Palestine, Origen met another traveling Christian whom he took to be a heretic because of his views on free will. Origen offered to debate the man publicly, but understandably the supposed heretic avoided the confrontation. Origen was therefore considerably annoyed when he arrived at Antioch, about two-thirds of his way home, to find that the person whom he had met at Ephesus had created a sensation among Christians there with a fictitious account of a debate he and Origen supposedly had at Ephesus, a debate in which Origen said that the devil ought to be saved. The imposter did not back down when Origen confronted him openly at Antioch, but he discredited himself when he refused to submit his dialogue to persons who knew Origen's style and could evaluate its authenticity. No doubt assuming that he had laid that matter to rest, Origen continued on to Caesarea. There he wrote five more books of his *Commentary on the Song of Songs*, a massive *Commentary on the Psalms*, and shorter commentaries on Proverbs and Ecclesiastes. He may also have written his twenty-five book *Commentary on the Minor Prophets* at this time if he did not write it in Athens. Only pitiful fragments remain of all these works.

The incident at Ephesus, though, continued to cause Origen trouble. The man he had met there was, as it turned out, a member of the church at Alexandria. On returning to his native city he gave Bishop Heraclas a copy of the debate that depicted Origen as a heretic and also informed him that Origen had spoken critically of him publicly. As we have already seen, there was no love lost between Origen and his former colleague as a teacher at Alexandria and, while he had not pursued Demetrius' vendetta against Origen, Heraclas had continued to consider him a heretic and thus prevented him from returning to his native city. The news from Ephesus, in addition to trouble he was having in Egypt, now persuaded Heraclas to act more forcefully. Heraclas took over from Demetrius a tradition according to which the bishop of Alexandria had jurisdiction over the church throughout Egypt. At Thmuis, a city on the eastern edge of the Nile Delta, that jurisdiction was being flouted by Bishop Ammonius, a supporter of Origen. Ammonius had entertained Origen on some occasion after Demetrius secured his condemnation, and Heraclas used this as a pretext to convene a synod at Thmuis that deposed Ammonius and appointed a new bishop, Philip, in his stead. But Ammonius did not choose to resign, and his congregation backed him, telling Philip that they could consider him their bishop only on Ammonius' death. Heraclas sought to meet this challenge to his authority in the time-tested way, by appealing for the support of the bishop of Rome. He therefore wrote a letter to the Roman Bishop Fabian informing him that Ammonius was hanging onto his see after being deposed for harboring a notorious heretic. Along with this letter he apparently sent a copy of the fictitious dialogue from Ephesus.

This action put Origen in a dangerous position since action by the bishop of Rome could easily threaten his now none-too-strong ties with the church in Palestine. As much as he despised bishops who threw their weight around in this way, he could not allow Heraclas' maneuver to go unchallenged. To approach Bishop Fabian effectively he needed powerful help, but Theoctistus and Alexander, who had backed him in his earlier crisis, were no longer so reliable. Origen therefore turned to the one influential Christian with whom he still had close relations, Ambrosius, who was at that time in Nicomedia. Nicomedia, on the Asian side of the Sea of Marmora, was the principal city in northern Asia Minor and, until Constantinople replaced it, a frequent seat of the imperial court. In the process of defending himself against Heraclas' charges, Origen wrote a series of letters, from which some fragments survive. He wrote to friends in Alexandria whom Heraclas had attempted to alienate from him, explaining that he had as much right to criticize Heraclas as the Hebrew prophets had to criticize the leaders of their time and explaining the circumstances of the dialogue in which he supposedly showed himself a heretic. He had never, he wrote, held that the devil should be saved, a ridiculous proposition on the face of it, but he did believe that to deny the devil any opportunity for salvation was impossible to square with the doctrine of free will. As to the devil's actual salvation, he would leave that to God. Origen also wrote to Firmillian, the bishop of Caesarea Mazaca, whom he had met during the persecution under Maximinus, soliciting his support. In addition, he wrote to Bishop Fabian, defending himself and mentioning that he had never intended *On First Principles*, the work that had made him notorious, to be accessible to the general public. He also wrote, no doubt using Ambrosius' connections, to the emperor Philip and to his wife, Severa. They might or might not have been secret Christians themselves, but they certainly could have been expected to influence Fabian. As it turned out, these efforts may not have been needed. Heraclas, like Demetrius, died before he was able to complete the process of engineering Origen's ruin, and Dionysius, who succeeded him as bishop in 247, was a former pupil of Origen who had no desire to continue the action against his teacher. While in Nicomedia, Ambrosius prevailed upon Origen to resume work on the *Commentary on John*. It was there that he composed the thirty-second and last book, where he expressed in the preface his fear that he might be unable to finish the commentary in his life on earth and spoke, in the course of the commentary, of "so-called bishops."

## The Exchange with Julius Africanus

While Origen was in Nicomedia with Ambrosius and his family, he received a remarkable letter in response to remarks he made in a real public debate, this time with a person called Agnomon in the letter (even if Agnomon, which means "senseless man," does not sound like anyone's real name), probably in Palestine. The writer was Julius Africanus, a resident of the city of Nicopolis in Palestine, a city that may have occupied the site of the village of Emmaus mentioned in Luke 24. Africanus, a Christian, was Nicopolis' principal citizen and had personally interceded with the Emperor Elagabalus to give it a civic charter. He had also been on intimate terms with Elagabalus' successor, Alexander Severus, whom he had assisted in establishing a public library at

Rome, possibly in the Pantheon. He was well-known during his life for his *Kestoi* or *Embroidered Girdles*, a work far more miscellaneous in character than even Clement's *Stromateis*. It apparently contained information on topics ranging from aphrodisiacs to military tactics. A more influential work was his *Chronographies*, a work which attempted to coordinate the chronology of the Bible with that of Greco-Roman antiquity. In it Africanus set forth his belief that the world would last 6000 years and that 5500 had passed since creation when Christ was born. If Origen believed in chronologies of such a scale, and there is reason to think he did since in the *Commentary on the Song of Songs* he used shortness of the time the world exists as an argument against reincarnation,[16] his belief in a cycle of worlds becomes somewhat more plausible. In addition to the letter to Origen, a letter of Africanus survives that was written to an otherwise unknown Aristides. In it he set forth his contention, backed by what he alleged to be reliable local traditions, that the levirate marriage of Joseph's father explains the discrepancy between the genealogies of Christ in the Gospels of Matthew and Luke. According to Africanus, Joseph's natural father and his legal father were half brothers, sons of the same mother, and both descendants of David but by different lines. When one of the brothers died, the other took his wife to raise up children for him according to the provisions of the Jewish law. Matthew gives Jesus' natural descent through the second brother, Jacob, and Luke gives his legal descent through the first brother, Heli. Both genealogies are therefore correct even though they differ. Africanus' theory, even if far-fetched, remains a plausible way of reconciling the two genealogies, and it seems to have impressed Origen.

Julius Africanus applied his critical abilities and wide knowledge to better effect in his letter to Origen.[17] Origen, he wrote, had in his discussion with the so-called Agnomon, referred to the story of Daniel and Susanna, which belongs to the Septuagint version of the book of Daniel as if it were an integral part of the book. Was he not aware that the passage that contained the story was a forgery, interpolated in the book of Daniel when it was translated into Greek? Julius, out of courtesy, had refrained from expressing his misgivings at the time, but he had gotten the arguments against the passage together in the meantime and thought that Origen would have a hard time answering them. He would indeed. Julius' letter, though quite brief, raises all the principal textual, linguistic, stylistic, and historical arguments against the authenticity of the passage. Textually, the story is questionable because it did not belong to the Hebrew text of Daniel. (This is why Jerome, and the Protestant reformers who relied on him, excluded the passage from Daniel and placed it in the Apocrypha.) Linguistically, it is questionable because it is written in good idiomatic Greek, not the translation Greek of the rest of the Septuagint, and even employs two Greek puns. Stylistically, it is questionable because its plot could come from a Greek comedy and because it depicts Daniel differently from the way he is depicted in the authentic part of the book. Daniel acts not, as elsewhere, on the basis of dream visions but on the basis of a sudden inspiration, and he quotes from another book of the Bible, something neither the real Daniel nor any of the prophets were accustomed to do. Historically, it is questionable because it depicts the Jewish people in exile as having the right to pass a capital sentence, and that on a person who can only be the wife of their king since Susanna's husband's name was Joakim (Jehoiakin) and no one but a captive king in such circumstances could have a private garden for his wife to bathe in.

Origen's reply was longer than Africanus' letter but less cogent. Origen acknowledged the force of his correspondent's arguments but sought to demonstrate that, nonetheless, the story of Daniel and Susanna was an integral part of the original Hebrew book of Daniel. The argument, like Africanus' on the Gospel genealogies, was probably as good an argument as could be made in such a desperate case. Origen was, first of all, at pains to have it known that he, the compiler of the *Hexapla*, was quite aware that the story of Daniel and Susanna, along with other parts of Daniel as well as sections in other books, was not in the Hebrew Bible. He was nonetheless reluctant to abandon passages in the Septuagint received by the church just because the Jews did not accept them. In the case of the story of Daniel and Susanna, he suggested that the Jews had excised it from their manuscripts because it cast aspersions on their elders. He argued that a number of historical allusions in the New Testament to events not actually described in the Old must point to other Jewish excisions. As for the style, he denied that he could tell any difference between it and that of the rest of the book. The play on words was a problem, but puns can sometimes be translated effectively. In the case at hand, he himself had consulted a learned Jew, who told him there was no way of knowing if the Greek pun corresponded to one in Hebrew, as Hebrew equivalents for two of the words were not in the Bible and hence not known. The story might resemble a Greek comedy, but so did the Joseph stories where there was also a variety of ways God spoke to his servant. Africanus, furthermore, could not be sure that the Jews could not pass capital sentence while in captivity or that Joakim, the husband of Susanna, was their king. Africanus had alluded to the book of Tobit in his description of the abject condition of the Jewish people during the Babylonian captivity, but the Jews no more accept Tobit than they do the story of Daniel and Susanna. Besides, there are in fact rich Jews in Tobit, as there are in the book of Nehemiah, which the Jews do accept. As for prophets quoting each other, Julius Africanus was obviously unaware of the identity of Isaiah 2:2–4 and Micah 4:1–3, where one prophet must have been quoting the other, and there are other cases. Although Origen's answer does include some special pleading, it nonetheless answers Africanus' objections on entirely critical grounds, without appealing to dogma. We shall see Origen doing the same thing in a far larger work, his response to the pagan philosopher Celsus.

### Commentary on Matthew

Having done his best to secure Ambrosius' help, Origen returned to Caesarea. Perhaps he did not enjoy being under the constant eye of his patron. In the letter to Julius Africanus, in addition to conveying Ambrosius' greetings to his correspondent, he mentions that Ambrosius had read the entire letter and corrected what he chose to. At Caesarea Origen continued his exegetical work with a five-volume *Commentary on Luke* and a twenty-five-volume *Commentary on Matthew*. Only fragments, as usual, of the *Commentary on Luke* have come down to us, but eight books of the *Commentary on Matthew* have survived in Greek and a good deal more in a reliable, anonymous Latin translation, known as the *Series Commentary on Matthew*. We thus have a continuous commentary from Matthew 13:36 to 27:66, about half of the Gospel. The *Commentary on Matthew*, as we have already seen, is a rich source of information on Origen's understanding of ecclesiastical leadership and of the sacraments. Compared with the *Commentary on John*, especially the early parts of that work, it is terse and restrained. There are few of the long digressions ranging through word association over the entire Bible that are such a prominent feature in the earlier work. There is also a less openly critical attitude toward the letter of the text, and there are fewer doctrinal speculations of the sort that would shock more simple readers. There is also relatively little historical information, Origen's explanation of the *corban,* where he alludes to inquiries among Jewish scholars, being a major exception.[18] At the same time, the *Commentary on Matthew* testifies to the continuity of Origen's thought, which was already mature when he wrote *On First Principles.* Origen continued to allegorize, and he continued to lay heavy stress on the harmony of the Old and New Testaments, free will, and the beneficence of God. God is still primarily a healer, and Origen interpreted all of the healings in the Gospel as symbols of spiritual cures that the Logos continues to work. Origen also laid his customary stress on privileged, spiritual understanding of the Bible. Not only did Jesus' privileged treatment of the disciples constantly demonstrate this, so did some of Jesus' parables, such as the parable of the treasure hidden in a field (Matt. 13:44), where the field symbolized the Bible and the treasure its hidden meaning.[19]

One of the more interesting features of the *Commentary on Matthew* is its tendency to psychologize the Gospel's apocalyptic eschatological imagery. Thus, when the Gospel predicts that Christ will come "on the clouds of heaven with power and great glory" (Matt. 24:30), it refers to his appearance to the perfect in their reading of the Bible.[20] Likewise, the two comings of Christ, the first in humility and the second in glory, symbolize Christ's coming in the souls of the simple when they receive the rudiments of Christian doctrine and his coming in the perfect when they find him in the hidden meanings of the Bible.[21] The trials and tribulations the world must endure before the second coming symbolize the difficulties the soul must overcome before it is worthy of union with the Logos. The imminence of the second coming refers to the imminent possibility, for each individual, of death. Perhaps more radically, the two men laboring in a field, one of whom is taken and the other left when the Messiah comes (Matt. 24:40), represent good and bad influences on a person's will, which fare differently when the Logos is revealed to that person.[22] Although Origen did not openly deny the vivid apocalyptic expectations such passages originally expressed and still did for many Christians, he tended by psychologizing them to make them irrelevant. Although that was far from Origen's intention, the outcome of his work was to make the church feel distinctly more at home in the world.

The speculative themes of *On First Principles* are muted but not absent. Origen interpreted the parable of the tares in Matthew 13 so as to make it consistent with his own universalistic eschatology. In the parable the world is a field in which the Son of Man sows good seed and the devil sows evil seed. Both are allowed to grow until the harvest when the tares produced by the evil seed are gathered and burned and the wheat produced by the good seed is gathered and stored. When the tares are gathered and cast into the furnace, people will "weep and gnash their teeth. Then the righteous will shine like the sun in the kingdom of their Father" (Matt. 13:42–43). Origen interpreted the seeds not as persons but as opinions. At the consummation of the age the angels will root out all evil opinions and destroy them, and those who harbored such opinions will weep and gnash their teeth in remorse. The shining of the righteous as the sun, not as stars differing in glory, symbolizes the disappearance of any difference between rational spirits in the final consummation.[23] Origen also suggested that the preexistence of souls is the reasonable inference from the apparent unfairness of the parable of the vineyard in Matthew 20, where the laborers hired just before sundown receive the same wages as those hired in the morning who worked through the heat of the day.[24] We also find the doctrine that the world cannot be infinite or God could not know it.[25] At the same time Origen was careful to repudiate a doctrinal speculation of which some accused him but which he did not in fact hold, namely, the transmigration of souls into new bodies in this world.[26]

Origen's views on the resurrection of the body were particularly sensitive during his lifetime, and his treatment of that issue in the *Commentary on Matthew* is cagey. The Gospel mentions that the Sadducees, a Jewish sect, denied the resurrection. Origen compared them with the persons Paul argued against when he defended the resurrection of the dead in 1 Corinthians 15. There Paul wrote, "If for this life only we have hoped in Christ, we are of all men most to be pitied" (1 Cor. 15:19), and ventured that without such hope Christians might as well "eat and drink" rather than endure suffering for their faith. Origen's opponents must have likened his views to those of the Sadducees and cited Paul against him on the debilitating effect denying the resurrection would have on Christian morality. Origen was at pains to show the irrelevance of their criticism. The Sadducees, and Paul's opponents for that matter, he pointed out, denied not only "what the more simple customarily call the resurrection of the flesh," but the immortality of the soul as well. It is their refusal to allow for any form of life after death where souls could be rewarded or punished for their deeds in this life that by Paul's reasoning must lead to a concern for only the pleasures of the moment, not the denial of a specific understanding of that life. Those who deny the view held by the many that we shall reassume our present bodies but affirm that the soul is immortal and that we shall assume an ethereal body better than this one do not endanger morality. Whatever its merits, denying a fleshly resurrection is not open to that criticism. Origen hastened to add that he did not deny that "all flesh shall see the salvation of God" or other biblical passages that seem to affirm the resurrection of the flesh. The superficial impression the passage gives is that Origen affirmed the resurrection of the flesh but wanted to be fair to those who did not. In fact, however, he nowhere explicitly affirmed it, and by associating the resurrection of the flesh with the many and the more simple he gave the clear impression to anyone at all familiar with his thought that he rejected it.[27]

## Celsus' *True Doctrine*

During these years at Caesarea, perhaps in 248, Origen received from Ambrosius a copy of *The True Doctrine*, a treatise which Celsus, a pagan philosopher, had written against Christianity some seventy or so years earlier. Ambrosius asked Origen to refute Celsus' book, which he considered a threat to the faith of Christians. He may also have found influential pagans ominously turning to it as the Roman millennium approached to explain the empire's perilous condition. Origen had not heard of the book, and Ambrosius is the first Christian we know to have read it. Origen, therefore, reasonably hesitated to advertise the book by refuting it. He pointed out that Jesus himself did not deign to respond to his accusers, and Paul did not list "argument" among the things that might conceivably separate us from the love of God in Christ.[28] Nevertheless, Ambrosius evidently found Celsus' arguments disturbing, so

Origen undertook the refutation that did, in fact, preserve such fragments of *The True Doctrine* as have come down to us. He initially planned to refute only Celsus' main arguments, quoting his own words where necessary, but he had not completed a single codex before a passage written purportedly from a Jewish perspective convinced him a more detailed refutation was in order. Origen did not alter what he had already written, but from that time on he answered each of Celsus' charges in detail. This detailed refutation, in eight books, is the treatise we know as the *Contra Celsum* (Latin for *Against Celsus*).[29] As it happens, it is the only large-scale work by Origen that survives intact in Greek.

Origen preserved enough of Celsus' *The True Doctrine* to give us a fascinating glimpse of second-century Christianity through the eyes of a hostile but fair-minded pagan observer. Origen's refutation also enables us to see how he distinguished Christianity from the Greek philosophical tradition he himself relied on so heavily and, as Henry Chadwick has observed, how he satisfied himself that his own faith was reasonable.[30]

All we know about Celsus is what we can infer from the *Contra Celsum*. He was an able polemicist, he knew Greek literature and philosophy well, and he knew Christianity and Judaism better than a pagan could be expected to. Origen believed that Celsus had been dead for some time, and internal evidence from *The True Doctrine* points to around 180 as the time of its composition. Origen thought that Celsus was an Epicurean, probably because he identified him with the Epicurean philosopher Celsus, a friend of the satirist Lucian, who wrote a treatise *On Magic*. This identification poses no chronological problem, and, since Lucian's friend shared his zeal against superstition, it is easy to picture him writing against Christianity. Nonetheless, the author of *The True Doctrine* was probably another man with the same common name since he was evidently a Platonist rather than an Epicurean. Celsus announced, at the end of *The True Doctrine*, that he planned to write a sequel, a treatise on the right way to live, evidently a pagan equivalent of Clement's *Pedagogue* to follow the pagan equivalent of his *Exhortation to the Greeks*, but no trace of such a work has survived.[31]

Celsus seems to have learned about Christianity by reading as well as by personal observation, but his references are so vague that we cannot tell just what he did read. He certainly read parts of the Bible, and since he was evidently familiar with the sorts of arguments they used, he had probably read a work by one of the second-century apologists, perhaps Justin or Aristides. He also knew writings of the Simonians and Ophites, obscure Gnostic groups that had all but vanished by Origen's time. Celsus naturally considered such works Christian; it was not his task to distinguish true from false doctrine. From his perspective, Christianity appeared to be a multitude of sects at odds with each other who had nothing in common but the name of Christ.[32] Celsus did distinguish Christianity from Judaism, though, and so firmly that Origen faulted him for being unaware of the Ebionite Christians who kept the law of Moses.

Philosophically, Celsus was a conventional Middle Platonist. He believed in an utterly transcendent, impassible, and beneficent God, who, while ultimately responsible for the ordered existence of the material world and for its direction, had no direct dealings with it. God operated through the daemons, inferior spiritual beings, to create and guide the world. Matter, the substratum of which the universe is formed, is independent of God. It is the ultimate source of evil, which is an inevitable consequence of material existence. Although Celsus considered Plato the clearest exponent of this understanding of God and God's relation to the world, he like other Middle Platonists did not consider Plato its author. Rather, nations like the Egyptians, Indians, and Persians had taught it since time immemorial. Unlike Numenius, Celsus did not count the Jews among the exponents of this ancient and venerable doctrine. Human beings, by dint of unsparing moral and intellectual discipline, can come to know the transcendent God. Such knowledge is indescribable and comes, as Plato taught, "like a light in the soul kindled by a leaping spark."[33]

God's nature is ineffable, so there can be no single authoritative doctrine. Those who cannot contemplate God directly through philosophy know God symbolically through mythology and worship God indirectly in the traditional cults of their ancestors. Although he embraced cultic polytheism, Celsus was arguably a more consistent monotheist than Origen, who considered the Logos a second god. Celsus reconciled philosophical monotheism to traditional pagan polytheism by identifying the pagan gods with the daemons of Platonism. He found exhilarating the sheer multiplicity of myths and cults that had arisen because God allotted different daemons to govern the various nations of the world and because those nations described ultimate reality in different ways. Pagans do not dishonor God when they worship the daemons as gods. Because God is utterly perfect and self-sufficient, it is blasphemous to suggest that such worship makes God jealous. Worshiping the daemons is, in fact, the richest and most adequate way to worship the one transcendent God. As we worship the daemons, each like the sun or Athena with its own characteristics, our praise of God becomes fuller and more perfect.[34] Besides, the daemons themselves deserve and demand our gratitude for their role in creating and governing the world. Celsus considered the ancient myths and rituals an integral part of the legacy of Hellenism, a legacy he held in awe. He fervently supported the Roman Empire as the guardian of Hellenism from the barbarians and as the patron of traditional religion and considered it entirely appropriate to worship the emperor's genius.

Celsus did not consider the ancient myths literally true, but he was no rationalist in the modern sense. He believed in God's providence and in the reality of miracles and inspired oracles. He warned, however, that manifestations of the supernatural are in themselves ethically neutral. We do well to gain knowledge of the future from Apollo and healing from Asclepius, but it is bad, even though entirely possible, to obtain the same things through magic. Critical reasoning, not miracles, is the only criterion for evaluating religious claims. Knowledge of God may, as Plato taught, be hard to obtain and impossible to describe once obtained, but only the intellect can obtain it at all. Only imposters would circumvent the intellect by demanding implicit faith.

Celsus was convinced, seeing things as he did, that Christianity was alien to Hellenism and a threat to it. The beauty, nobility, and rationality of the Greek tradition were, for him, not so much standards of taste as standards of value. A religion that worshiped the uneducated son of a Jewish carpenter, a person who died an agonizing and degrading death, a person who would never even have been heard of had not a handful of fanatics from the scum of society claimed that he had appeared to them after death—such a religion had nothing in common with Homer and Plato.

Philosophy may not fully account for Celsus' vehemence, but it provided him with a standpoint from which to attack Christianity and arguments against its doctrines, beginning with its doctrine of God.

Celsus' reading of the Bible convinced him that Christians worshiped a crudely anthropomorphic and bloodthirsty deity. The very first chapter implied that God had a human form when it said that God made humanity "in his image."[35] Because they could conceive no way of seeing their corporeal God except through corporeal eyes, Christians taught the resurrection of the body. (Who in his right mind, Celsus asked, would want to reanimate a corpse?)[36] Moreover, Christians blasphemously turned God into a bogey who threatens to bring fire to the earth like a torturer or like a cook.[37] It seems, in fact, that Celsus could give the Bible no credit. If the God of the Bible wished to be revealed to humanity, it was only because God wanted to show off like the newly rich.[38] In order to make such charges plausible, Celsus disallowed allegorical interpretation of the Bible even though he freely availed himself of allegory to interpret other myths.

Besides depicting God so discreditably, Christians taught philosophically indefensible doctrines about God's relation to the material world. They taught that God fashioned the world. This breached God's transcendence and made God directly responsible for the evil inherent in materiality.[39] Worse, they taught that God actually assumed a human body. The Incarnation confused the sensible and intelligible modes of reality and was an absolutely incomprehensible change on God's part from a better state to a worse.[40]

Christians might object that God did this out of love for the human race, but Celsus replied that this was an arrogant claim. Why should God care for the human race more than for all the rest of creation? Why, in particular, should God be especially concerned for that tiny portion of humanity who are rightly believing Christians? Christians are like bats, ants, frogs, or worms, who say:

> God shows and proclaims everything to us beforehand, and He has even deserted the whole world and the motion of the heavens, and disregarded the vast earth to give attention to us alone; and He sends messengers to us alone and never stops sending them and seeking that we may be with Him for ever.[41]

They even say, "Since some among us are in error, God will come or will send His Son to consume the unrighteous, and that the rest of us frogs may have eternal life with Him."[42] Why should human beings get such attention? They are rational, but so are the daemons, who are far more powerful and do not suffer the indignity of being clothed in grossly material bodies. Nor are Christians the only rational bodily creatures. Birds must be rational since they foretell the future, and elephants must be rational since they honor their oaths.[43] If Christians do not in fact teach that God abandoned the direction of the universe to assume a human body on earth, they find themselves on the horns of a dilemma. What becomes of their criticism of pagan polytheism if they themselves worship Jesus Christ as a second god?

> If these men worshipped no other God but one, perhaps they would have had a valid argument against the others. But in fact they worship to an extravagant degree this man who appeared recently, and yet think it is not inconsistent with monotheism if they also worship His servant.[44]

Compromising their shrilly proclaimed monotheism was, in Celsus' opinion, the least absurd thing about the Christians' worship of Christ. If, as Christians claimed, God intended to be revealed by becoming a human being, God would not have done so late in the history of the world and in an obscure corner of it. Nor would God have been revealed through a person like Jesus. Born to a family of artisans and physically unimpressive, Jesus accomplished nothing notable and died wretchedly.[45] Jesus may indeed have performed the paltry miracles his followers ascribed to him but only by magic.[46] He plagiarized, mostly from Plato, such of his teachings as were at all worthwhile. For example, he found in the *Crito* Socrates' eloquent argument that we should not harm those who harm us and vulgarized it into an admonition to turn the other cheek. Jesus also cheapened Plato's saying that it is impossible for an outstandingly good man to be exceptionally rich into the saying that it is harder for a camel to go through the eye of a needle than for a rich man to enter the kingdom of God.[47] Christian claims that Jesus rose from the dead are worthless. They admit that Jesus appeared only to his own followers, and they are the sort of people most likely to be deceived by sorcery or hallucination: a hysterical woman and some ignorant fishermen.[48] If Jesus had really wished to prove that he was divine, Jesus would have appeared alive to his persecutors and to all people everywhere.[49] It is Jesus' humility and degradation Celsus found disgusting. Celsus did not object rationalistically that water and blood could not have flowed from Jesus' side as he hung dead on the cross, but he snickered that Jesus' veins did not contain ichor, the life-fluid of the Olympian gods.[50] If Christians absolutely had to invent a new doctrine, they would have done better to have worshiped Hercules, Asclepius, or Orpheus, whose triumphs over death make finer stories. Even Jonah or Daniel in the Bible would have been a nobler object of adoration than Jesus.[51]

Celsus took advantage of the Jews' refusal to believe in Jesus. He asked:

> What God that comes among men is disbelieved, and that when he appears to those who were waiting on him? Or why ever is he not recognized by people who had been long expecting him?[52]

And why did they not believe in him? Celsus had a hypothetical Jew give the answer. To begin with, the Jew argued, our prophet said in Jerusalem that God's son would come to judge the holy and punish the unrighteous, but Jesus did neither of these things. A few biblical prophecies could conceivably apply to Jesus, but they could apply equally well to many others.[53] In addition, Jesus' birth and moral character were not those of God's offspring. His mother was a poor woman who made her living by spinning. According to Celsus' hypothetical Jew, her husband expelled her from his house when he discovered that she was pregnant by a Roman soldier named Panthera, Jesus' real father. Jesus eventually learned magic as he worked as a laborer in Egypt and returned to his native land to practice magic and charlatanry.[54] Besides, Celsus added later in his own voice, Jesus could not have been the Messiah predicted in the Jewish Scriptures because his teaching contradicts Moses, who supposedly received the law from God: Moses ordered the people of Israel to massacre their enemies, but Jesus told his followers to love theirs.[55]

Christians, like the notorious impostors of the mystery cults, propagated their disgusting and ludicrous doctrines by demanding uncritical acceptance. They went about saying "Do not ask questions; just believe," "Thy faith will save thee," and "The wisdom in the world is an evil, and foolishness a good thing." Such sayings invite people to be taken in by the first charlatan who comes along.[56] When sensible pagans object that the person Christians claim to have been God's son died as a criminal, Christians brazenly respond that that is all the more reason for believing in him.[57] Of course, they can only persuade slaves, women, and children, or, at best, simple artisans, with such methods, so they make a virtue out of necessity and proclaim, "Let no one educated, no one wise, no one sensible draw near."[58] Admittedly, some truths are too sublime to be expressed in words, but that does not excuse irrationality. Plato, who spoke eloquently about God's ineffability, took care to avoid giving anyone a pretext for removing theology from the scope of rational discussion. He did not arrogantly claim that he had discovered anything new or that he had obtained a special revelation from heaven; he confessed that he derived his doctrines by critical inquiry.[59] By demanding faith, Christianity, in Celsus' opinion, gave the surest indication of its incompatibility with Hellenism.

The main problem with Christian worship, another area where Celsus found fault, was that Christians did not honor the daemons in the rituals their ancestors used. Beyond that, Christian worship violated standards of order and seemliness. Unlike pagan mysteries, like the Eleusinian, which restrict their clientele to respectable people, Christians take perverse delight in inviting the most depraved people to join them:

> Those who summon people to the other mysteries make this preliminary proclamation: Whosoever has pure hands and a wise tongue. And again, others say: Whosoever is pure from all defilement, and whose soul knows nothing of evil, and who has lived well and righteously. Such are the preliminary exhortations of those who promise purification from sins. But let us hear what folk these Christians call. Whosoever is a sinner, they say, whosoever is unwise, whosoever is a child, and, in a word, whosoever is a wretch, the kingdom of God will receive him.[60]

Of course Christians have to open their doors to such people since no one else will come.[61] Christian claims that they call sinners to repent and amend their lives are illusory; it is impossible to alter the character of people who are naturally or habitually vicious.[62] Christians also worship in a tawdry fashion; no doubt because they want to keep their society secret, Christians lack altars, images, and temples.[63]

The charge that the Christian church was a secret society was grave. Celsus did not necessarily consider religious secrecy reprehensible, but in their case it implied political subversiveness. The first words Origen quoted from The True Doctrine charged Christianity with violating Roman law by existing as a secret society.[64] Celsus returned to this political accusation at the end of his book, where he called Christian refusal to swear by the emperor's genius an act of obstinate fanaticism.[65] Nor was this simply an offense to patriotic citizens; it revealed an attitude toward authority that, if unchecked, would be the empire's ruin. Christian unwillingness to serve in the army or in positions of civic responsibility also evidenced their subversiveness; the barbarians would be only too glad if everyone followed their example. The fate of the Jewish people amply refutes their claim, absurd on the face of it, that God could protect the empire without anyone's fighting for it. Their powerlessness and inability to call any land their own demonstrate the impotence of the God who vowed to protect them.[66] Celsus darkly predicted that a future emperor would come to his senses and destroy the Christians before they destroyed him,[67] but he did not take such pleasant hopes too seriously. Resigning himself to the continued existence of Christianity, he exhorted Christians, even if they persisted in their foolish beliefs, at least to set aside their hatred of the empire and join pagans in its defense.[68]

## Origen's Reply to Celsus

*The True Doctrine* called for a sophisticated and erudite response, and the *Contra Celsum* met that demand. Origen's treatise, though, was not tightly organized. He simply responded to each topic as it presented itself in Celsus' work. It is therefore useless to give a synopsis of the *Contra Celsum*, especially since *The True Doctrine* itself had no obvious organization we can ascertain. Origen's refutation had four separable but interrelated elements, all of them present throughout the *Contra Celsum*. (1) He sought to undermine Celsus' plausibility. (2) He repudiated certain charges altogether. (3) He admitted that certain charges accurately portray Christian beliefs but challenged Celsus' interpretation of them. (4) He attacked the paganism of which Celsus had instituted himself as representative and defender.

Origen's attempt to undermine Celsus' credibility is the least impressive of these elements. Throughout the first half of the *Contra Celsum*, Origen lost no chance to brand Celsus as an Epicurean. Origen, as we have seen, had plausible grounds for this, but he did it tendentiously. Epicureanism was, by Origen's time, thoroughly discredited, not because of its inflexible dogmatism or its implausible physics, but because its materialism, denial of divine providence, and ethics of pleasure were deemed impious. By identifying Celsus as an Epicurean, Origen impugned his character and presented some of his most telling objections to Christianity, particularly his observations on God's role in creation and on the Incarnation as the cavils of a virtual atheist.[69] But Origen found it increasingly implausible to present the author of *The True Doctrine* as an Epicurean, and, halfway through the book, shortly after allowing that Celsus the Epicurean might have been a different person of the same name,[70] he let the topic drop.

Origen's attempts to discredit Celsus by exposing his ignorance of the subject are fairer. In two cases he actually pointed out serious problems in the Bible which Celsus had overlooked: the inability of Noah's ark, if built according to the specifications in Genesis, to hold all the animals it was supposed to and the disparity between the genealogies in Matthew and Luke.[71] (If Origen had not found Julius Africanus' arguments convincing, he probably would not have mentioned the latter.) Origen also challenged, with a grammarian's skill, Celsus' characterization of his hypothetical Jew. A real Jew, he wrote, would at least have been able to discuss Old Testament prophecies intelligently. Who, after all, was the prophet in Jerusalem who predicted that God's son would come? Origen could not find him.[72] A real Jew would have been able to cite the Old Testament knowledgeably, but he probably would not, like Celsus' Jew, have cited Euripides. Neither would he have used rationalistic arguments against the miracles in the New Testament that are just as effective against those in the Old.[73] Such criticism probably prejudices the reader against Celsus, but *ad hominem* arguments settle nothing. Celsus' charges were still serious even if he could have presented them more capably.

Origen's repudiation of some of Celsus' charges as inapplicable, although the modern reader may find them less than candid, are more vital to the *Contra Celsum*. Origen himself despised no less than Celsus much that Celsus objected to in Christianity, but Celsus was not misinformed. Except when he was clearly handling Gnostic ideas, Origen, in repudiating Celsus' accusations, was tacitly repudiating the views of most Christians. Most of them, as we have seen, did believe that the resurrection of the body meant the restoration of the body to its earthly condition, and Origen had to present his spiritualizing view cautiously.

Most of them, similarly, if we take Origen's complaints in other writings seriously, conceived of God as an irascible old man in the sky. When a contemporary of Celsus, the Christian apologist Theophilus of Antioch, confronted the charge that Christians taught a wrathful God he wrote: "By all means! He is wrathful against those who do wicked things."[74] Origen's repudiation of Celsus' charges thus answers an outside critic and attacks at the same time the simple Christians who gave him such grounds for attacking the church.

According to Origen, the crude concept of the resurrection which Celsus ascribed to Christians was only a straw man. He misunderstood a doctrine, "which, while preached in the churches, is understood more clearly by the intelligent."[75] Origen presented his own interpretation as the true and philosophically defensible doctrine of the resurrection: the resurrection of the body is a way of speaking symbolically about the continuity of a seminal principle. Origen also taxed Celsus with deliberately ignoring the symbolic character of biblical language that describes God in human terms. As for God's wrath, which Celsus found so objectionable, it is not an emotional reaction but "something which He uses in order to correct by stern methods those who have committed many terrible sins."[76] "Correct," used instead of "punish," is the key word. As for the threats of a future punishment by fire, these are utterances in which "the Logos, accommodating himself to what is appropriate to the masses who will read the Bible, wisely utters threatening words with a hidden meaning to frighten people who cannot in any other way turn from the flood of iniquities."[77]

Origen was especially eager to repudiate Celsus' accusation that Christians denigrated reason and education even though Clement of Alexandria's patient struggle to justify pagan philosophy to his fellow Christians and Tertullian's glorification of what he took to be the irrational paradoxes in Christian doctrine lend considerable credibility to Celsus' charges. Christians, Origen admitted, encourge people to accept doctrine on faith, but this is not because they cannot provide a rational justification for those doctrines. If the masses had the aptitude and inclination to pursue philosophy, the demand for faith would be unnecessary, but, as it is, Christians have no choice but to present their doctrine as a truth to be accepted on faith.[78] Instead of attacking Christians, Celsus would have been well advised to look to his own house. Most people who prefer one philosophical sect to the others do so out of blind faith. Few indeed examine the claims of all the schools to ascertain which is most sound. Instead, they adhere dogmatically to the first sect they happen to light on.[79] Origen's treatise, which kept strictly to rules of rational discourse, is itself the aptest refutation of Celsus' charge that Christianity is obscurantist. Celsus, according to Origen, was no more justified in his charge that Christians discouraged education. Christians, in fact, encourage the study of literature and philosophy as a preparation for the investigation of the deeper mysteries of the Bible.[80] Again, Origen's own evident familiarity with literature and philosophy, not at all inferior to his opponent's, makes his defense plausible.

It would be unfair to accuse Origen of a lack of candor in thus repudiating the views of the majority of Christians: what did they know? He did not consider Christianity a sociological phenomenon but the way to attain knowledge of God. The views of the spiritually advanced are the necessary standard. When Celsus attacked positions held by the benighted majority of Christians, he just demonstrated his ignorance of the deeper doctrines and his incompetence to discuss Christianity. Because Celsus failed to distinguish simpler from spiritual Christians, Origen took it upon himself to vindicate Christian esotericism. In trying to make them appear subversive, Celsus accused Christians of keeping their doctrines secret. Origen responded that the doctrines of Christianity were no secret; most people knew them far better than they did the opinions of the philosophical sects. Christians do not even try to hide their doctrine of the resurrection, for all the mirth it gives to pagans who misunderstand it. Nevertheless, Christianity, like the philosophy of Pythagoras, has doctrines withheld from the majority.[81] Although Christians invite all and sundry to their mysteries in order to make them whole, they reserve the truly mystical doctrines for the minority who can demonstrate real purity and detachment from earthly preoccupations.[82] This is not deceitful. Where higher doctrines might harm the simple, the philosophers themselves approve the concealment of higher truth by means of a medicinal lie.[83] From Origen's point of view, therefore, much of Celsus' argument is irrelevant; if he had known the deeper doctrines, he would have had far less to quarrel about.

Although in many cases he considered Celsus' charges beside the point, Origen could not dismiss entirely Celsus' attack on the Christian doctrine of God. Christians did believe that God created the world and that God had a special concern for the human race. Neither could he pretend that Celsus' charge that Christians allegorized the Bible without justification and worshiped in a tawdry fashion were based on sheer misinformation. Most of all, Origen could not avoid the issue at the heart of Christianity's quarrel with paganism: the two sides' radically different views of the person and mission of Jesus Christ. Origen easily responded appropriately to all these charges because he had most of the arguments he needed already at hand. Apologists, first Jews then Christians, had been defending their traditions and practices for centuries when Origen wrote, and he knew all their arguments well. In other cases, Origen could use stock arguments in the controversy between rival philosophical schools. Thus, when Celsus took the Academic position that the world does not exist for the benefit of the human race, Origen answered with Stoic arguments to the contrary.[84] Origen also used arguments he himself had developed against Gnosticism, defending the goodness of the God of the Old Testament and the consistency of the Old Testament with the New. He also used an argument Clement originated and he had developed in *On First Principles* to provide an empirical basis for the authority of the Bible, an argument he called, borrowing a phrase from Paul, a "demonstration of the Spirit and of power" (1 Cor. 2:4).

The "demonstration of the Spirit and of power" is the backbone of the *Contra Celsum*. It argues that we cannot now witness Jesus' miracles and resurrection from the dead, nor can we now verify that Christ's life corresponded exactly to Old Testament prophecies, but the effects we can observe now in the Christian community must have an adequate cause. This enabled Origen to throw back in his face Celsus' sneers at Christianity's obscure and barbaric origin. Origen made a virtue of Jesus' lowly birth with an illustration from Plato, an anecdote about Themistocles, the Athenian general who defeated the Persians at Salamis, and an inhabitant of the tiny island of Seriphos:

> The Seriphian in Plato reproached Themistocles after he had become famous for his generalship, saying that he had not won his fame by his own character, but from the good luck to have had the most famous city in all Greece as his home. From Themistocles, who was openminded and saw that his home had also contributed to his fame, he received the answer: "I would never have been so famous if I had been a Seriphian,

nor would you have been a Themistocles if you had had the good luck to be an Athenian.'' But our Jesus, who is reproached for having *come from a village,* and that not a Greek one, who did not belong to any nation prominent in public opinion, and who is maligned as the son of *a poor woman who earned her living by spinning* and as having left his home country *on account of poverty* and *hired himself out as a workman in Egypt,* was not just a Seriphian, to take the illustration I have quoted, who came from the least and most insignificant island, but was a Seriphian of the very lowest class, if I may say so. Yet he has been able to shake the whole human world, not only more than Themistocles the Athenian, but even more than Pythagoras and Plato and any other wise men or emperors or generals in any part of the world.[85]

Just as Jesus' obscurity and lowly birth become the best reasons for taking his message seriously, the same is true with his disciples. If Jesus had chosen as emissaries people with training in rhetoric and philosophy, it would not be too astonishing that they spread the Christian message throughout the world. For people who were at best barely literate to accomplish this is a sign of extraordinary power.[86]

Christianity's success in overcoming its obscure origins and gaining adherents throughout the world, and that in the face of contempt and persecution, was a remarkable testimony to the power of its message, but it did not necessarily prove it true. What compels conviction is Christianity's effect on the character of believers. Sexual continence where paganism is powerless makes this obvious. Troops of Christian virgins, inspired only by the love of God, drive away all lust by their prayers to God. Contrast them with the priest of Demeter at Eleusis, from whom ritual purity demands sexual continence. Does the goddess he serves enable him to restrain himself? No, he must depend on a drug to make him impotent.[87] Nor is sexual continence the only ethical ideal God enables Christians to achieve. Thousands of them with no formal education live lives of courage, temperance, and justice, ideals the philosophers only dream of achieving.[88] Although Origen, as we have seen, despaired over the decline in Christian commitment and moral standards since the last serious persecutions, he did not hesitate to hold the church up to pagans as a community on an obviously higher moral plane than the society around them. It is astonishing, given Origen's ordinary contempt for the more simple, that precisely the impact of Christianity on the unlettered masses is, for him, its most impressive achievement.

Plato's philosophy, admittedly, contains much that is useful, but it can never influence humanity much because only a handful of intellectuals can make sense of it. Epictetus has perhaps done more good than Plato, because ordinary people can profit from his simple style.[89] Nothing, though, can compare with the impact of Christianity on uneducated people, and a religion that can change them dramatically for the better must be powerful indeed. Thus Origen, the archetypal intellectual, argued that Christianity must be true, not because it is logically compelling, but because it works.

Origen had relatively little to argue with in Celsus' doctrine of God. He heartily agreed that God was utterly transcendent and had no human attributes. Nonetheless, he rejected Celsus' contention that God, creator of the soul, did not create the body because it was inappropriate for God to deal with matter. Origen countered Celsus with the Stoic argument that the intricacy of the bodies of animals, where each organ is perfectly adapted to its function, implies divine design.[90] Stoic arguments, as mentioned earlier, also countered Celsus' contention that Christians made God too exclusively concerned with the human race.[91] Origen met Celsus' charge that a God involved in the creation of the material world would, thereby, be responsible for evil with the argument against Marcion: the material world is good in itself, even though God permits what we perceive as evil in order to chastise the disobedient and persuade them to return to God.[92]

Origen's real quarrel with Celsus on the subject of God was over Jesus Christ. He sought to disarm Celsus' criticism that for God to become human was intolerable since it entailed God's changing and changing for the worse at that. God does not change, Origen replied. The Bible affirms that. But in the Incarnation God is revealed to us through the Logos.[93] This is a marvel but not a paradox. We have cleaved to the flesh for so long that we have become fleshly, so how, except by assuming flesh, could the Logos effectively reveal God to us? This did not demean God; it ennobled us. Once we have known the incarnate Logos, we advance beyond the flesh to a spiritual recognition, as Paul said: "Yea, though we have known Christ after the flesh, yet now henceforth know we him no more" (2 Cor. 5:16 KJV).[94] Nor does the Incarnation mean that the Logos originated from a woman's womb. The Logos has always existed but, for our sake, united with a human soul and body. It is true that we worship this soul and body when we worship Christ so that in a sense we worship Christ's flesh, but that is appropriate since the body and soul of Christ have acquired divine attributes by their union with the Logos.[95] Celsus should not have scoffed at the time and place of the Incarnation. It is not as if the Logos had neglected the human race until recently; God has always inspired people to obtain reason and truth. Nevertheless, the Logos fittingly appeared as human when the Roman peace made it possible for God's message to spread unimpeded and among the people to whom that coming was predicted.[96] The doctrine of two divine hypostases negates Celsus' contention that consistent monotheists could not worship Christ as a second god. The Logos, Origen argued, has received from God the right to divine honor. By honoring the Logos we honor God and the Logos' attributes.[97]

There is no incongruity, Origen argued, in claiming that Jesus of Nazareth was the incarnate Logos. The founder of the Christian church, with its wide dispersion, high moral standards, and ability to raise ordinary people to the apprehension of spiritual things, must have had divine power.[98] A person of such influence could not have been a bastard, but the Panthera story does indirectly show that his birth was extraordinary since it was not possible to pass off Joseph as his father.[99] Neither could a person who practiced magic have influenced followers for good as Jesus did. There is only one grain of truth in that slander: evil demons cannot abide Jesus' name.[100] It is absurd to contend that Jesus, a Galilaean Jew, plagiarized Plato. Their teachings are similar because the Logos, incarnate in Jesus, at times inspired Plato.[101] Celsus considered Jesus' unimpressive appearance unworthy of God, but "his body differed in accordance with the capacity of those who saw it" since he appeared in aspects appropriate to the spiritual advancement of those who saw him. To some he did appear "without form and comeliness," but to the inner circle he appeared in glory on the mount of the transfiguration.[102] Furthermore, there is nothing unworthy of deity in Jesus' death. It is an example, in accord with the ideals of Greek philosophy, of how to bear adversity.[103] It would not have suited Jesus' redemptive purpose for him to have disappeared from the cross as Celsus said he would have had he really been divine. Only our ability to be joined with Christ in his death enables us to be born to new life.[104] Jesus did not appear after the resurrection to those who persecuted him because they did not deserve to see him in glory.[105] It is not remarkable that the Jews as a nation failed to recognize their promised Messiah. From the time of Moses when they worshiped the golden calf to the present they have shown themselves unfaithful to God.[106] Their claim that Jesus did not fulfill all the messianic prophecies is worthless because they do not know that some prophecies refer to Christ's first coming in humility and others, not yet fulfilled, refer to his second coming in glory.[107]

In their debate over Christ, Origen and Celsus had different presuppositions about what is appropriate for God to do. Origen defended the church's position ably, but he would not have convinced anyone who shared Celsus' feeling for the incompatibility of divinity with degradation and death. In their debate about allegory, Origen and Celsus shared the same presuppositions, and this enabled Origen to get the better of the argument. Allegory was vital to Origen's defense of the Christian doctrine of God and of Christianity's departure from Jewish practices. The fundamental principle, as in the case of the Incarnation, is God's condescension:

> Just as when we are talking with little children we do not aim to speak in the finest language possible to us, but say what is appropriate to the weakness of those whom we are addressing, and, further, do what seems to us to be of advantage for the conversion and correction of the children as such, so also the Logos of God seems to have arranged the scriptures. . . . There was no need for the multitude that the words put into God's mouth, which were intended to be addressed to them, should correspond to His real character.[108]

When Celsus attempted to show that Jesus contradicted Moses, Origen like a schoolmaster scolded him for having "fallen into a very vulgar error concerning the meaning of the Bible," failing to recognize anything but its literal meaning.[109] This aggressiveness was appropriate since Celsus had no good reason for rejecting biblical allegory. The merits of allegory as such were not at issue—had that been the case, Origen would have found himself more hard pressed—but the limits of its applicability. Celsus considered Christian allegory a paltry attempt to hide the Bible's barbarities and to avoid the law of Moses, but he took allegory for granted in the interpretation of Homer and Hesiod because they belonged to the Greek literary heritage that he revered.

Christian apologists before Origen defended allegorical interpretation of the Bible but considered allegory inappropriate for interpreting
Greek myths because of their association with pagan idolatry. Only
Clement of Alexandria showed some appreciation for the symbolism of
Greek mythology. Had Origen followed his predecessors' example, he
and Celsus would simply have talked past one another, but he took a
different tack. He accused Celsus of a double standard, allowing allegory in the interpretation of Greek literature but disallowing it in the
interpretation of the Bible.[110] Christians, he wrote, had no such double
standard. He quoted Plato's myth of the birth of Eros (love) from Poros
(means) and Penia (need), which he likened to the Bible's myth of the
Garden of Eden, which Celsus ridiculed. He then wrote:

> If readers of this were to imitate the malice of Celsus (which no Chris-
> tian would do) they would ridicule the myth and would make a mock
> of so great a man as Plato. But if they could find Plato's meaning by
> examining philosophically what he expresses in the form of a myth,
> they would admire the way in which he was able to hide the great doc-
> trines as he saw them in the form of a myth on account of the multitude,
> and yet to say what was necessary for those who know how to discover
> from myths the true significance intended by their author.[111]

Yet Origen, while accepting Plato's myths, attacked mercilessly
Hesiod's stories of the castration of Uranus and the creation of Pandora.
He did not deny that these were allegorical, but he considered their
crudity and immorality unacceptable. In doing so he had Plato on his
side:

> The truth is . . . that it is the legends of the Greeks which are not only
> *very stupid*, but also very impious. For our scriptures have been written
> to suit exactly the multitude of the simple-minded, a consideration to
> which no attention was paid by those who made up the fictitious stories
> of the Greeks. For this reason it was not mere ill will which led Plato to
> banish from his Republic myths and poems of this character.[112]

Origen is saying that the moral character of the literal stories, the criterion that led Plato to condemn Homer and Hesiod, is the criterion that
justifies biblical allegory.

In order to prove that the Bible met Plato's standard, Origen had to
meet Celsus' objections to some of its stories. He therefore had to
present the literal level more positively than he had in *On First Princi-*

*ples*, where he complained that the letter of the Bible could leave the impression that God was worse than the most savage and unjust of men.[113] Origen did not worry about the story of the expulsion from the Garden of Eden, which Celsus ridiculed because it implied that God was unable to control what happened and because of details like the talking snake. The story of Lot's incest with his daughters after the destruction of Sodom, which Celsus denounced as unspeakably crude, had to be defended. Here Origen turned to Stoic ethics. The Stoics allowed that even incest would be permissible in one case: a world conflagration where only one father and daughter survived to continue the human race. He argued that Lot's daughters, when they saw the fiery destruction of the cities on the plain, mistakenly thought that the whole world had been destroyed, and that this misunderstanding mitigated their crime.[114]

Celsus has called the allegories of the Bible "more shameful and preposterous than the myths." Again Origen called him up short. Had Celsus, he asked, actually read the genuinely philosophical allegories of the Bible by two Jews, Philo and Aristobulus, or by the pagan philosopher Numenius? He obviously did not know what he was talking about.[115] Nor was allegory, as Celsus claimed, artificial when applied to the Bible. Paul repeatedly allegorized the Old Testament, and the Psalmist prayed for allegorical understanding in the words, "Open my eyes, that I may behold wondrous things out of thy law" (Ps. 119:18).[116] Origen's defense of allegory may not and probably should not satisfy us, but it effectively refuted Celsus because it applied standards from his own philosophical tradition.

Origen's contemporaries probably would have found his defense of the church's worship the most compelling part of the book since it dealt with an issue that went to the heart of the religious sensibilities of the age. Celsus' principal charge aganist Christianity was that it led people to abandon the worship of the daemons in the cults of their ancestors. Jews, about whom Celsus had nothing else good to say, at least followed genuinely ancient ancestral customs in worship, but Christians, adherents of a new and universal religion, obviously did not. Origen answered this charge in the manner of earlier Christian apologists. In the first place, he argued, following ancestral customs is not always good. Would Celsus approve if Scythians committed parricide or if

Persians committed incest? In both cases their ancestral customs allow these things. Would he want the Taurians and Libyans to honor the daemons with human sacrifice? That is their ancestral custom.[117] Since, presumably, even Celsus would not approve of such things, he cannot consistently condemn Christians out of hand for abandoning their ancestral worship. In the second place, Origen contended, worship of daemons is positively wicked. (The fact that "demon" always signifies an *evil* spirit to us is a testimony to the triumph of the Christian position Origen championed over Celsus' understanding of "daemon" as simply "spiritual being.") He emphatically rejected Celsus' view that beings whom the pagans worshiped as daemons belonged to the same spiritual reality that Christians worshiped under different names. Origen affirmed that there were spiritual beings inferior to God and superior to human beings who administer the universe on God's behalf, but Origen called them "angels" rather than "daemons" and considered the difference in terminology vital. Names are not indifferent, he wrote. Just as the names of God have real power to accomplish good, so the names of the daemons have real power to do evil.[118] The fact that magicians call upon the names of the pagan daemons is a sign of the inherently evil character of the names and of the beings they signify.[119] Unlike the daemons who harm those who fail to worship them, the angels approve of us better if we do not sacrifice to them but worship God instead.[120] Christians, who worship God through the Logos, do not have to worry though about the daemons' jealousy since the angels protect them.[121] Because those who do sacrifice to daemons put themselves in their power, Christians avoid doing so at all costs.[122]

Origen's response to Celsus' attacks on the actual conduct of Christian worship makes clear the contrast in their religious sensibilities. Origen considered it actually praiseworthy for the church to invite sinners into its fellowship since it did so in order to reform them. Nor were such reforms illusory. Philosophy should have taught Celsus that even without the direct assistance of the Logos it is possible to abandon habitual sin. Socrates found Phaedo a male prostitute and made him a philosopher worthy to expound his noblest doctrine, and Xenocrates turned Polemo, who had once disrupted his lectures with a troop of flute-girls and revellers, into his successor as head of Plato's Academy.[123] The Christian church fulfilled its mission not by being a club for the respectable but by being a hospital for sinners.

Worship without temples, images, altars, and impressive ceremonial, which Celsus considered tawdry, Origen considered glorious. Christianity, in Origen's opinion, came as close as humanly possible to truly spiritual worship, a worship utterly divorced from material aids. "We say, " he wrote, "that a man offers worship in this life with the due rites if he remembers who is the Creator, and what things are dear to Him, and if he does everything with regard to what God loves."[124] He was pleased that Christians had no shrines. One physical place cannot be holier than another; holiness belongs to rational creatures not to places.[125] Origen found it problematic that Christians did consecrate Sunday and the two fast days, Wednesday and Friday, for special worship and that they had two annual feast days, Easter and Pentecost, not that they lacked an elaborate ceremonial calendar. These days are only symbols for processes that go on continually in true Christians. Sunday, which he called the Lord's Day, is an example: "The perfect man, who is always engaged in the words, works, and thoughts of the divine Logos, who is by nature his Lord, is always living in His days and is continually observing the Lord's Day."[126] Only the need to provide the more simple with regular reminders has compelled the church to set certain days aside for particular purposes.[127] As for altars, images, and temples, Christians do very well without them. What they do have are the spiritual realities these outward things merely symbolize. The Christian altars are in the minds of the righteous, from which ascend "intelligible incense," that is, "prayers from a pure conscience." Likewise, Christian images are their virtues, each of which is an image of its archetype among the aspects of the Logos.[128] The Christian temples are their own bodies, consecrated, as Paul taught, to God's service.[129] Christians do not engage in cultic sacrifice as the pagans do, but they have, in the bread called "eucharist," a more worthy symbol of their thankfulness to God.[130] Here again Origen had a good case. One reason for Christianity's eventual triumph may be that its worship harmonized much better with the ideals of philosophy than the traditional pagan cults did. It is ironic that that triumph transformed Christian worship, within a few centuries, into something far closer to Celsus' ideal than to Origen's.

We also find irony in Origen's response to Celsus' charges that Christians were unpatriotic. The Christians' refusal to honor the emperor's genius struck Celsus as one indication of a profound lack of civic-mindedness that manifested itself more dangerously in their refusal to serve as magistrates or soldiers. Origen defended the Christian refusal to honor the emperor's genius forthrightly. Either the emperor's genius is nothing at all, in which case it is dishonest to honor it, or it is a daemon, in which case such honor would be wicked. Admittedly it is unlawful to refuse such honor, but God's law, or, as the philosophers put it, natural law, supersedes the emperor's law.[131] Christians, he explained, do not serve as magistrates because those with administrative ability have a higher calling and citizenship in the church. Origen followed a cardinal principle in apologetics, to compare the ideals of one's own side with the other side's practice. He described the church's leaders as humble, competent, and reluctant to exercise power in contrast with secular magistrates who rarely exemplified such virtues.[132] It is hard to believe that the bishops he described so glowingly in the *Contra Celsum* were the same people he was excoriating in his *Commentary on Matthew*, a work written for Christians.

Origen's position on Christian service in the army was just as uncompromising. It is hard to assess the position, if there was one, of the Christian church as a whole on this issue although obviously Celsus had reason to believe when he wrote that it opposed having its members serve in the army. The issue was not pressing in the second and third centuries because there was no conscription ordinarily, and the army drew most of its recruits from rural districts where there were few Christians. (There were many Christians in one out-of-the-way rural recruiting area, the region of Commagene on the upper Euphrates river, and Christians from there were in the army when both Celsus and Origen were writing.) Origen's older contemporary, Tertullian, condemned service in the army, but he also testified to the presence of Christians in it. Certain sayings of Jesus forbade fighting and killing, but it is hard to tell whether they or the pervasive immorality and paganism of army life were the basis of Christian opposition to service in the army.[133] Origen, however, clearly taught that Jesus' prohibition of violence ruled out service in the army. He dismissed on this ground Celsus' charge that

Jesus' followers were revolutionaries, and he explicitly included the right to wage defensive war among the provisions of the Old Testament that Jesus abrogated.[134] If everyone were to be like the Christians, he answered Celsus, the emperor would have nothing to fear since the barbarians themselves would be mild, law-abiding Christians.[135] However, the barbarians would not have to become Christians for a Christian empire to be safe:

> If as Celsus suggests all the Romans were convinced and prayed, they would be superior to their enemies, or would not even fight wars at all, since they would be protected by divine power which is reported to have preserved five entire cities for the sake of fifty righteous men.[136]

The fate of the Jews proves nothing. They lost their national existence, not because God could not protect them, but because God justly punished them for their role in the death of Christ.[137]

But Origen did not seriously expect the Roman Empire to become Christian, and he admitted that hopes of universal peace probably could not be fulfilled on this earth.[138] In the meantime, the Roman empire was beneficial. God, in fact, brought it into existence to facilitate the spread of the gospel. God showed approval of the Roman Empire when the Logos became incarnate during the reign of Augustus, the emperor who completed the process of bringing many kingdoms under one authority.[139] Origen thus did not altogether rule out war. He recognized the legitimacy of just wars, and he tacitly approved of wars for the defense of the empire.[140] But Christians, he maintained, should not fight in those wars. All Christians are priests, and like pagan priests they must keep themselves undefiled by bloodshed if they are to make sacrifice on the army's behalf. By destroying by their prayers the daemons who stir up strife, they serve the empire more effectively than they could with arms in their hands:

> We who offer prayers with righteousness, together with ascetic practices and exercises which teach us to despise pleasures and not to be led by them, are cooperating in the tasks of the community. Even more do we fight on behalf of the emperor. And though we do not become fellow-soldiers with him, even if he presses for this, yet we are fighting for him and composing a special army of piety through our intercessions to God.[141]

Celsus would not have found this reassuring. Such sentiments would have confirmed his fear that Christianity was corroding the empire's strength. Christian attitudes about service in the army gradually changed after Constantine, who had discovered in the Christian God a powerful God of battles, made Christianity the empire's favored religion and purged the army of its pagan cults. The same is true of Christian willingness to serve as magistrates once their religion became an asset. Christians, nonetheless, did not cease to consider the soul's eternal salvation a higher goal than society's temporal welfare. Some modern historians, beginning with Edward Gibbon in *The Decline and Fall of the Roman Empire*, have taken a page from Celsus and blamed the triumph of Christianity for the loss of an ethic of civic service that, they claim, materially contributed to the empire's fall.

Although in the *Contra Celsum* Origen put most of his effort into rationally refuting attacks on Christianity, he did not hesitate to launch a counterattack against Celsus' high-minded, philosophical paganism. We have already seen how he contrasted Christianity's success in speaking to all kinds of people and reforming their lives with the ineffectiveness of the best Greek philosophy to do such things. Origen's most serious charge was not that pagan philosophy was ineffective but that it idolatrously worshiped daemons. Plato, for example wrote of how Socrates (Origen mercifully withheld their names) went down to the Piraeus to pray to Artemis and how he sacrificed a cock to Asclepius just before his death.[142] Because they are not idolaters, simple Christians put the greatest philosophers to shame:

> I believe that because God saw the arrogance or the disdainful attitude towards others of people who pride themselves on having known God and learnt the divine truths from philosophy, and yet like the most vulgar keep on with the images and their temples and the mysteries which are a matter of common gossip, He chose the foolish things of the world, the simplest of the Christians, who live lives more moderate and pure than many philosophers, that He might put to shame the wise, who are not ashamed to talk to lifeless things as if they were gods or images of gods.[143]

This collusion with popular idolatry is all the worse because the philosophers know better. Celsus damned himself and all of them by quoting from Heraclitus a saying that summed up the irrational folly of idolatry:

"Those who approach lifeless things as gods are like a man who holds conversation with houses."[144] Idolatrous polytheism genuinely horrified Origen, so much so that he ascribed to Satan (albeit transformed into an angel of light) two sentences in Plato's *Phaedrus* (again he did not mention the author by name) that seemed to sanction it.[145] This was a real weakness in pagan philosophy since it had never been able either to adapt to popular religion or to reform it. We have seen how important the Christian repudiation of idolatry was to one converted pagan with a philosophical background in Clement's *Exhortation to the Greeks*.[146]

At issue here is not the validity of Platonism but its compatibility with pagan worship. Adolf Harnack, the great historian of Christian doctrine, supposedly said that during the period of the early church Christianity and paganism had two mythologies but only one theology. This is not entirely true, but it helps very much to illuminate the *Contra Celsum*. Origen and Celsus championed variant forms of Platonism. They agreed that there was one transcendent God, who is the ultimate source of all that has ordered existence. They agreed that there is a continuum of being extending downward from this transcendent God through rational spirits, animals, and plants, to inert objects. They agreed on a fundamental distinction between sensible and intelligible reality. They also agreed that the human intellect has the capacity, given rigorous discipline, to contemplate the transcendent God. They agreed that myth and symbol are an appropriate way to express this ultimate reality in terms from which ordinary people can benefit. They also had no fundamental quarrel over moral values. Their only irreconcilable difference, aside from matters of sensibility, was over the Incarnation, which could have no place in Celsus' theology. Origen, of course, thought of himself as simply defending the church's tradition, but his own understanding of that tradition was so imbued with Platonism that in effect he was arguing that Christianity is more compatible with Platonism than paganism is.

In making that argument, Origen could call upon an ancient tradition that was uncompromisingly monotheistic, a genuinely spiritual worship, and high moral standards to prove that Christianity is superior to paganism. He went farther than that though, and here the Incarnation does play a role. He argued that the grace of God, accessible in the incarnate Logos, Jesus Christ, makes Platonism for the first time a practical, as opposed to a merely theoretical wisdom. This is what Celsus could not understand:

> He ridicules our teachers of the gospel who try to elevate the soul in every way to the Creator of the universe, and who show how men ought to despise all that is sensible and temporary and visible, and who urge them to do all they can to attain to fellowship with God and contemplation of intelligible and invisible things, and to reach the blessed life with God and the friends of God.[147]

Nor is this merely fortuitous; Moses and the prophets were, in effect, Platonists before Plato, who taught the distinction between the sensible and the ideal worlds long before the person who supposedly discovered that distinction came along:

> The very ancient doctrine of Moses and the prophets is aware that the true things all have the same name as the earthly things which are more generally given these names. For example, there is a "true light," and a "heaven" which is different from the firmament, and "the sun of righteousness" is different from the sun perceived by the senses. In general, in contrast to sensible things, none of which are real, the scripture says, "God, his works are true."[148]

In contrast with pagan Platonism, which is hobbled by idolatry, Christianity enables its adherents to shut the eyes of sense in prayer and ascend in soul beyond the sensible world to God.[149] Although Origen's *Contra Celsum*, just by the fact that a Christian could write it, did more than any other work of its time to make Christianity intellectually respectable, it defended it as Platonism for the masses.

## Porphyry

Origen's *Contra Celsum* was the most powerful blow yet struck by any Christian in the controversy with paganism and remains the greatest apology written in Greek. It is therefore ironic that Origen, as an old man, had occasion to meet a youth from Tyre who was to write *Against the Christians*, the most powerful counterargument from the pagan side. The youth, after Origen met him, changed his good Phoenician name, Malchus, to Porphyry and emerged as a prolific author with a wide range of interests. Porphyry (c. 232–c. 303) studied with Plotinus and wrote his biography and edited his writings. He also wrote a history of philosophy, literary critical works including the allegorical interpretation of the cave of the nymphs in Homer already mentioned, works on logic that became standard textbooks for a long time, and specialized treatises in the natural sciences. In 448 the now Christian empire ordered all copies of *Against the Christians* burnt, but fragments of it survive. Porphyry was, unlike Celsus, a penetrating biblical critic, an ability he could conceivably have gained as a student of Origen. He is famous for demonstrating, in advance of modern biblical scholarship, which did his work over for him, that the book of Daniel was written during the Maccabaean revolt of the second century B.C. rather than, as the book itself proclaims, in the Persian period. In a fragment of *Against the Christians* that has survived, Porphyry discussed Origen, whose Christian Platonism he found utterly irrational and baffling. The passage is one of the few first-hand accounts of him we possess and pays a backhanded tribute to his philosophical erudition. Porphyry identified Origen as the person most responsible for Christian allegorical interpretation of the Bible, a procedure he attacked as vehemently, and perhaps as inconsistently, as Celsus had:

> But this kind of absurdity must be traced to a man whom I met when I was still quite young, who had a great reputation, and still holds it, because of the writings he has left behind him, I mean Origen, whose fame has been widespread among the teachers of this kind of learning. For this man was a hearer of Ammonius, who had the greatest proficiency in philosophy in our day; and so far as a grasp of knowledge was concerned he owed much to his master. . . . Origen, a Greek educated in Greek learning, drove headlong towards barbarian recklessness; and making straight for this he hawked himself and his literary skill about; and while his manner of life was Christian and contrary to the law, in his opinions about material things and the Deity, he played the Greek, and introduced Greek ideas into foreign fables. For he was always consorting with Plato, and was conversant with the writings of Numenius and Cronius, Apollophanes and Longinus and Moderatus, Nicomachus and the distinguished men among the Pythagoreans; and he used also the books of Chaeremon the Stoic and Cornutus, from whom he learnt the figurative interpretation, as employed in the Greek mysteries, and applied it to the Jewish writings.[150]

Porphyry seems to have thought, almost certainly mistakenly, that Origen was reared as a pagan, but the picture of the old man, thoroughly Christian in his manner of life, consorting continually with Plato and the principal authors of the Middle Platonic school, and applying allegory to the Bible rings true.

## Persecution and Death

In the course of his *Commentary on Matthew* Origen had occasion, probably in 248 or 249, to comment on Matthew 24:9, "Then they will deliver you up to tribulation, and put you to death; and you will be hated by all nations for my name's sake." In interpreting it, he mentioned that there had not yet been a general persecution of Christians but that, when such a persecution did come, the words of the following verse, "and then many will fall away," would also be fulfilled.[151] At the same time he had cause to ponder Celsus' prediction that an emperor would arise who would finally decide to eradicate Christianity. Within a year or two, both predictions were fulfilled. The church was, during the reign of Philip the Arab, enjoying a period of unprecedented prosperity, and Christians much younger than Origen, who was in his early sixties, could not even remember a time when persecution was a serious threat. At the same time, Origen must have been aware of increasing tension. Doubtless the celebration of the millennium of the founding of Rome, considering the sorry state the empire found itself in at the time, contributed to pagan resentment. Might it not be that the growing numbers of Christians, who flaunted their contempt for the gods who had made Rome great, were responsible for the empire's decline? Was there not needed a reaffirmation of old-fashioned patriotism and piety if the empire was to regain its strength to meet dangers within and without? When he expressed his misgivings about a coming persecution in the *Commentary on Matthew*, Origen may already have heard about ominous events that occurred in Alexandria in 248. There pagan mobs went on the rampage against Christian persons and property, killing at least four who refused to sacrifice to the gods. Although one Alexandrian apparently lapsed, others showed that the spirit of martyrdom Origen imbibed in his youth was still strong. Apollonia, an aged Christian virgin roughed up by the mob, found herself threatened with being thrown into a bonfire if she did not pray to the pagan gods. She asked for a moment to consider and, as soon as she was released, jumped into the fire of her own accord.[152] If such an atrocity could happen when the emperor was favoring Christians, what would happen when that favor was withdrawn?

Christians did not need to wait long to find out. In 249 the general from Illyria, Decius, overthrew Philip and replaced him as emperor.

Decius was the sort of emperor for whom Celsus had been looking. Determined to restore the empire's inner strength, Decius immediately began to persecute Christians.[153] One of the first acts of his reign was to order the arrest of prominent Christian leaders. Fabian, the bishop of Rome, died at this time, as did Babylas, the bishop of Antioch, and Alexander, the bishop of Jerusalem, once a friend of Clement and Origen. Two important church leaders managed to escape this initial phase of the persecution, Bishop Cyprian of Carthage and Bishop Dionysius of Alexandria, Origen's former pupil. It may be that Origen was also imprisoned at this time. If not, he was jailed during the second phase of Decius' persecution, which was a nightmare for Christians. Early in 250 Decius issued a proclamation commanding all free inhabitants of the empire to acquire, on pain of death, a properly validated certificate stating that they had sacrificed to the gods. A few of these certificates have actually been found in Egypt, impressive legal documents stating in all cases that their possessors were life-long worshipers of the gods.

The edict's effect was immediate and devastating. Thousands of Christians were not the stuff of martyrs. In one North African town so many appeared the first day that the magistrates had to tell many Christians to come back and sacrifice the next day. Other Christians desperately sought to avoid the choice between apostasy and martyrdom. Some acquired certificates fraudulently, and others simply laid low. Only a relatively small number were actually imprisoned or died for their faith. Bishop Dionysius of Alexandria, in a letter to Bishop Fabius of Antioch, Babylas' successor, described what happened when the edict ordering sacrifice was promulgated in his city.[154] The entire Christian community, already on edge, was terrified. Many eminent Christians, who could not hope to avoid detection, came forward immediately to sacrifice, and others were forced to do so by mobs of pagans. Some approached the sacrifices pale with fear, as if, Dionysius wrote, they themselves were about to be the victims in the sacrifice rather than the ones sacrificing. Others ran eagerly toward the sacrifices as if trying to show that they had never been Christians at all. Some Christians refused to sacrifice and were imprisoned. Of them, some forswore themselves under torture or simply under the threat of it, but a certain number remained faithful to the end and were executed, often cruelly.

Fortunately for the Christians, the Roman government did not have the technical means to conduct a truly efficient persecution. Many pagan magistrates did not share the emperor's hatred for Christians, and the persecution abated as he left Rome to meet a more critical danger than the Christians, a horde of Goths who had crossed the Danube and were ravaging the Balkan provinces. It ceased entirely when Decius fell in battle in 251, only two years after gaining power. The persecution, as it turned out, harmed the church more by occasioning sharp divisions over how to treat those who had sacrificed or had obtained certificates, most of whom were clamoring for readmission to communion, than by actually terrorizing its members.

Origen survived the persecution a broken man. His last known works were letters describing his imprisonment. While in prison he received a letter on martyrdom, like that which he himself had once sent to Ambrosius, from Dionysius, the new bishop of Alexandria. This may have made up somewhat for past injuries. Origen's judge was not interested in putting him to death but in securing his recantation. He therefore attempted to break his will by torturing him upon a rack and threatening him with fire. Disciplined by a life of asceticism, Origen did not succumb. He was denied, however, the crown of martyrdom. This is unfortunate since if Origen had died in prison it would have been much harder for subsequent generations to condemn him. Origen simply fades from history after his release from prison; we assume that he died within a few years, perhaps in 253. One tradition has it that he retired to Tyre and died there. Certainly he deserved better of the church than to be left to die in obscurity, but he may have expected nothing more. He had nevertheless met and overcome the greatest test a Christian of his time could face and had conclusively demonstrated that his own devotion to Christ was not purely theoretical.

# X
# A Permanent Legacy

## Origen's Achievement

The inclusiveness of Origen's interests, the extent of his accomplishments, the coherence of his thought, the breadth of his influence, and the intensity of the controversy that has continued to surround him make Origen a figure of unquestionably great historical importance. This survey of Origen's life and thought has, if it has been successful, provided the evidence for the appreciation of the first three of these items. It is not within the scope of this book to examine in any detail Origen's influence and the controversies surrounding him, but a brief survey of the reception of Origen's thought in the Christian tradition is in order to show the full extent of Origen's importance and in order to show how it is that his actual works have come down to us in the state they have. Finally, it seems appropriate to suggest ways in which Origen is not simply a figure of historical importance but an author who still speaks to us today.

Origen's interests were so inclusive as to make him practically a microcosm of the spiritual life of the third century. Central, of course, was the Christian tradition, which provided him with the Bible as interpreted according to the rule of faith, an ethic of heroic asceticism, and a disciplined community committed to its ideals. A Hellenistic literary education provided him with critical procedures for analyzing the Bible's text and contents. General education in mathematics and the natural sciences provided him with a picture of the cosmos. The Gnostic schools of Basilides, Valentinus, and Marcion forced him to struggle with the issues of free will and theodicy and spurred him to create a coherent theological system answering to theirs. Middle Platonism, it-

244

self an eclectic school drawing on all of Greek philosophy except
Epicureanism, provided him with the conceptual tools and the vision of
reality from which he constructed his Christian theological system. Judaism provided him access to the text of the Old Testament and to the
Hellenistic and rabbinic traditions of interpreting it. If we must understand Origen to understand the development of Christian thought, we
must understand the intellectual world in which he lived in order to
understand Origen.

The extent of Origen's accomplishments as a writer is such as to
rank him with Varro and Augustine as one of the most prolific writers of
antiquity. Perhaps only a fellow Alexandrian, the first-century literary
scholar Didymus Chalcenterus ("Brass-guts"), who supposedly wrote
so many books he could not even remember them all, wrote more than
Origen. In the course of this writing he examined the text of the entire
Old Testament and commented in detail on most of the verses of the
Bible in a manner that combined an overall theological vision, a match-
less familiarity with the entire Bible, and great critical sensitivity. He
also wrote works which laid the basis for systematic theology in the
Christian tradition, established the intellectual dominance of the catholic ecclesiastical tradition over Gnosticism and put it on a par with the
best pagans had to offer, and provided lasting inspiration for contempla-
tives. As we have seen, Origen's method of composition, dictating to
stenographers and revising little while relying on his elephantine memory for most details, enabled him to achieve this astonishing output.
This method also meant that his works are often repetitive, diffuse, and
stylistically undistinguished. They are, however, never dull for those
willing to make the effort required to read them. We are constantly
aware in reading Origen of the presence of a powerful and fascinating
mind shaping and transforming all with which it deals. We always
know, even in tedious passages (one might say, especially in such passages) that Origen is up to something, and the desire to discover what it
is and how he will pull it off rivets our attention. In addition to being a
writer, Origen was also, of course, a skilled teacher, preacher, and
debater, as well as a revered spiritual guide.

What is perhaps as remarkable as the extent of Origen's accomplishments as a writer and as a person is the coherence of his thought.
Although we can speak of Origen's contributions as a teacher, a theolo-

gian, a preacher, an interpreter of the Bible, a contemplative ascetic, or a spiritual guide, all of these areas of activity are simply aspects of a single overriding concern, the attainment of the transforming knowledge of God. For this reason we cannot do justice to any single aspect of Origen's work without a comprehension of the whole. Previous treatments of Origen's thought have never done justice to this, the most remarkable aspect of it.[1] Origen's interpretation of the Bible, for example, makes no sense if we do not understand that it is a process of contemplating the deep mysteries of God. Nor can we understand his contemplation unless we see it as a fully intellectual activity. Because the knowledge of God transforms the contemplative into the likeness of God, and it is God's nature to be beneficent, the contemplative spontaneously seeks, like God, to help others toward the knowledge of God, addressing them at their appropriate level of comprehension as a preacher and teacher. In the process, the contemplative seeks to guard them from error and from sin as well as to teach them the truth. Although, as we shall see, Origen's thought provided a vast storehouse from which later generations took what they found to be useful, no one was fully able to appropriate what was most valuable in it.

## The Origenist Tradition and Its Enemies

Origen died in obscurity, and it took some time for his influence to be fully felt. His copy of the *Hexapla*, his correspondence, and, it seems, his personal library remained in the possession of the church at Caesarea, but there seems to have been no continuous Origenist tradition there. For such a school, we must look back to Alexandria, where Dionysius, who survived the persecution under Decius as well as a later persecution in 257 under the Emperor Valerian, was bishop until his death in 264. Dionysius was not uncritical of Origen, but he was far more sympathetic toward him than were his two predecessors. As a student of Origen, he became a fine theologian and biblical scholar. He shared Origen's rejection of the popular Christian expectation of an earthly millennial reign of Christ and, as a result, questioned the authenticity of the Revelation of John, which speaks of such a millennium. Origen had simply treated the book symbolically, but Dionysius marshalled an impressive sheaf of historical and literary evidence to prove that Revelation was not by the same author as the Gospel and letters of

John and, hence, given the consensus that those books were by the Apostle John, not of apostolic authorship or a proper part of the New Testament.

Two Alexandrians, Theognostus (d. c. 282) and Pierius (d. c. 309), self-consciously continued Origen's theological and exegetical tradition at Alexandria. Pierius, whose contemporaries knew him as "the younger Origen," educated Pamphilus (c. 240–309), a wealthy native of Beirut who eventually settled in Caesarea and reestablished the Origenist tradition there. The gradual spread of Origen's influence was not without opposition. Two bishops, Peter (d. 311), the bishop of Alexandria, and Methodius (d. c. 311), who seems to have been bishop of a city called Olympus in Lycia, the southwesternmost part of Asia Minor, led the opposition to Origen. Methodius, the more important figure, seems to have drawn heavily on Origen but rejected those elements in his theology that conflicted with the ecclesiastical tradition as commonly understood. The only work of his that survives intact is his *Symposium*, an imitation of Plato's dialogue in which a party of consecrated Christian virgins discuss chastity. He also wrote defending the doctrine of free will. He attacked Origen in a treatise *On the Resurrection* which reaffirmed the resurrection of the flesh as traditionally understood. Most of these figures died as a result of the Great Persecution initiated by the Emperor Diocletian and continued, in the Greek-speaking east, by his successors Galerius and Maximinus Daia. During that persecution Pamphilus, while imprisoned at Caesarea, wrote, with the collaboration of a younger scholar, Eusebius (c. 260–c. 340), who survived the persecution and became bishop of Caesarea, an *Apology for Origen* as a response to charges Peter and Methodius brought against him. The first volume of this work survives in a translation into Latin by Rufinus. It defended Origen as orthodox and presented him as a model Christian. Because in the process of defending Origen Pamphilus affirmed his denial of eternal punishment, the *Apology* itself was controversial.

The early fourth century marks the great watershed in the history of early Christianity and the beginning of a period in which Origen's work achieved such influence as to leave a permanent mark on the Christian tradition. The decade that preceded the Council of Nicaea in 325, the first council at which bishops from the entire Christian church met to discuss issues of doctrine and ecclesiastical order, was a period of dizzying change in which the church passed from persecution to peace to patronage. Constantine, the Christian convert who eventually took over the entire empire, not only put an end to persecution but quickly began to shower the church with favors. At the center of these events and chronicling them for posterity was Eusebius of Caesarea, Pamphilus' student and fellow-admirer of Origen. Drawing on the *Apology* and on Origen's works, especially his correspondence, Eusebius composed the so-called "Life of Origen" which occupies the greater part of the sixth book of his pioneering *Ecclesiastical History*. Most of the information we have about Origen comes from this book, which is especially valuable because it copiously cites documents like Porphyry's *Against the Christians* which have otherwise disappeared. The account of Origen in the *Ecclesiastical History* is not, however, entirely reliable because it is strongly biased toward Origen and conceals to a large extent the controversy surrounding him during his life and because Eusebius sometimes drew unfounded conclusions from evidence he had or passed on dubious traditions.

The Origenist tradition continued in Egypt where its principal spokesmen were Didymus the Blind (c. 313–98) and Evagrius Ponticus (346–99). Didymus, the author of a number of commentaries, more fully carried on Origen's preoccupation with the interpretation of the Bible. Evagrius took a greater interest in the speculative and contemplative aspects of Origen's thought and adapted it to the needs of the monastic movement which had emerged strongly in the course of the fourth century. Didymus, who lived in Alexandria, taught Gregory of Nazianzus (329–89), Rufinus of Aquileia (c. 345–410), and Jerome (c. 342–420), three figures who spread Origen's influence and preserved his works. Evagrius, who began his ecclesiastical career as a protégé of Gregory of Nazianzus, eventually settled in Nitria, an important monastic colony in the Libyan desert south of Alexandria. From there Evagrius' Origenistic ascetic theology spread rapidly throughout the Christian world. His works were rapidly translated into Syriac, the language of Christians in what is now Syria and Iraq, and spread from there to Armenia.[2] Evagrius influenced western monasticism through his disciple, John Cassian (c. 360–435), one of the founders of the Latin-speaking monastic tradition, whose writings profoundly influenced Benedict of Nursia (c. 480–c. 550), whose *Rule* ordered the regular reading of Cassian's works.

Didymus and Evagrius are the last figures of any distinction as theologians whom we can legitimately call Origenist. Other important theologians, while remaining appreciative of Origen, tended to be selective in what they adopted from him. Thus Cassian, whose understanding of contemplation and of the relation of the human will to God's grace was genuinely Origenist, had little interest in Origen's speculative concerns. As a result, Origen's understanding of contemplation became less intellectual and more affective as it entered the contemplative tradition in the West. Gregory of Nazianzus, who referred to Origen as "the whetstone of us all," was more interested in Origen's contributions to theology and was careful to avoid the more controversial aspects of his thought. Gregory was one of three theologians from Cappadocia, a region now in central Turkey, known collectively as the Cappadocian Fathers. The other two are Basil (c. 330–79), the bishop of Caesarea Mazaca, and his younger brother Gregory (c. 330–c. 395), the bishop of the little town of Nyssa. Basil, known as "the Great," was influential as a theologian and ecclesiastical politician in the controversy that eventually produced a definitive definition of the doctrine of the Trinity and was also a monastic writer and organizer. His ascetic writings have the normative role for Greek orthodox monks that Benedict's Rule has for those in the western tradition. Basil and Gregory of Nazianzus collaborated in 358–59 on the *Philocalia*, an anthology of Origen's work that preserves fragments of a number of works, including *On First Principles*, now lost in Greek. Gregory of Nyssa, now considered the greatest of the three as a theologian, was more deeply imbued with the spirit of Christian Platonism and, like Origen, whom he also admired, had strong universalizing tendencies.

Athanasius (c. 296–373), the bishop of Alexandria from 328, joined the Cappadocians in his concern for the doctrine of the Trinity, in particular for the correct definition of the relation between God the Father and God the Son. This was as much a political as a theological issue for two generations from the Council of Nicaea in 325 to the First Council of Constantinople in 381. The primary motive behind Constantine's summoning of the Council of Nicaea was the disunity that threatened the Greek-speaking half of the church due to controversy over the views of Arius (c. 250–c. 336), a presbyter in the church at Alexandria. Arius, relying among other things, on the subordinationist strain in Origen's Christology, denied that Christ was God in the same sense that God the

Father was. Arius preferred to view Christ as "the first born of all creation," a created divine being who, unlike God the Father, had a beginning in time. The council of Nicaea condemned Arius' views, upheld his excommunication by the church at Alexandria, and affirmed that Christ was fully divine, being "of one substance," with God the Father. A reaction, however, soon set in, with many in the church and in the imperial court favoring Arius' views or, at least, finding the "of one substance" formula unpalatable because it smacked of the Sabellian failure to distinguish adequately the three divine hypo-stases. Against Arius, who appealed to Origen's subordinationism, his affirmation, that is, of Christ the Son's inferiority to God the Father, Athanasius appealed to Origen's doctrine of eternal generation and to his understanding of redemption. If, as Origen taught, Christ was born from God the Father rather than created by God, then Christ would have the same substance as God the Father, especially since Christ shared with God the Father the property of not being subject to the category of time. Moreover, Athanasius argued, a created being like the Christ of Arius, not being divine himself, could not assist us to the ultimate goal of redemption in Origen's theology, the attainment of likeness to God. Although Origen was not directly responsible for the doctrine of the Trinity eventually reaffirmed in the "of one substance" formula of Nicaea at Constantinople in 381, his theology established the questions at issue and suggested the general framework of the eventual solution.

Although the greatest theologians whose work contributed to the defeat of Arianism at Constantinople looked gratefully to Origen as a theological mentor, the definitive establishment of the doctrine of the Trinity eventually contributed to the church's official rejection of him. Shortly after the Council, Epiphanius (c. 315–403), bishop of Salamis (now Famagusta), the chief city of Cyprus, published a scathing denunciation of Origen in his *Panarion* or *Medicine-Chest for All Heresies*. He depicted Origen as the main source of the recently defeated Arian heresy and spread slanders about Origen's character, including a story that he had sacrificed to Sarapis at Alexandria after being threatened with rape by an Ethiopian and another that he took a memory drug. Epiphanius' work had no immediate effect, but he bided his time.

In the meantine, Origen's method of biblical interpretation spread to the Latin-speaking West. A vital figure in this process was Ambrose (c.

339–97), the bishop of Milan. Ambrose, a brilliant orator of noble birth, dominated the western church during the later part of the fourth century and even forced emperors to yield to the power of his personality. Ambrose admired the Cappadocians and gained from them an appreciation of Origen's allegorical interpretation of the Bible, which he practiced extensively in his preaching at Milan. Ambrose, in turn, introduced the allegorical interpretation of the Bible to Augustine of Hippo (354–430), the theologian from North Africa who was to shape western theology profoundly for more than a thousand years. Augustine was an ambitious young rhetorician of Christian origins who had subsequently embraced and become disillusioned with the Gnostic theology of the Manichees when he heard Ambrose preaching at Milan. Until that time he had believed that the Christian Bible was unspeakably crude and fantastic. He described Ambrose's effect on him in his *Confessions:*

> Although I took no trouble to learn what he said, but only to hear how he said it . . . yet, along with the eloquence I prized, there also came into my mind ideas which I ignored; for I could not separate them . . . . First of all, his ideas had already begun to appear to me defensible; and the Catholic faith, for which I supposed that nothing could be said against the onslaught of the Manichaeans, I now realized could be maintained without presumption. This was especially clear after I heard one or two parts of the Old Testament explained allegoric-ally—whereas before this, when I had interpreted them literally, they had "killed" me spiritually. However, when many of these passages in those books were expounded to me thus, I came to blame my own despair for having believed that no reply could be given to those who hated and scoffed at the Law and the Prophets.[3]

This was precisely the same effect Origen himself had had upon Ambrose's namesake a century and a half earlier. Although Augustine's theological perspective differed in significant ways from Origen's, his immensely influential handling of biblical symbolism was in the Origenist tradition.

Another important avenue for the influence of Origenist exegesis was through two scholarly monks from the Latin-speaking West who settled in the Holy Land, Rufinus on the Mount of Olives just outside Jerusalem and Jerome at Bethlehem. Both men had studied, although Jerome only briefly, with Didymus the Blind at Alexandria, and both began their careers as passionate admirers of Origen, whose works they first translated into Latin. Jerome translated almost eighty of Origen's homilies. Rufinus translated many homilies along with Origen's *Commentary on Romans*, part of his *Commentary on the Song of Songs*, and his treatise *On First Principles*. Ultimately, however, the two men, who had been friends since their youth, became enemies when they took different sides in what historians refer to, somewhat misleadingly, as the First Origenist Controversy.[4] In 393 Epiphanius, whose *Panarion* had not had the desired effect, went on a crusade against Origenism. He was especially influential among the monks in the Holy Land, where he had been an abbot before becoming a bishop, so he sent a representative there to procure abjurations of Origenism. Jerome, somewhat surprisingly, complied promptly with Epiphanius' demand. He would later claim that he had only been familiar with Origen's homilies and had not known about the heretical doctrines in *On First Principles* until Epiphanius called them to his attention. Rufinus, with the backing of his bishop, John of Jerusalem, renounced any errors of which Origen might be accused but refused to abjure him. This resulted in an estrangement between Jerome and John, who as bishop of Jerusalem had jurisdiction over Bethlehem, which the mediation of Bishop Theophilus of Alexandria (d. 412) settled in 397. Since Jerome was a genius at invective, this estrangement had become a *cause célèbre* throughout the Christian world by the time it was settled.

The true controversy began a year later, in 398, when Rufinus, who had returned in the meantime to his native Italy, published a translation of the first two books of *On First Principles*. This translation, which Rufinus soon completed, was venturesome in itself, since Latin-speaking readers had not been exposed to the more speculative aspects of Origen's thought. What ignited the controversy, though, was Rufinus' indiscreet preface, in which he claimed to be following Jerome's example in translating Origen and in emending theologically offensive passages in the process. Jerome bitterly resented the suggestion that he was still an admirer of Origen and that his translations were less than accurate. He responded with an attack on Rufinus in a letter to friends at Rome and with his own, purportedly strictly literal translation of *On First Principles*, which was, as we can tell by comparing both versions with existing Greek fragments, as biased in its accentuation of Origen's alleged deviations from orthodoxy as Rufinus' was in its concealment of them. Unfortunately, only fragments of the work remain. A literary controversy over Origen continued in the West for some years, but while the controversy left Origen with the reputation for being somewhat suspect, it damaged his reputation in the West relatively little. The translations of his works continued to be read, and his indirect influence continued to be felt on Jerome, whose commentaries and whose great *Vulgate* translation of the Bible depended much on Origen's inspiration.

More significant for the ultimate fate of Origen's works were developments in the Greek-speaking East. In 399 the largely Coptic-speaking monks of the Egyptian desert, whom Athanasius had turned into powerful allies of the bishop (now known as the Patriarch) of Alexandria during the Arian Controversy, reacted violently to a pastoral letter from Theophilus urging them, in good Origenistic fashion, to forswear anthropomorphic concepts of God. The monks had prayed all their lives to an old, and very large, man in the sky, and they took Theophilus' letter as a proposal that they become atheists. Theophilus, always an astute politician, saw that he could not afford to alienate the monks and did an adroit about face. Although he did not cease to read Origen with pleasure, he became the avowed champion of orthodoxy against Origen's supposedly deadly heresies. In the process he attacked the small minority of literate monks in the Origenist tradition of Evagrius Ponticus, who died before he could become the focus of controversy. Theophilus attacked Evagrius' followers at Nitria and hounded the most eminent of them, four saintly brothers known as the Tall Brothers, out of Egypt. The Tall Brothers went to Constantinople, where they pleaded their case against Theophilus before the powerful Empress Eudoxia (d. 412) and the Patriarch John Chrysostom (c. 347–407). John Chrysostom was no Origenist, being a product of the independent theological tradition of Antioch, but he was sympathetic to the Tall Brothers' situation, which embroiled him in controversy with Theophilus. John was the greatest preacher of his day and a person of unquestioned integrity, but he was no politician, and the charge of harboring Origenist heretics aided Theophilus in securing his deposition and banishment. Chrysostom, who died in exile in 407, was soon revered as a saint, but the controversy which Epiphanius initiated and Theophilus stirred up left a permanent stain on Origen's reputation. The end of the fourth century marks the end of the period when Origen's works exerted an enormous direct influence on the theology, exegesis, and spirituality of Greek-speaking Christendom although their indirect influence continued to be immense.

With the breakdown of Roman imperial power in the West over the course of the fifth century, Latin- and Greek-speaking Christianity drifted increasingly apart, and Origen's reputation fared differently in the two areas. In the West he was read and respected but somewhat suspect. His reputation was not helped by the regard in which his *Commentary on Romans* was held by Pelagius, the British theologian who had the poor judgment to attack Augustine's understanding of divine grace. Nevertheless, Origen remained influential in the monastic tradition. The two so-called "Renaissances" during the Middle Ages in the West, those of the ninth and twelfth centuries, both involved revivals of Origenism. The ninth century produced, in the Irish theologian John Scotus Erigena (c. 810–c. 877), a Platonistic systematist with a vision of the world fully as grand as that of *On First Principles,* which helped inspire it. The monastic theologians of the Cistercian movement in the twelfth century also read and appreciated Origen. The great masterpiece of Medieval mysticism, the *Sermons on the Song of Songs* by Bernard of Clairvaux (1090–1153) would be unthinkable without Origen's commentary on the same book in Rufinus' translation. Still more imbued with Origenism was Bernard's close friend, William of St. Thierry (c. 1085–1148), who wrote on the nature of humanity and the relation between love and knowledge. The scholastics of the following centuries, however, had little use for Origen, and interest in him languished until the fifteenth century. The scholastics perpetuated his memory largely in debates over whether or not Origien, along with Samson, Solomon, and Trajan, could have been saved. Two nuns claimed to have had visions that settled the matter in his favor.

In the East, Origenism remained popular, and controversial, among monks in Palestine and Syria. Eventually controversy among monks over Origen brought him to the attention of the Emperor Justinian I (483–565), who was, among other things, an amateur theologian. Justinian secured the condemnation of Origen, along with his disciples Didymus and Evagrius, at the Second Council of Constantinople in 553, three hundred years after Origen's death. In the Byzantine world Origen remained under a cloud until the fourteenth century, and this resulted in the disappearance of most of his works that were not translated from

Greek. The steady encroachment of the Turks, however, led to a renewed interest in Origen's *Contra Celsum* as the principal defense of Christianity written in Greek.

A lasting revival of interest in Origen, and a renewal of the controversy surrounding him, occurred in the Renaissance.[5] John Cardinal Bessarion (1403–72), a refugee from the Greek East, brought to Italy the renewed interest in Origen as the author of the *Contra Celsum*, which was printed in a Latin translation by Cristoforo Persona (c. 1416–85) in 1481. Persona was a humanist who ended his life as curator of the Vatican library. By that time Origen's homilies and *Commentary on the Song of Songs* had already appeared in print twice, the first time in 1468. A serious controversy occurred in 1487 when John Pico della Mirandola (1463–94) issued, among nine hundred theses for debate, the thesis that "it is more reasonable to believe that Origen was saved than it is to believe that he was damned." A papal commission condemned Pico's position on the grounds that a council had condemned Origen, but not before airing the issue had made Origen more familiar. Pico, as a self-styled Platonist with strong interests in esoterism, found Origen's speculative theology highly congenial, as did other humanists, although in his defense of him he stressed Origen's willingness to defer to the church.

The most important figure in the Renaissance revival of interest in Origen was the great Dutch humanist Erasmus (c. 1469–1536), who valued Origen above all other Christian authors. In a 1518 letter to John Eck, he wrote that a single page of Origen taught him more Christian philosophy than ten pages of the revered Augustine. Erasmus particularly admired Origen's style for its lack of the rhetorical flourishes characteristic of so many other Patristic authors. He made Origen more accessible by translating in 1527 the portion of the *Commentary on Matthew* that only survived in Greek and by publishing in 1536, as the last major accomplishment of his life, the most complete edition of Origen's works that had appeared so far. Erasmus made heavy use of Origen's chapter on freedom of the will from *On First Principles* in his own most important theological work, *On Free Will*, which he published in 1524. He wrote the treatise to combat what he considered an overemphasis on God's grace, to the expense of human moral responsibility, in the works of Martin Luther (1483–1546). Luther's response, his own most carefully constructed theological treatise, *On the Bondage of the Will* (the title comes from a phrase he found in Augustine), was as much a refutation of Origen as it was of Erasmus.

Origen's emphasis on the importance of human effort in the achievement of salvation and his denigration of faith made him far less congenial to the Reformation than he had been to the Renaissance. Certain aspects of his thought, however, appealed to the Protestant Reformers and to their predecessor, the Czech reformer Jan Hus (c. 1372–1415). Hus found Origen an inspiration in his own attempt to redefine the church as a spiritual reality rather than as an officially-constituted hierarchy, and insofar as the sixteenth-century reformers followed Hus in that respect, they also found Origen useful. The Swiss reformer, Ulrich Zwingli, (1484–1531), also found Origen useful in arriving at his symbolic understanding of the eucharist and in his understanding of worship. Luther, however, found Origen's position on grace hopelessly defective and would have nothing to do with him. This occasioned a remark, absurd outside the context of his own theology, that "in all of Origen there is not a single word about Christ," and the boast "I have put Origen under the ban."

## Origen in the Modern World

In the period between the Renaissance and the nineteenth century the French polymath, Pierre Daniel Huet (1630–1721), who eventually became bishop of Avranches in Normandy, was the most significant person for the transmission of Origen's legacy. Huet published a critical edition of Origen's exegetical works in 1668 to which he attached *Origeniana*, a thorough and sympathetic examination of Origen's life, doctrine, and works that is still valuable. Not long after Huet's death, Charles Delarue (1685–1739) published, in 1733, what is still the fullest critical edition of Origen's works. Interest in Origen increased dramatically when nineteenth-century German church historians began to free the study of the history of Christian thought from dogmatic or apologetic considerations. The greatest of these historians, Adolf Harnack (1851–1930), whose magisterial *History of Dogma* first appeared in 1886, summarized Origen's thought and assigned him a central, if not altogether positive, role in the development of Christian thought. The twentieth century has witnessed an extraordinary rebirth of interest in and appreciation of Origen among Catholic theologians, including Karl Rahner, Hans Urs von Balthasar, Jean Cardinal Daniélou, and Henri Cardinal de Lubac. There is currently a wealth of critical studies on Origen in German, French, and English to which the notes and bibliography in this book can give only a meager testimony. Origen's place is secure as a major figure in the history of the church.

But is Origen's interest for us entirely historical? The philosophical and scientific presuppositions with which any theology today must come to terms are certainly different from those which Origen took into consideration, so there is scarcely any chance that his system will be renewed in its entirety. Origen, however, dealt creatively with issues that any Christian theology must confront. Two such issues stand out as ones where his efforts were so fruitful that he provides a model today: theodicy and the role of the intellect in religion.

Marcion, as we have seen, raised the issue of theodicy in an acute form for Origen by denying that the God of the Old Testament was the same God as the God and Father of Jesus Christ in the New Testament. How was it possible to believe that the all-powerful Creator of the universe, the God who called the people of Israel and revealed the divine will to them, was both just and good? How could a good God, moreover, be so wrathful against some rational creatures as to condemn them to everlasting punishment? Origen is distinctive among the great formative theologians in the Christian tradition in his decision to make the beneficence of God a primary datum in theology, and he did so in such a way as neither to sentimentalize God nor to trivialize evil. Origen's doctrine that this world and all the difficulties we face in it are simply God's way to persuade all creatures to return to a free and loving unity with God gives all of life meaning as a part of God's plan, yet scrupulously respects the integrity of the individual. Origen also relieves Christianity of the embarrassment which has always beset the Augustinian tradition which dominates the western Christian tradition: how to account for a good God's punishing people eternally for sins they could not help committing. In Origen's theology all of God's punishment is a loving chastisement intended to bring souls to God as swiftly as possible and cure them of their sin. Surely Origen's system is no more difficult to adjust to today's view of the world than is that of Augustine and his followers.

The role of the intellect in religion has been a particular problem for the modern era when it seems more and more as if the application of critical reason, whether in the natural sciences or in the interpretation of the Bible, poses a threat to established religious convictions. This is simply not a problem for Origen, for whom the unimpeded application of the intellect in all areas is precisely the way to come to a fuller knowledge of God. Even though it may run the risk of scandalizing the more simple, Origen refuses to retreat into obscurantism. If the Christian revelation is true, then there are reasonable answers to the Gnostics, to the Jews, and to pagans like Celsus. If the Bible is God's word, then the more accurately it is known, the more critically it is examined, the more of God it will reveal. More importantly, the intellect itself can be the prime means of experiencing the reality of God. Willian R. Inge, dean of St. Paul's, London, summed up the value of this side of Origen in a plea for a greater appreciation of Origen's work:

> What would the Church be without its thinkers and its mystics, who believe that those who seek the pearl of great price will be led by the Holy Spirit into all truth? Even their errors are more instructive than the docile orthodoxy of those who say they believe whatever the Bible says, or what Holy Church teaches. To disparage reason is blasphemy against the Holy Spirit, whose gifts are wisdom and understanding, counsel and might, knowledge, and the fear of the Lord. In this faith Origen lived, worked, suffered, and died.[6]

# APPENDIX

# Origens

One of Plotinus' fellow students when he studied under Ammonius Saccas was a man named Origen. Plotinus had such respect for this man, who wrote three philosophical treatises, that he fell silent in embarrassment when Origen turned up at one of his lectures at Rome, saying that he did not wish to speak when someone was present who knew already what he was going to say. Was the Origen whom Plotinus respected as a colleague the same Origen as the Christian theologian? That is unlikely, even though the alternative explanation, that two men named Origen studied under Ammonius at different times, is scarcely attractive on the face of it. Bearing in mind that we must not multiply Origens beyond necessity, there are compelling reasons for believing that there were, indeed, two of them who studied under Ammonius.

Porphyry, who knew that our Origen had studied under Ammonius Saccas, is also the source of our information about Plotinus' relationship with his colleague, Origen the philosopher, information contained in his *Life of Plotinus*. That work provides us four reasons for postulating two Origens:

(1) Porphyry did not say that the Origen whom Plotinus knew was a Christian, and the natural assumption the reader makes is that he was not.

(2) The titles of the works Porphyry ascribed to Origen the Platonist do not correspond to any works we know of by Origen the Christian. It is just conceivable that our Origen wrote three religiously neutral philosophical treatises—he attracted pagans to his philosophical lectures at Caesarea, so he must have been capable of objectivity—but such activ-

ity flies in the face of the attitude he displayed in all his extant works.

(3) Porphyry states that Origen the Platonist wrote his treatises during the reign of Gallienus, who was technically a colleague with his father Valerian from 253 on, but ruled in his own right only from 260 to 268, by which time our Origen was almost certainly dead.

(4) Plotinus could have studied under Ammonius for as long as nine years and still have taken up his studies with him after our Origen left Alexandria permanently, and there is no reason to think that our Origen was ever in Rome to drop in on a lecture when Plotinus was teaching there. Origen left Alexandria in 233, never, as far as we know, to return. Plotinus, according to Porphyry, studied with Ammonius for an undisclosed number of years before he joined Gordian III's ill-fated invasion of Persia in 242. He went to teach at Rome somewhat later. Although Origen did travel to Rome on one occasion we know of, that was before he had left Alexandria permanently.

There remains the possibility that there were two Origens, but that Porphyry confused the Christian Origen with the man of the same name who had studied with Plotinus under Ammonius. This is highly doubtful since Porphyry had met our Origen and he knew Plotinus intimately. Furthermore, his statement in *Against the Christians* that Origen studied with Ammonius Saccas scarcely helped him prove, as he attempted to in the treatise as a whole, that Christians were ignorant and irrational. Eusebius, the church historian, confused matters further, it appears, by confusing Ammonius Saccas with the Christian bishop, Ammonius of Thmuis, but that is beside the point. We are left with the conclusion that our Origen and another man, a pagan, of the same name, studied under Ammonius Saccas, but that our Origen did so perhaps two decades before Plotinus did and probably never met his greatest contemporary.

# Bibliography

**Works by Origen in English Translation**

*The Commentary on John*
> (Books 1, 2, 4, 5, 6, 10 only) Translated by Allan Menzies. *Ante-Nicene Fathers*, vol. 10. Original supplement to the American edition. Reprint ed., Grand Rapids, Mich.: Wm. B. Eerdmans Publishing Company, 1974.

*The Commentary on Matthew*
> (Fragments of Books 1, 2, 10—14) Translated by John Patrick. *Ante-Nicene Fathers*, vol. 10. Original supplement to the American edition. Reprint ed., Grand Rapids, Mich.: Wm. B. Eerdmans Publishing Company, 1974.

*The Commentary on the Song of Songs*
> Translated by R. P. Lawson. *Ancient Christian Writers*, vol. 26. Westminster, Md.: The Newman Press, 1957.

> (Prologue only) Translated by Rowan A. Greer. *An Exhortation to Martyrdom, Prayer and Selected Works*. New York: Paulist Press, 1979.

*Contra Celsum*
> Translated by Henry Chadwick. Cambridge: At the University Press, 1953, 1965, paper, 1980.

> Translated by Frederick Crombie. *Ante-Nicene Fathers*, vol. 4. Reprint of Edinburgh Edition, 1885, Grand Rapids, Mich.: Wm. B. Eerdmans Publishing Company, 1976.

*Dialogue with Heraclides*
> Translated by Henry Chadwick. Library of Christian Classics, vol. 2. *Alexandrian Christianity*. Philadelphia: The Westminster Press, 1954.

*Exhortation to Martyrdom*
> Translated by Henry Chadwick. Library of Christian Classics, vol. 2. *Alexandrian Christianity*. Philadelphia: The Westminster Press, 1954.

> Translated by Rowan A. Greer. *An Exhortation to Martyrdom, Prayer, and Selected Works*. New York: Paulist Press, 1979.

Translated by John J. O'Meara. *Ancient Christian Writers*, vol. 19. Westminster, Md.: The Newman Press, 1954.

*Homilies on Genesis and Exodus*
Translated by Ronald E. Heine. *Fathers of the Church*, vol. 71. Washington, D.C.: Catholic University of America Press, 1982.

*Homilies on Numbers*
(Homily 27 only) Translated by Rowan A. Greer. *An Exhortation to Martyrdom, Prayer and Selected Works*. New York: Paulist Press, 1979.

*Homilies on the Song of Songs*
Translated by R. P. Lawson. *Ancient Christian Writers*, vol. 26. Westminster, Md.: The Newman Press, 1957.

*Letters to and from Julius Africanus and to Gregory*
Translated by Frederick Crombie. *Ante-Nicene Fathers*, vol. 4. Reprint of Edinburgh Edition, 1885, Grand Rapids, Mich.: Wm. B. Eerdmans Publishing Company, 1976.

*On First Principles*
Translated by G. W. Butterworth. London: S. P. C. K., 1936; New York: Harper & Row, Publishers, Harper Torchbooks, 1966.

Translated by Frederick Crombie. *Ante-Nicene Fathers*, vol. 4, Reprint of Edinburgh Edition, 1885, Grand Rapids, Mich.: Wm. B. Eerdmans Publishing Company, 1976.

(Book 4 only) Translated by Rowan A. Greer. *An Exhortation to Martyrdom, Prayer and Selected Works*. New York: Paulist Press, 1979.

*On Prayer*
Translated by Rowan A. Greer. *An Exhortation to Martyrdom, Prayer and Selected Works*. New York: Paulist Press, 1979.

Translated by John J. O'Meara. *Ancient Christian Writers*, vol. 19. New York: Paulist Press, 1954.

Translated by John Ernest Leonard Oulton. Library of Christian Classics, vol. 2. *Alexandrian Christianity*. Philadelphia: The Westminster Press, 1954.

*Philocalia*
Translated by George Lewis. Edinburgh: T. & T. Clark, 1911.

## Important Works about Origen

GENERAL

Henry Chadwick. *Christianity and the Classical Tradition*. Oxford: Clarendon Press, 1966.

Jean Daniélou. *Origen*. Translated by Walter Mitchell. London & New York: Sheed and Ward, 1955.

Eugène de Faye. *Origène; sa vie, son oeuvre, sa pensée*. 3 vols. Paris: Ernest Leroux, 1923, 1927, 1928.

LIFE AND WORK

Pierre Nautin. *Origène: sa vie et son oeuvre*. Paris: Beauchesne, 1977.

THEOLOGY

Marguerite Harl. *Origène et la fonction révélatrice du Verbe Incarné*. Paris: Editions du Seuil, 1958.

Hal Koch. *Pronoia und Paideusis; Studien über Origenes und sein Verhältnis zum Platonismus*. Berlin: Walter de Gruyter & Co., 1932; reprint ed., New York: Garland Publishing, 1979.

SCRIPTURAL INTERPRETATION

R. M. Grant. *The Earliest Lives of Jesus*. New York: Harper & Bros., 1961.

R. P. C. Hanson. *Allegory and Event*. Richmond: John Knox Press, 1959.

SPIRITUALITY

Walther Völker. *Das Vollkommenheitsideal des Origenes*. Tübingen: J. C. B. Mohr, 1930.

FURTHER BIBLIOGRAPHY

Henri Crouzel. *Bibliographie critique d'Origène*. Stenbrugis: Abbatia Sancti Petri, The Hague: Martinus Nijhoff, 1971. (Second vol. in preparation)

# Notes

INTRODUCTION: Alexandria

1. E. M. Forster, *Alexandria: A History and a Guide*, 2nd ed. (Garden City, N. Y.: Doubleday & Co., Doubleday, Anchor Books, 1961) is an engaging introduction to the city and its history.
2. On Alexandrian scholarship see Rudolph Pfeiffer, *A History of Classical Scholarship from the Beginnings to the End of the Hellenistic Age* (Oxford: the Clarendon Press, 1968); John Edwin Sandys, *A History of Classical Scholarship*, 3 vols. (Cambridge: At the University Press, 1906–1908), vol. 1; and Samuel Sambursky, *The Physical World of the Greeks*, trans. Merton Dagut (London: Routledge and Kegan Paul, 1956).
3. Dio Chrysostom *Discourses* 32.35–36. On Alexandrian trade see M. P. Charlesworth, *Trade-routes and Commerce of the Roman Empire* (Cambridge: The University Press, 1924), and Mikai Rostovtsev, *The Social and Economic History of the Roman Empire*, 2 vols., 2nd ed. (Oxford: At the Clarendon Press, 1941, 1957), 1:273–99.
4. See the introduction to Victor A. Tcherikover's *Corpus Papyrorum Judaicarum*, 2 vols. (Cambridge, Mass.: Harvard University Press, 1957), vol. 1.
5. See Harold Idris Bell, *Egypt, from Alexander the Great to the Arab Conquest; a Study in the Diffusion and Decay of Hellenism* (Oxford: At the Clarendon Press, 1948).
6. Edward Gibbon, *The Decline and Fall of the Roman Empire*, ed. J. B. Bury, 7 vols. (London: Methuen & Co., 1896), 1:78. Modern historians are less impressed than Gibbon was with the age he so glowingly described but there is no question that the age that followed witnessed a decline from it. See Arnold Hugh M. Jones, *The Later Roman Empire 284–602*, 3 vols. (Oxford: Basil Blackwell, 1964), 1:1–36; Roger Rémondon, *La crise de l'empire romain de Marc Aurèle à Anastase*, 2nd ed. (Paris: Presses universitaires de France, 1970); Géza Alföldi, "The Crisis of the Third Century as Seen by Contemporaries," *Greek, Roman and Byzantine Studies* 15 (1974): 89–111; and Ramsay MacMullen, *Roman Government's Response to Crisis*, A.D. *235–337* (New Haven: Yale University Press, 1976).

CHAPTER I: The Church (c. 185–c. 201)

1. Pierre Nautin, *Origène: sa vie et son oeuvre* (Paris: Beauchesne, 1977), presents this reconstruction. This book largely follows, on the basis of an examination of the evidence, Nautin's account.

2. Two sources, outside of Origen's works, for the reconstruction of second-century worship in this chapter are the *Didache* and *The First Apology of Justin, the Martyr,* both accessible in *Early Christian Fathers,* ed. and trans. Cyril C. Richardson (New York: The Macmillan Company, paper, 1970). The other is Hippolytus' *Apostolic Tradition,* trans. Gregory Dix (London: S.P.C.K., 1937).

3. See the *Letter of Aristeas,* intro., trans., and notes by Herbert T. Andrews in R. H. Charles, ed., *The Apocrypha and Pseudepigrapha of the Old Testament in English* (Oxford: At the Clarendon Press, 1913), 2:83–122.

4. The *Epistle of Barnabas,* ascribed to Paul's sometime companion, explains that the ritual laws of the Old Testament were never intended to be taken literally: the clean and unclean animals, for example, are really symbols of different kinds of people. *The Shepherd of Hermas* is a compilation of commandments, parables, and visions supposedly vouchsafed to a Roman prophet. Its purpose is moral edification. Both are accessible in the Loeb Classical Library series, *The Apostolic Fathers,* 2 vols. (Cambridge, Mass.: Harvard University Press, 1913). The *Apocalypse of Peter* is an apocalyptic book that is remarkable for its disgusting pictures of hell, and which ultimately influenced Dante. The *Acts of Paul* is a fanciful continuation of the apostle's life, after the Acts of the Apostles leaves off. The extant fragments of both books, along with the other apocryphal New Testament books mentioned here, are available in Ernst Hennecke and Wilhelm Schneemelcher, editors, *The New Testament Apocrypha,* 2 vols. (Philadelphia: The Westminster Press, 1963).

5. Eusebius *Ecclesiastical History* 6.2.9, trans. with intro. and notes by Hugh Jackson Lawlor and John Ernest Leonard Oulton, 2 vols. (London: S.P.C.K., 1927, 1928), 1:178. Used by permission.

6. Ibid., 6.2.10–11 (trans. Lawlor and Oulton, 1:178).

7. R. P. C. Hanson discusses the canon of faith and its relation to the Bible in *Tradition in the Early Church* (London: SCM Press, 1962; Philadelphia: The Westminster Press, 1963).

8. J. N. D. Kelly, *Early Christian Doctrines,* rev. ed. (San Francisco: Harper & Row Publishers, 1977) is a definitive treatment of the doctrinal issues here summarily discussed.

9. Hippolytus *Refutation* 9.7.

10. See C. J. Cadoux, *The Early Church and the World* (Edinburgh: T. & T. Clark, 1925), and Robert M. Grant, *Early Christianity and Society* (San Francisco: Harper & Row Publishers, 1977), for discussion of Christian ethics in the context of Greco-Roman society. See also the relevant sections of G.E. M. de Ste Croix, *The Class Struggle in the Ancient World from the Archaic Age to the Arab Conquests* (Ithaca, N.Y.: Cornell University Press, 1981).

11. Ignatius *Epistle to the Romans,* 2, 4, trans. author, accessible in Richardson, *Early Christian Fathers,* pp. 103–104. All unattributed citations are the author's translations.

12. See W. H. C. Frend, *Martyrdom and Persecution in the Early Church* (Oxford: Basil Blackwell, 1965; Garden City, N.Y.: Doubleday & Company, Inc., Anchor Books, 1967), for a history of Roman persecution and the Christian response to it.

13. This work is in Richardson, *Early Christian Fathers*, pp. 149–58. Herbert Musurillo also translated it, along with the other genuine early acts of martyrs, in *Acts of the Christian Martyrs* (Oxford: Clarendon Press, 1972). Perhaps the genre's degeneration, once persecution ceased, into fantasy and sensationalism accounts for the undue neglect of these testimonies to early Christian piety.

14. Plato *Republic* 2.361e.

15. Hippolytus *Apostolic Tradition* 4.

16. The early chapters of Kenneth E. Kirk's *The Vision of God* (London: Longmans, Green, and Co., 1931), contain a penetrating discussion of early Christian rigorism. See also Oscar D. Watkins, *A History of Penance* (London: Longmans, Green, and Co., 1920), vol. 1.

17. Pierre Nautin, *Lettres et écrivains chrétiennes du deuxième et troisième siècles* (Paris: Presses universitaires de France, 1952), provides valuable insights into the workings of the church in this period.

Chapter II: Grammar and Gnosis (c. 201–11)

1. This discussion of ancient education depends heavily on the splendid work by H.-I. Marrou, *A History of Education in Antiquity*, trans. George Lamb (New York: Sheed & Ward, 1956).

2. For a sympathetic account of the Olympian religion, see Walter Otto, *The Homeric Gods: the Spiritual Significance of Greek Religion*, trans. Moses Hadas (London: Thames and Hudson, 1954).

3. Heraclitus *Homeric Problems* 69 (trans. author), Félix Buffière, ed., *Allégories d'Homère*, Budé series (Paris: Société d'Edition «Les Belles Lettres», 1962).

4. Two easily accessible editions of Lucian's works are Lucian, *Satirical Sketches*, trans. Paul Turner (Harmondsworth, Middlesex: Penguin, 1961), and Lucian, *Selected Works*, trans. Bryan A. Reardon (Indianapolis: Bobbs-Merrill, 1965).

5. There are a number of useful works on Greco-Roman religion. Among them are Harold Idris Bell, *Cults and Creeds in Graeco-Roman Egypt* (Liverpool: At the University Press, 1954); André J. Festugière, *Personal Religion among the Greeks* (Berkeley and Los Angeles: University of California Press, 1954); Johannes Geffcken, *The Last Days of Greco-Roman Paganism*, trans. Sabine MacCormack (1920; rev. ed., 1929; Amsterdam: North-Holland Publishing Company, 1977); and A. D. Nock, *Conversion: the Old and New Religion from Alexander the Great to Augustine of Hippo* (Oxford: Oxford University Press, 1933).

6. See R. E. Witt, *Isis in the Graeco-Roman World* (Ithaca, N. Y.: Cornell University Press, 1971).

7. See Plutarch *De Iside et Osiride*, ed. and trans. with intro. and comm. by J. Gwyn Griffiths (Cambridge: University of Wales Press, 1970).

8. Nock, *Conversion*, p. 118.

9. For theurgy see Hans Lewy, *Chaldaean Oracles and Theurgy: Mysticism, Magic, and Platonism in the Later Roman Empire*, ed. and rev. by Michel Tardieu (Paris: Etudes Augustiniennes, 1978).

10. See Franz Cumont, *Astrology and Religion among the Greeks and Romans* (New York: G. P. Putnam's Sons, 1912; reprint ed., New York: Dover Publications, 1960).

11. *Corpus Hermeticum* 1.15, ed. and trans. Walter Scott, *Hermetica: The Ancient Greek and Latin Writings which Contain Religious or Philosophic Teachings Ascribed to Hermes Trismegistus*, 2 vols. (Oxford: At the Clarendon Press, 1924–25), 1:123.

12. Hans Jonas, *The Gnostic Religion*, 2nd ed. (Boston: Beacon Press, 1958, 1963), is the best general introduction to Gnosticism. Other useful works are the introduction to Werner Foerster, *Gnosis: A Selection of Gnostic Texts*, 2 vols. (Oxford: At the Clarendon Press, 1972), vol. 1; Robert M. Grant, *Gnosticism and Early Christianity*, 2nd ed. (New York: Columbia University Press, 1959, 1966); and Elaine Pagels, *The Gnostic Gospels* (New York: Random House, 1979, Vintage Books, 1981).

13. See Eusebius *Ecclesiastical History* 6.2.12–15.

14. Quoted in Clement of Alexandria *Excerpts from Theodotus* 78 (trans. Foerster, *Gnosis*, 1:230).

15. Foerster, *Gnosis*, 1:59–83, assembles the principal Patristic testimonies to Basilides' teaching. See also Gilles Quispel, "Gnostic Man: The Doctrine of Basilides," in *Gnostic Studies*, 2 vols. (Istanbul: Nederlands Historisch-Archeologisch Intituut in het Nabije Oosten, 1974), 1:103–133.

16. For the teachings of Valentinus see Foerster, *Gnosis*, 1:121–61, and Quispel, "The Original Doctrine of Valentinus," in *Gnostic Studies*, 1:27–36.

17. *The Gospel of Truth*, trans. George W. MacRae, in *The Nag Hammadi Library in English*, ed. James M. Robinson (San Francisco: Harper & Row, Publishers, 1977), pp. 37–49. The phrase quoted here is on p. 38.

18. The letter is translated in Foerster, *Gnosis*, 1:154–61. See Quispel, "La Lettre de Ptolémée à Flora," in *Gnostic Studies*, 1:70–102.

19. These fragments are translated in Foerster, *Gnosis*, 1:162–83.

20. *The Tripartite Tractate*, trans. Harold W. Attridge and Dieter Mueller, *Nag Hammadi Library*, pp. 54–97. The relation of the Son to the Father is discussed on p. 55 and elsewhere in the first part of the treatise. Quispel suggests that Heracleon could be the author in "From Mythos to Logos," in *Gnostic Studies*, 1:158–69.

21. See *Nag Hammadi Library*, pp. 82–84.

22. See Edwin C. Blackman, *Marcion and His Influence* (London: S.P.C.K., 1948), and Adolf Harnack, *Marcion: das Evangelium vom Fremden Gott*,

2nd ed. (Leipzig: J. C. Hinrichs'sche Verlag, 1921, 1924). Harnack provides a reconstruction, insofar as one is possible, of Marcion's works.

23. See Origen *Contra Celsum* 5.4 and 5.61.

24. Allain Le Boulluec suggests Origen knew Irenaeus' work in "Ya-t-il
    des traces de la polémique antignostique d'Irénée dans le *Péri Archôn*
    d'Origène?" in *Gnosis and Gnosticism: Papers read at the Seventh Inter-
    national Conference on Patristic Studies (Oxford, September 8th–13th
    1975)*, ed. Martin Krause (Leiden: F. J. Brill, 1977), pp. 138–47.

CHAPTER III: Platonism (211–15)

1. Eusebius, who allowed only one year between persecutions, was evidently mistaken, thinking that Laetus and Aquila held office in succession. See, Nautin, *Origène*, pp. 32–33, 36–39.

2. All our information comes from the sixth book of the Eusebius' *Ecclesiastical History* and from an allusive autobiographical notice in Clement
   *Stromateis* 1.21.144–45. See Nautin, *Lettres et écrivains chrétiennes*, pp.
   105–44.

3. See H.-I. Marrou's introduction to his edition, with translation into
   French, of *Le Pédagogue*, 3 vols. (Paris: Editions du Cerf, 1960–70), vol.
   1, for a discussion of the work's structure.

4. Clement did not actually read Seneca, who wrote in Latin, but the close-
   ness of their arguments probably indicates an eventual common source in
   Stoic ethics.

5. Plato *Epistle* 2.314b, quoted in Clement *Stromateis* 1.1.14. The works of
   Clement (except for parts which deal in any way with sex, which the
   Victorian editors prudently printed in Latin) are accessible in English
   translation in *Ante-Nicene Fathers* (reprint ed., Grand Rapids, Mich.:
   Wm. B. Eerdmans Publishing Company, 1974), vol. 2. The *Exhortation
   to the Greeks* and *Who Is the Rich Man Who Is to Be Saved?* along with a
   fragment of a baptismal homily, are translated by G.W. Butterworth,
   *Clement*, Loeb Classical Library (Cambridge, Mass.: Harvard University
   Press, 1919). Books 3 and 7 of the *Stromateis* are accessible in *Alexandrian Christianity*, ed. John Ernest Leonard Oulton and Henry Chadwick
   (Philadelphia: The Westminster Press, 1954). The translation of book 3 in
   the latter volume makes up the major omission in the *Ante-Nicene Fathers*
   volume.

6. Clement *Stromateis* 5.8.

7. Ibid., 4.2.4.

8. Ibid., 6.9.71.

9. Salvatore R. C. Lilla, who also demonstrates the influence of Gnosticism
   and Philo, demonstrates conclusively in *Clement of Alexandria: A Study
   of Christian Platonism and Gnosticism* (London: Oxford University Press,
   1971), that Clement's philosophy was Platonist rather than, as Clement
   himself claimed, eclectic.

10. A good introduction is Samuel Sandmel, *Philo of Alexandria* (New York: Oxford University Press, 1979).

11. Plato *Theaetetus* 176b, trans. F. M. Cornford, in *The Collected Dialogues of Plato*, ed. Edith Hamilton and Huntington Cairns (Princeton: Princeton University Press, 1961), p. 881, quoted in Clement *Stromateis* 2.22.136.

12. Clement *Stromateis* 4.22.136.

13. Ibid., 7.16.104; 7.1.1.

14. Ibid., 6.15.126.

15. Ibid., 7.16.96.

16. Ibid., 3.6.46.

17. Ibid., 7.12.70; 3.16.101.

18. Ibid., 2.20.108–109.

19. Ibid., 4.10.

20. Ibid., 4.4.15.

21. Ibid., 2.19.97; 7.9.53.

22. Ibid., 6.13.106; 7.12.77; 4.25.157–59; 7.7.36.

23. Ibid., 6.13.106.

24. Ibid., 2.19.96; 6.17.161.

25. Ibid., 7.13.82.

26. Ibid., 4.5.18, in which he cites Plato *Republic* 9.591d.

27. Ibid., 6.18.167.

28. Ibid., 1.11. *Stoikheia*, the Greek word Clement interpreted as "elements," had a wide range of meaning, and its meaning in Colossians is not at all clear. The Revised Standard Version, followed here, translates it "elemental spirits," the Authorized Version "rudiments."

29. Ibid., 6.8.67; 1.5.28.

30. Ibid., 1.18.89. Clement interpreted Paul's negative *oukhi*, a word that ordinarily introduces a question to which an affirmative response is expected, as if it were the simple negative *ouk*.

31. See appendix.

32. Porphyry *Life of Plotinus* 10, trans. Stephen MacKenna, Plotinus *The Enneads*, 4th rev. ed. (London: Faber and Faber Limited, 1969), p. 8.

33. Justin Martyr *Dialogue with Trypho* 1 discusses experiences with philosophy. The detail about the cloak comes from the *Acts of Justin*.

34. See Eusebius *Ecclesiastical History* 6.19.14.

35. A.-J. Festugière, *Contemplation et vie contemplative selon Platon* (Paris: J. Vrin, 2nd ed., 1950, 1975), p. 5, trans. author.

36. The best introduction to Origen's philosophical background is P. Merlan's section, "Greek Philosophy from Plato to Plotinus," in *The Cambridge History of Later Greek and Early Medieval Philosophy*, ed. A. H. Armstrong (Cambridge: At the University Press, 1977), pp. 14–132. For more detail see John Dillon, *The Middle Platonists* (London: Duckworth, 1977).

37. Numenius *Fragments* 8, ed. Edouard des Places (Paris: Société d'Editions «Les Belles Lettres», 1973), p. 51.

38. Arrian *Discourses of Epictetus* 1.7, trans. W. A. Oldfather, Loeb Classical Library, 2 vols. (London: William Heinemann: 1925), 1:59.
39. Plato *Timaeus* 28c— 29a (trans. Benjamin Jowett, in *Collected Dialogues*, p. 1162). The term here translated "artificer" is *dêmiourgos*, "demiurge," the term Gnostics would use to refer to the Old Testament Creator God.
40. Ibid., 29e—30a.
41. Plato *Phaedo* 81e; *Phaedrus* 250c.
42. Plotinus *Ennead* 2.9.18, trans. A. H. Armstrong, Loeb Classical Library, 6 vols. (Cambridge, Mass.: Harvard University Press, 1966), 2: 297.
43. Plato *Republic* 10.612e—613a (trans. Paul Shorey, *Collected Dialogues*, p. 837).
44. Plato *Gorgias* 525b (trans. W. D. Woodhead, *Collected Dialogues*, p. 305).
45. Plato *Republic* 2.380a–b.
46. Plato *Republic* 6.486a (trans. Paul Shorey, *Collected Dialogues*, p. 722).
47. Plato *Laws* 12.966c (trans. A. E. Taylor, *Collected Dialogues*, p. 1511).
48. Plato *Phaedrus* 247c.
49. See, for example, Plato *Phaedo* 69c–d.
50. Pointing this out is one merit of Hans Jonas' fine chapters on Origen in *Gnosis und spätantiker Geist*, 2 vols. (Göttingen: Vandenhoeck & Ruprecht, 1934), 2.1.171–223. See also Andrew Louth, *The Origins of the Christian Mystical Tradition: From Plato to Denys* (Oxford: Oxford University Press, 1981).

CHAPTER IV: Christian Scholarship (215–22)

1. Eusebius *Ecclesiastical History* 6.14.10, and Jerome *Illustrious Men* 61. Nautin's attempt *Le dossier d'Hippolyte et de Méliton dans les florilèges dogmatiques et chez le historiens modernes* (Paris: Editions du Cerf, 1953), to show that Hippolytus was not, in fact a Roman theologian are unconvincing.
2. Quoted from Kelly, *Early Christian Doctrines*, p. 123, which should be referred to for a more comprehensive treatment of the issues discussed here.
3. Origen *Homilies on Jeremiah* (Greek series) 20.2. This work is not accessible at this time in an English translation. Two modern series, both incomplete, present it and most of Origen's other works in the original Greek or (in the case of ancient translations) Latin texts. These are *Die griechischen christlischen Schriftsteller* and *Sources chrétiennes*. The latter is less complete but has the advantage of presenting the works with a facing translation in French. The fullest edition of Origen's works is still the 1733 Delarvel edition reprinted in Jacques Paul Migne, *Patrologia Graeca*. Pierre Nautin's *Origène*, pp. 241–60 contains a comprehensive list of the current editions of works by Origen not included in the three editions mentioned above.

4. Origen *Exhortation to Martyrdom* 36. See Nautin, *Origène*, pp. 74–75.
5. Origen *Commentary on John* 5.8. This translation and all other unattributed translations are by the author.
6. This description of Origen's text-critical labors depends on Nautin's original but convincing treatment of the subject in *Origène*, pp. 303–61. For other views see Sidney Jellicoe, *The Septuagint and Modern Study* (Oxford: At the Clarendon Press, 1968), pp. 100–146.

CHAPTER V: A Theological System (222–30)

1. See Franz H. Kettler, *Der ursprüngliche Sinn der Dogmatik des Origenes* (Berlin: Alfred Töpelmann Verlag, 1966).
2. Nautin, *Origène*, translates these fragments into French on pp. 264–75.
3. The fragments of this work are collected in *Origenes Werke*, ed. Ernst Klostermann, in *Die Griechische christlichen Schriftsteller* (Leipzig: J. C. Hinrichs'sche Buchhandlung, 1901), 3:325–79.
4. See Didyme l'Aveugle, *Sur la Genèse, texte inédit d'après un papyrus de Toura*, intro., ed., trans., and notes by Pierre Nautin and Louis Doutreleau, 2 vols. (Paris: Editions du Cerf, 1976 and 1979).
5. See Eric Junod's discussion in the introduction to his *Sources chrétiennes* edition of this fragment in Origène, *Philocalie 21–27, sur la libre arbitre* (Paris: Editions du Cerf, 1976).
6. See, for example, Plotinus *Ennead* 2.3, "Are the Stars Causes?"
7. G. W. Butterworth's masterful translation, Origen, *On First Principles* (London: S.P.C.K., 1936; New York: Harper & Row, Publishers, Harper Torchbooks, 1966), includes all the putative Greek fragments along with Rufinus' translation. Used by permission.
8. See, particularly, *Origeniana*, the proceedings of the first international colloquium on Origen Studies (Bari: Istituto di literatura cristiana antica, Università di Bari, 1975) for articles by Marguerite Harl, "Structure et cohérence du *Peri Archon*," pp. 11–32, and Gilles Dorival, "Remarques sur la forme du *Peri Archon*," pp. 33–45.
9. For a translation of this work, see Gilbert Murray, *Five Stages of Greek Religion* (New York: Columbia University Press, 1925), pp. 241–67; (Garden City, N.Y.: Doubleday & Co., Doubleday Anchor Book, 1955), pp. 191–212.
10. The new edition of *On First Principles* in the *Sources chrétiennes* series, 4 vols. (Paris: Editions du Cerf, 1978, 1980), ed. and trans. Henri Crouzel and Manlio Simonetti, presents the work in its original structure.
11. Origen *On First Principles* preface 7 (trans. Butterworth, pp. 4–5).
12. Ibid., preface 10 (p. 6), quoting the Septuagint reading of Hos. 10:12.
13. See Plotinus *Ennead* 5.1.6, "the eternally achieved engenders eternally an eternal being," (trans. MacKenna, p. 374).
14. Compare Plotinus *Ennead* 5.3.11 (trans. MacKenna, p. 393):
    The Intellectual-Principle [Plotinus' second hypostasis] is established in multiplicity; its intellection, self-sprung though it be, is in

the nature of something added to it . . . and makes it multiple: the utterly simplex, and therefore first of all beings must, then, transcend the Intellectual-Principle.

15. Origen *Commentary on John* 1.119.
16. Ibid., 2.113–14. Compare Plato *Timaeus* 30c–31a.
17. Ibid., 1.30. Origen probably found this concept, known as "sober intoxication," in Philo; it is a commonplace in his homilies.
18. Plotinus *Ennead* 5.3.1 (trans. MacKenna, p. 374).
19. Origen *Commentary on John* 2.2.17–18. The effect of the Greek construction is approximated by writing "the Word was god."
20. Ibid., 2.3.20.
21. Augustine *City of God* 10.29.
22. Origen *On First Principles* 2.6.2. (trans. Butterworth, p. 109).
23. See Frances M. Young, *The Use of Sacrificial Ideas in Greek Christian Writers from the New Testament to John Chrysostom* (Cambridge, Mass.: Philadelphia Patristic Foundation Ltd., 1979), pp. 167–82.
24. Numenius *On the Good* fr. 4a (trans. des Places, p. 45).
25. Origen *On First Principles* 1.6.2. (trans. Butterworth, p. 53). For passages in Paul, in addition to Phil. 2:10–11, which Origen interpreted in a universalistic sense, see Romans 8 and 1 Corinthians 15.
26. Ibid., 1.7.3. (trans. Butterworth, p. 61).
27. Ibid., 1.7.3,2,5. quoting Phil. 1:23 (trans. Butterworth, p. 61, 60, 63).
28. Ibid., 2.8.3. Compare *The Gospel of Truth* 34 in Robinson, *Nag Hammadi Library*, p. 45.
29. Ibid., 2.9.7, quoting Mal. 1:2–3 in the version of Rom. 9:13.
30. So, at any rate, if Didymus the Blind followed Origen in his *Commentary on Genesis* 106–8 (trans. Nautin, pp. 248–55).
31. It is curious that John Hick, *Evil and the God of Love* (London: Macmillan, 1966) does not deal with Origen, who exemplifies far better than Irenaeus himself the "Irenaean" theodicy that Hick presents as an alternative within the tradition of Christian theology to the dominant theodicy of Augustine.
32. Origen *On First Principles* 2.3.3 (trans. Butterworth, p. 87).
33. See, for instance, Origen *Commentary on John* 1.178, where he interpreted the subjection of the world to vanity in Romans 8 as its subjection to bodily existence, and *Exhortation to Martyrdom* 3, where he praised the prospective martyr's eagerness to commune with God apart, not only from his earthly body, but from any body.
34. Jerome *Against John of Jerusalem* 25–26. Nautin, who quotes the entire passage in French in *Origène*, pp. 298–301, argues (ibid., pp. 296–98) that this passage, long thought to come from Origen's treatise *On the Resurrection*, actually is from his *Stromateis*.
35. See Georg Anrich, "Clemens und Origenes als Begründer der Lehre vom Fegfeuer," *Theologische Abhandlungen: eine Festgabe zum 17. Mai*

*1902 für Heinrich Julius Holtzmann*, ed. W. Nowak (Tübingen: J. C. B. Mohr [Paul Siebeck], 1902), pp. 95–120.

36. See Plato *Phaedrus* 245c; *Laws* 10.904c.
37. See Plotinus *Ennead* 3.2, "Providence."
38. Epictetus *Discourses* 1.1.10–12 (trans. Oldfather, 1:9,11).
39. Origen *On First Principles* 3.1.13 (trans. Butterworth, p. 182).
40. Ibid., 4.1.1 (p. 257).
41. Plato *Phaedrus* 246a (trans. R. Hackforth, *Collected Dialogues*, p. 493).
42. Plotinus *Ennead* 3.5.9 (trans. MacKenna, p. 200).
43. Ibid., 1.1.12; 4.3.27–32.
44. For a discussion of the role of myth and allegory in Greek philosophy and in Christianity, see Jean Pépin, *Mythe et allégorie: les origines grecques et les contestations judéo-chrétiennes*, 2nd ed. (Paris: Etudes Augustiniennes, 1976).
45. Origen *On First Principles* 4.2.1 (trans. Butterworth, p. 271).
46. Ibid., 4.2.3, quoting Luke 11:52.
47. Ibid., 4.2.6.
48. Ibid., 4.2.7 (trans. Butterworth, p. 282).
49. Ibid., (trans. Butterworth, pp. 283–84).
50. Ibid., 4.4.10 (trans. Butterworth, p. 327).

CHAPTER VI: Controversy (230–34)

1. Especially since Nautin, *Origène*, pp. 366–68, has shown that Eusebius' language in *Ecclesiastical History* 6.19.16 depends on Origen's description of his conflict with Demetrius in Origen *Commentary on John* 6.2.
2. See Lee I. Levine, *Caesarea Under Roman Rule* (Leiden: E. J. Brill, 1975).
3. Nicholas de Lange, *Origen and the Jews* (Cambridge: Cambridge University Press, 1976) discusses Origen's indebtedness to Jewish thinkers and his attitude to Jews in his work.
4. On Antioch see Glanville Donney, *A History of Antioch in Syria from Seleucus to the Arab Conquest* (Princeton: Princeton University Press, 1961), and D. S. Wallace-Hadrill, *Christian Antioch: A Study of Early Christian Thought in the East* (Cambridge: Cambridge University Press, 1982).
5. Pausanius *A Description of Greece*, Loeb Classical Library, trans. W. H. S. Jones, 4 vols. (Cambridge, Mass.: Harvard University Press, 1918, 1926, 1933, 1935), with a companion vol. by R. E. Wycherley, rev. ed. (Cambridge, Mass.: Harvard University Press, 1955). R. E. Wycherley, *The Stones of Athens* (Princeton: Princeton University Press, 1978), reconstructs the Athens Origen saw.
6. See Nautin, *Lettres et écrivains chrétiennes*, pp. 121–34.
7. Origen *Commentary on John* 6.2.
8. Adolf Harnack, *The Mission and Expansion of Christianity* (New York: G. P. Putnam's Sons, 1908), 1: 463, and Walter Bauer, *Orthodoxy and*

*Heresy in Earliest Christianity* (Philadelphia: Fortress Press, 1971) pp. 53–55 present the relevant information on this issue.

9. See Rudolf Sohm, *Kirchenrecht* (Leipzig: Dunker and Humblot, 1892), vol. 1, on forms of authority in the early church. Sohm's formulation of charisma influenced Max Weber, who made it an important sociological category. See Joseph Wilson Trigg, "The Charismatic Intellectual: Origen's Understanding of Religious Leadership," *Church History* 50 (March 1981) 5–19, for a fuller discussion of this issue. Used by permission.

10. See Clement *Stromateis* 7.7.36; 4.25.157–59.
11. Origen *Homilies on Leviticus* 6.5.
12. Ibid., 1.4; 9.8–9.
13. Origen *Commentary on John* 1.3.
14. Ibid., 13.47.
15. Origen *Commentary on Matthew* 11.5.
16. See Origen *Commentary on John* 13.18 and *Homilies on Leviticus* 4.6.
17. Origen *Homilies on Isaiah* 6.4.
18. Origen *Commentary on John* 32.17.
19. Origen *On First Principles*, Preface 3.
20. Origen *Commentary on Matthew* 14.11–12.
21. Origen *Contra Celsum* 3:48; 6.7.
22. Origen *Homilies on Numbers* 22.4.
23. Origen *Homilies on Genesis* 16.5.
24. Origen *Commentary on Matthew* 11.15.
25. Ibid., 16.20.
26. Origen *Homilies on Numbers* 9.1, referring to Num. 16:31–33.
27. See Origen *Series Commentary on Matthew* 10; also *Commentary on John* 32.12.
28. See Origen *On Prayer* 28.8–10.
29. Origen *Commentary on Matthew* 12.14. See also *Contra Celsum* 6.77.
30. Origen *Homilies on Leviticus* 14.2–4; *Homilies on Judges* 2.5; *Commentary on Matthew* 12.12.
31. The first explicit reference to presbyters as priests is in *Syriac Didascalia* 9. This is a work that seems to date from the middle of the third century. At about that time Cyprian of Carthage in his correspondence customarily referred to bishops as priests.

CHAPTER VII: Exegesis and Prayer (234–38)

1. A fragment quoted by Lawlor and Oulton in Eusebius *Ecclesiastical History*, 2: 213–14.
2. Origen *Commentary on John* 19.27.40ff.
3. Origen *Commentary on John* 5.5.
4. Ibid., 13.3.15—13.5.39.
5. Ibid., 1.15.89.

6. Ibid., 28.20.171–77; 6.4.21; 13.48.316ff.
7. Ibid., 32.24.310–11.
8. Ibid., 10.16.141.
9. Ibid., 10.18.172–216. Origen provides an allegorical interpretation of all of the circumstances of the triumphal entry with his characteristic ingenuity.
10. Ibid., 10.3.10.
11. Ibid., 10.5.28.
12. Ibid., 13.55.379.
13. Ibid., 10.28.107.
14. Ibid., 6.2.34.
15. Ibid., 6.30.153.
16. See Robert M. Grant, *The Earliest Lives of Jesus* (New York: Harper & Bros., 1961).
17. Origen *Commentary on John* 6.40.204ff.
18. See Marguerite Harl, "Origène et la sémantique du langage biblique," *Vigiliae Christianae* 26 (1972): 161–87, for a discussion of this issue in connection with Origen's treatment of Paul's word "law" in the Epistle to the Romans.
19. Origen *On Prayer* 2.1, trans. John Ernest Leonard Oulton, *Alexandrian Christianity*, ed. Henry Chadwick and John Ernest Leonard Oulton (Philadelphia: The Westminster Press, 1954), p. 239. Used by permission of the Westminster Press.
20. Ibid., 13.2–4.
21. Ibid., 27.2.
22. John Calvin *Institutes of the Christian Religion* (1559 ed.), 20.3.2.
23. Origen *On Prayer* 12.2.
24. Ibid., 14.6—15.1.
25. Ibid., 11.2.
26. Ibid., 11.4–5.
27. Ibid., 23.2.
28. Ibid., 25.1 (trans. Oulton, p. 289).
29. Ibid., 29.17 (trans. Oulton, p. 319).
30. Origen *Exhortation to Martyrdom*, 3 (trans. Henry Chadwick, *Alexandrian Christianity*, p. 394).
31. Ibid., 47 (trans. Chadwick, pp. 426–27).

CHAPTER VIII: Teaching and Preaching (238–44)

1. See Nautin, *Origène*, pp. 155–61 and 183–97 for a discussion of the author's identity. For an opposing view, see the introduction in Henri Crouzel's edition of the *Speech of Appreciation, Remerciement à Origène* (Paris: Editions du Cerf, 1969). Crouzel's position has not changed in the light of Nautin's objections.
2. [Gregory Thaumaturgus?] *Speech of Appreciation* 5.63.

3. For Origen's view on the value of philosophy in the education of Christians, see Origen *Contra Celsum* 3.58.
4. [Gregory Thaumaturgus?] *Speech of Appreciation* 7.93–99.
5. Ibid., 7.100–108.
6. Ibid., 8.109–110.
7. Ibid., 8.114.
8. Ibid., 9.124 (see Nautin, *Origène*, p. 192, n. 16) and 9.116. See also 12.149, where the author alludes to Plato's *Theaetetus*.
9. Ibid., 12.148–49. See Nautin, *Origène*, p. 192, n. 17. One Platonist who held this doctrine was Hierocles, who may, like Origen, have learned it from Ammonius Saccas.
10. Ibid., 13.151–53.
11. Ibid., 13.154.
12. Ibid., 16.196.
13. Ibid., 15.174.
14. Ibid., 7.85–87.
15. See Chapter VI above.
16. [Gregory Thaumaturgus?] *Speech of Appreciation* 2.10.
17. Ibid., 15.173.
18. Ibid., 4.42. The reference to Isa. 9:6 (as it appears in the Septuagint version). See Origen *Contra Celsum* 5.53.
19. See Porphyry *Life of Plotinus* 10 and Plotinus *Ennead* 3.4.
20. Crouzel includes Origen's letter to Gregory in his edition of the *Speech of Appreciation*, and Nautin prints it in its entirety and discusses it in *Origène*, pp. 155–61.
21. See Maurice Wiles, *The Divine Apostle: the Interpretation of St. Paul's Epistles in the Early Church* (London: Cambridge University Press, 1967), pp. 111–21.
22. See Eusebius *Ecclesiastical History* 6.33.
23. Henry Chadwick's translation of this work, with an excellent introduction and notes, is in Chadwick and Oulton, *Alexandrian Christianity*, pp. 430–55.
24. See Nautin, *Origène*, pp. 389–409.
25. See Origen *Homilies on Genesis* 10.1.
26. Origen *Homilies on Jeremiah* (Greek series) 4.3.
27. The best discussion of Origen's preaching is in the introduction by Pierre Nautin to the *Homilies on Jeremiah* in the *Sources chrètiennes* edition: Origène, *Homélies sur Jérémie*, ed. and trans. Pierre Husson and Pierre Nautin (Paris: Editions du Cerf, 1976), pp. 100–91.
28. Origen *Homilies on Jeremiah* (Greek series) 2.3.
29. Ibid., 1.2 and 3. The quotation is from 1 Cor. 5:5.
30. Origen *Homilies on Joshua* 8.2.
31. Ibid., 1.7. The quotation is from Josh. 11:23.
32. Origen *Homilies on Genesis* 15.2, 3.

33. Ibid., 1.9, 10.
34. See Origen *Dialogue with Heraclides* 148–50, and *Contra Celsum* 5.29, referring to Matt. 7:6.
35. Origen *Homilies on Jeremiah* (Greek series) 14.1.
36. In the following paragraphs I am relying heavily on Marcel Simon's *Verus Israel: étude sur les relations entre chrétiens et juifs dans l'empire romain (135–425)* (Paris: Editions de Boccard, 2nd ed., 1964).
37. Origen *Contra Celsum* 1.55. On the dialogue between Jason and Papiscus see ibid., 4.52.
38. See Nicholas de Lange, *Origen and the Jews*, pp. 86–87.
39. Origen *Homilies on Leviticus* 7.5.
40. Origen *Homilies on Jeremiah* (Greek series) 12.13. See also de Lange, *Origen and the Jews*, pp. 75–79.
41. David J. Halperin, "Origen, Ezekiel's Merkabah, and the Ascension of Moses," in *Church History* 50 (1981): 261–75.
42. See Origen *Homilies on Exodus* 6.6.
43. Origen *Homilies on Leviticus* 8.9.
44. Origen *Homilies on Judges* 4.1.
45. Origen *Homilies on Leviticus* 7.6.
46. Origène, *Sur la Pâque*, ed. Octave Guérand and Pierre Nautin (Paris: Editions Beauchesne, 1979), henceforth referred to as Origen *On the Passover*.
47. Ibid., 1. For a discussion of the Quartodeciman controversy see pp. 96–100 of Nautin's introduction to his and Guérand's edition. Nautin's view that Melito's *On the Passover* was originally a treatise has not met widespread acceptance.
48. Ibid., 40.
49. Ibid.
50. Ibid., 17–21.
51. Ibid., 26–30.
52. Ibid., 34.
53. Ibid., 23–24.
54. Ibid., 30–32.
55. Origen *Homilies on Luke* 33.5.
56. Origen *Homilies on Leviticus* 9.4.
57. See, for example, Origen *Homilies on Luke* 2.1.
58. Origen *Homilies on Leviticus* 4.2.
59. Origen *Homilies on Luke* 21.4.
60. Origen *Homilies on Numbers* 12.4 and *Homilies on Ezekiel* 6.5.
61. Origen *Commentary on Matthew* 15.15.
62. Origen *Series Commentary on Matthew* 16 and *Commentary on the Song of Songs* 2.
63. Origen *Homilies on Joshua* 1.1.
64. Ibid., 15.5.

65. Origen *Homilies on Leviticus* 9.7.
66. Origen *Homilies on Jeremiah* (Greek series) 2.3.
67. Origen *Commentary on John* 32.2–14.
68. Ibid., 6.32–33.
69. Origen *Homilies on Exodus* 13.3. On Origen's eucharistic teaching see Lothar Lies, *Wort und Eucharistie bei Origenes: zur Spiritualisierungs-tendenz des Eucharistieverständnisses* (Innsbruck: Tyrolia Verlag, 1978).
70. Origen *Homilies on Leviticus* 7.5.
71. Origen *Series Commentary on Matthew* 85.
72. Origen *Commentary on Matthew* 11.14.
73. Origen *Homilies on Leviticus* 13.5.
74. Origen *Commentary on Matthew* 16.7 and *Series Commentary on Matthew* 85.
75. Origen *Commentary on Matthew* 11.1–2.
76. Origen *Homilies on Exodus* 13.3.
77. Origen *Homilies on Numbers* 16.9.
78. Origen *Fr. on I Corinthians*, ed. by C. Jenkins, *Journal of Theological Studies* 9 (1908): 364.
79. Origen *Commentary on Matthew* 16.8.
80. Origen *Homilies on Leviticus* 14.2–4.
81. Origen *Commentary on Matthew* 17.24, referring to Matt. 22:14.
82. Ibid., 12.12
83. Origen *Homilies on Leviticus* 11.2 and *Homilies on Joshua* 5.6.
84. Origen *Homilies on Jeremiah* (Greek series) 12.5.
85. Origen *Homilies on Leviticus* 2.4.
86. Origen *Homilies on Ezekiel* 12.1.
87. Origen *Homilies on Psalm 37* 2.6.

CHAPTER IX: Standing Fast (244–53)

1. The account of Origen's life in this chapter follows Nautin's reconstruction of his biography in *Origène*, pp. 87–89, 91–98, 161–82, 435–41, a section in which his conclusions are, as usual, tentative but convincing.
2. The entire work is accessible in Origen, *The Song of Songs Commentary and Homilies*, trans. and annotated by R. P. Lawson, *Ancient Christian Writers*, vol. 26 (Westminster, Md.: The Newman Press, 1957), and the prologue alone in Origen *An Exhortation to Martyydom, Prayer and Selected Works*, trans. Rowan A. Greer (New York: Paulist Press, 1979), a volume in the Classics of Western Spirituality series. For convenience, the subchapter numbers in Lawson's translation are used when referring to passages, even though they are not in the standard editions.
3. Origen *Commentary on the Song of Songs*, prologue 1.
4. Ibid., 2. Porphyry *Life of Plotinus* 15 shows that Plotinus agreed with Origen that carnal love had no place in Plato's *Symposium*. Other works besides the Song of Songs which, according to Origen, the Jews restricted

were the opening chariot vision in Ezekiel, the description of the reconstructed temple at the end of the same book, and the creation narrative in Genesis. Since all three of these passages gave rise to cosmological speculations of a quasi-Gnostic character in Jewish tradition, it is reasonable to presume that this is why the Song of Songs was restricted, not because of its erotic suggestiveness.

5. Ibid., 3.
6. Charles Bigg, *The Christian Platonists of Alexandria* (Oxford: At the Clarendon Press, 1913), p. 173, aptly spoke of Origen's all-pervasive symbolism as a "sacramental mystery of nature."
7. Origen *Commentary on the Song of Songs* prologue 2.
8. Ibid. The reference is to Ignatius *Epistle to the Romans* 7.2. This is a controversial, if quite defensible, interpretation of Ignatius. There is a highly interesting discussion of this section of Origen's prologue in Anders Nygren, *Agape and Eros*, trans. Philip A. Watson, rev. ed. (Philadelphia: The Westminster Press, 1953), pp. 387–92. Nygren is, of course, responsible for making the distinction between *agapê* and *erôs* as radically opposed concepts a part of the current coin of theological discourse. Nygren finds in Origen's identification of the two in our passage a clear sign of his consistent synthesis of Christianity (*agapê*) with Platonism (*erôs*) elsewhere in his writings. Although he challenges Origen's interpretation of Ignatius, he is oddly silent about Origen's argument that *agapê* can refer to carnal love in the Septuagint. See also John M. Rist, *Eros and Psyche* (Toronto: University of Toronto Press, 1964).
9. Origen *Commentary on the Song of Songs* 3.15; 3.11.
10. Ibid., 3.3.
11. Ibid., 2.1.
12. Ibid., 1.1.
13. Ibid., 3.1.
14. Ibid., 1.5.
15. Ibid., 1.2.
16. Ibid., 2.5.
17. This letter, along with Origen's response and Origen's letter to Gregory, is translated by Frederick Crombie in Alexander Roberts and James Donaldson, eds., *The Ante-Nicene Fathers* (Grand Rapids, Mich.: Wm. B. Eerdmans Publishing Company, 1976), 4:385–94.
18. Origen *Commentary on Matthew* 11.9. Books 10–14 of this work are accessible in a translation by John Patrick in Allan Menzies, ed., *The Ante-Nicene Fathers*, vol. 10 (Original Supplement to the American Edition; reprint ed., Grand Rapids, Mich.: Wm. B. Eerdmans Publishing Company, 1974), pp. 411–512.
19. Ibid., 10.5.
20. Origen *Series Commentary on Matthew* 50.
21. Ibid., 32.

22. Ibid., 39,50,58.
23. Origen *Commentary on Matthew* 10.2,3.
24. Ibid., 15.35.
25. Ibid., 13.1.
26. Ibid., 13.1,2.
27. Ibid., 17.29, reference to Isa. 40:5.
28. Origen *Contra Celsum* preface 3,4.
29. There is an excellent translation of this work: Origen *Contra Celsum*, trans. with intro. and notes, by Henry Chadwick (Cambridge: At the University Press, 1953, 1965). Used by permission.
30. Henry Chadwick, in the introduction to his translation of Origen's *Contra Celsum*, p. ix.
31. Origen *Contra Celsum* 8.76.
32. Ibid., 3.10–12.
33. Ibid., 6.3, citing Plato *Epistles* 7.341c.
34. Ibid., 8.66.
35. Ibid., 5.27.
36. Ibid., 5.14; 7.34.
37. Ibid., 4.72; 5.14; 4.11.
38. Ibid., 4.6.
39. Ibid., 4.54.
40. Ibid., 4.14.
41. Ibid., 4.23 (trans. Chadwick, p. 199).
42. Ibid., 4.30 (trans. Chadwick, p. 205).
43. Ibid., 4.88.
44. Ibid., 8.12 (trans. Chadwick, p. 460).
45. Ibid., 1.28; 6.75; 2.37; 2.68; 2.24.
46. Ibid., 1.28.
47. Ibid., 7.58, comparing Plato *Crito* 49b–e to Luke 6:29 or Matt. 5:39 and 6.16 comparing Plato *Laws* 5.743a to Matt. 19:24 and parallels.
48. Ibid., 2.59–60.
49. Ibid., 2.63.
50. Ibid., 2.36.
51. Ibid., 7.53.
52. Ibid., 2.75 (trans. Chadwick, p. 123).
53. Ibid., 1.49–50.
54. Ibid., 1.28, 32, 38.
55. Ibid., 7.18.
56. Ibid., 1.9 (trans. Chadwick, p. 12).
57. Ibid., 3.48–55.
58. Ibid., 3.48 (trans. Chadwick, p. 162).
59. Ibid., 6.10.
60. Ibid., 3.59 (trans. Chadwick, p. 168).
61. Ibid., 3.65.

62. Ibid., 3.66.
63. Ibid., 8.55, 17.
64. Ibid., 1.1.
65. Ibid., 8.25.
66. Ibid., 8.69.
67. Ibid., 8.71.
68. Ibid., 8.74–76.
69. Ibid., 5.3.
70. Ibid., 4.54.
71. Ibid., 4.41; 2.32.
72. Ibid., 1.49.
73. Ibid., 2.34, 58.
74. Theophilus of Antioch *Ad Autolycum* 1.3.
75. Origen *Contra Celsum* 5.18 (trans. Chadwick, p. 277).
76. Ibid., 4.72 (trans. Chadwick, p. 241).
77. Ibid., 2.15 (trans. Chadwick, p. 275).
78. Ibid., 1.9.
79. Ibid., 1.10.
80. Ibid., 3.58.
81. Ibid., 1.7.
82. Ibid., 3.60.
83. Ibid., 4.19.
84. See Henry Chadwick, "Origen, Celsus, and the Stoa," in *Journal of Theological Studies* 48 (1947): 34–49.
85. Origen *Contra Celsum* 1.29 (trans. Chadwick, p. 29). The reference is to Plato, *Republic* 1.329e—330a. The italics are in the original and here and in a subsequent quotation represent what modern editors believe to be the fragments of *The True Doctrine*.
86. Ibid., 1.62.
87. Ibid., 7.48.
88. Ibid., 3.68.
89. Ibid., 6.2.
90. Ibid., 4.39ff.
91. Ibid., 4.73ff.
92. Ibid., 6.44.
93. Ibid., 4.14–16.
94. Ibid., 6.68.
95. Ibid., 3.41.
96. Ibid., 2.30.
97. Ibid., 8.12; 8.6.
98. Ibid., 2.51.
99. Ibid., 1.32.
100. Ibid., 1.6.
101. Ibid., 7.58.

102. Ibid., 6.77 (trans. Chadwick, p. 390).
103. Ibid., 2.42.
104. Ibid., 2.69.
105. Ibid., 2.64.
106. Ibid., 2.75.
107. Ibid., 1.56.
108. Ibid., 4.71 (trans. Chadwick, p. 240).
109. Ibid., 7.18 (trans. Chadwick, p. 409).
110. Ibid., 4.38.
111. Ibid., 4.39 (trans. Chadwick, p. 215). The passage in question is Plato *Symposium* 203b–e.
112. Ibid., 4.50 (trans. Chadwick, p. 225). The reference is to Plato *Republic* 2.379c,d.
113. Origen *On First Principles* 4.2.1. See Chapter V.
114. Origen *Contra Celsum* 4.45.
115. Ibid., 4.51 (trans. Chadwick, p. 226).
116. Ibid., 4.49–50.
117. Ibid., 5.27.
118. Ibid., 1.25.
119. Ibid., 7.69.
120. Ibid., 8.36.
121. Ibid., 7.70, 8.36.
122. Ibid., 7.69.
123. Ibid., 3.67.
124. Ibid., 8.57 (trans. Chadwick, p. 495).
125. Ibid., 4.59. Origen's statement leaves open the possibility of Christian veneration of the tombs of martyrs, which would later emerge as full-fledged holy places.
126. Ibid., 8.22 (trans. Chadwick, p. 468).
127. Ibid., 8.23.
128. Ibid., 8.17 (trans. Chadwick, p. 464).
129. Ibid., 8.19, reference to 1 Corinthians 3.
130. Ibid., 8.57.
131. Ibid., 8.65; 1.1.
132. Ibid., 8.75.
133. See Adolf Harnack, *Militia Christi*, trans. and intro. David McInnes Gracie (Philadelphia: Fortress Press, 1981), and John Helgeland, "Christians and the Roman Army from Marcus Aurelius to Constantine," in *Aufstieg und Niedergang der römischen Welt* II. 23.1 (1979): 724–834.
134. Origen *Contra Celsum* 3.7; 7.26. See also 5.33.
135. Ibid., 8.68.
136. Ibid., 8.70 (trans. Chadwick, p. 506), reference to Genesis 18.
137. Ibid., 8.69.
138. Ibid., 8.72.

139. Ibid., 2.30.
140. Ibid., 4.82.
141. Ibid., 8.73 (trans. Chadwick, p. 509).
142. Ibid., 6.4, reference to Plato *Republic* 1.327a and *Phaedo* 118a.
143. Ibid., 7.44 (trans. Chadwick, p. 432), allusion to 1 Cor. 1:27.
144. Ibid., 1.5 (trans. Chadwick, p. 9), quoting Heraclitus, *fr.* B5 (Diehls).
145. Ibid., 8.4, quoting Plato *Phaedrus* 246e–247a, 250b, allusion to 2 Cor. 11:14.
146. See Chapter III above.
147. Origen *Contra Celsum* 3.56 (trans. Chadwick, p. 166).
148. Ibid., 7.31 (trans. Chadwick, p. 419), allusions to 1 John 2:8, Gen. 1:6–8, Mal. 4:2, and Dan. 4:34.
149. Ibid., 7.44.
150. Eusebius *Ecclesiastical History* 6.19.5–8 (trans. Lawlor and Oulton, 1:192).
151. Origen *Series Commentary on Matthew* 39.
152. Eusebius *Ecclesiastical History* 6.41.1–9.
153. See Frend, *Martyrdom and Persecution*, pp. 389–439 (pp. 285–323 Anchor ed.).
154. Eusebius *Ecclesiastical History* 6.41.

CHAPTER X: A Permanent Legacy

1. Eugène de Faye, in *Origène, sa vie, son oeuvre, sa pensée*, 3 vols. (Paris: Ernest Leroux, 1923, 1927, 1928), provided an impressive overall picture of Origen's life and thought characterized by a careful discrimination between sources and a pioneering attempt to place Origen in the intellectual context of his time. Walther Völker and subsequent writers on Origen's spirituality went off on a wrong track by dismissing de Faye's entirely apt description of Origen as an intellectual mystic. De Faye's work, however, has serious limitations. He was entirely unsympathetic with Origen's allegorical method, considering it an unfortunate delusion at best and, at worst, a deliberate subterfuge. He also had little sensitivity to the peculiar qualities of second-century Christianity and, as a result, was at a loss to explain how Origen could be a Platonist and a deeply committed Christian at the same time. De Faye was also unaware of the importance of Origen's training as a grammarian and his contacts with Judaism in forming his thought.

Hal Koch's *Pronoia und Paideusis; Studien über Origenes und sein Verhältnis zum Platonismus* (Berlin: Walter de Gruyter & Co., 1932, reprint ed., New York: Garland Publishing, 1979), easily the most insightful single work yet published on Origen's thought, provides a convincing explanation of how Origen could simultaneously be both a Platonist and an "almost fanatical" Christian. Koch's work, however, focuses narrowly on Origen's relationship to the Platonic tradition, and he did not attempt, except in a relatively brief but quite fine encyclopedia article ("Origenes," in *Paulys Real-Encyclopädie der classischen Altertums- wissenschaft)*, to provide an assessment of Origen's achievement as a whole.

Walther Völker's seminal work on Origen's spirituality, *Das Vollkom- menheitsideal des Origenes* (Tübingen: J. C. B. Mohr, 1930) is extremely helpful in its description of the way Origen integrated thought and action. Nonetheless, it fundamentally misconceives Origen's spirituality as an affective piety in the mold of Teresa of Avila and, in the process, provides no link between Origen's passion for scholarship and his quest for the knowledge of God.

Jean Daniélou's richly detailed *Origène* (Paris: La Table Ronde, 1948; Eng. trans., *Origen*, New York: Sheed and Ward, 1955) actually disguises the coherence of Origen's thought by treating his sacramental theology, apologetics, exegesis, theological system, and mysticism as separate and seemingly unrelated topics. Daniélou also downplays Origen's Platonism in order to demonstrate his commitment to the church and to the Christian tradition.

Henri Crouzel, whose massive erudition and prolific scholarship have made him the most influential Origen scholar now living, has carried still further Danielou's tendency to downplay Origen's Platonism. In *Origène et la philosophie* (Paris: Aubier, 1962) he took Origen's manifestly critical comments about philosophy in many of his works as proof that Origen could not himself have been a Platonist and attempted to show that Origen was not, in any meaningful sense, a systematic theologian. The prestige of Crouzel's views has made Origen appear in much current scholarly writ- ing as a very safe, respectable—and dull—theologian.

2. See Antoine Guillaumont, *Les «Kephalaia Gnostica» d' Evagre le Pontique et l'histoire d'origénisme chez les Grecs et chez les Syriens* (Paris: Editions du Seuil, 1962).

3. Augustine *Confessions* 5.14.24, trans. Albert C. Outler, *Confessions and Enchiridion*, Library of Christian Classics (Philadelphia: The Westminster Press, 1955), 7: 111.

4. For an account of this controversy, see J. N. D. Kelly, *Jerome* (New York: Harper & Row, 1975).

5. See Max Schär, *Das Nachleben des Origenes im Zeitalter des Human- ismus* (Basel: Helbing & Lichtenhahn, 1979).

6. William R. Inge, "Origen," in *Proceedings of the British Academy* 32 (1946): 144–45.

# Index